MAKERS OF MANAGEMENT

Also by David Clutterbuck

How to Be a Good Corporate Citizen
Businesswoman (with Marion Devine)
The Re-Making of Work (with Roy Hill)
New Patterns of Work
The Winning Streak (with Walter Goldsmith)
The Winning Streak Workout Book (with Walter Goldsmith)
Everybody Needs a Mentor (with Marion Devine)
The Marketing Edge (with Tony McBurnie)
Clore: The Man and His Millions (with Marion Devine)
Management Buyouts (with Marion Devine)
Turnaround (with Rebecca Nelson)
Just-in-time: A global status report (with Chris Voss)

by David Clutterbuck and Stuart Crainer

The Decline and Rise of British Industry

MAKERS OF MANAGEMENT

Men and Women who Changed
the Business World

David Clutterbuck
&
Stuart Crainer

MACMILLAN
LONDON

First published in 1990 by
MACMILLAN LONDON LIMITED
4 Little Essex Street London WC2R 3LF
and Basingstoke

Associated companies in Auckland, Delhi, Dublin, Gaborone,
Hamburg, Harare, Hong Kong, Johannesburg, Kuala Lumpur,
Lagos, Manzini, Melbourne, Mexico City, Nairobi, New York,
Singapore and Tokyo

A CIP catalogue record for this book is available from the
British Library

Typeset by Wyvern Typesetting Ltd, Bristol

Printed and bound in
Great Britain by
Billings Bookplan Ltd

Contents

Introduction

In any major area of human endeavour, there are a few giants – people who have broken the mould of conventional thinking to provide new insights, new challenges, new emotional thresholds. The great thinkers and movers of science, engineering, the arts and politics – to name but a few – have all been chronicled. Their motives have been explored in depth and their personalities subjected to scrutiny. There seems to be a fundamental human urge to try to understand what makes extraordinary people so extraordinary.

This book is the result of a fascination with the origins of new ideas in management. It attempts to answer a number of questions, including:

- Who were (and are) the giants of management thought?
- How did their ideas develop?
- Why did they have such an impact?

To find the answers, we embarked on a major research exercise. We started by trying to identify who were the key thinkers in management. We asked numerous consultants and academics across the world for their opinions – a survey sent to a thousand management development specialists, with the aid of the European Foundation for Management Development, was very helpful – and then we set about sorting the giants from the merely tall. Our selection of the most influential management thinkers will inevitably be controversial. Some famous names were regarded by some respondents as keepers of the Holy Grail, by others as one-idea windbags. Quite a few people suggested themselves.

Our course through this minefield inevitably left some casualties. We have tried to re-enlist this second tier of management 'gurus' within the general introductory chapters, which attempt to trace the development of some of the main themes of management via the many contributions to new thinking.

We attempted to interview not only all those major and minor characters who were still alive, but also working colleagues, who could provide clues into the nature of their thinking processes. In doing so, we learned that many of the first-line gurus were multi-talented – extraordinary individuals in more than one field of endeavour. We also learned that innovative thinking in management comes from a variety of backgrounds. Perhaps the only common factor is a restless diversity of interests.

We believe that anyone who is in any way involved with the practice or theory of management will find these profiles of interest and value. We say this partly from experience – our own fascination with the project grew and grew, until it extended monthly – and partly from a conviction that the key to understanding ideas is to understand the person behind them. Ideas absorbed at an intellectual level are frequently – perhaps typically – held in isolation and very difficult to apply to practical problems today. Ideas absorbed emotionally as well as intellectually rapidly become part of the pattern of thinking and exert a more rapid and intense influence on problems. We hope that our profiles of management thinkers will provide some of that emotional insight, alongside the intellectual theory. Our aim has been to make both available within one volume.

Makers of Management rapidly assumed a life of its own. We see the project as a growing organism, a tree of knowledge that will bear fruit periodically. So we welcome your comments, suggestions and additions as the fertiliser for future editions.

David Clutterbuck and Stuart Crainer

CHAPTER 1

The Early Pioneers

Tracing the origins of management thinking is like digging up tap-roots. Every time you think you have reached the bottom, you find that there is a small branch going even deeper. In practical terms, it took management skills to erect the pyramids and the towers of Babylon, to organise an invading Mongol horde and to build the merchant ships that sailed the Mediterranean in Greek and Roman times. Yet no one spoke of management as a discipline in its own right, or as a topic worthy of study. You either had it or you didn't. Nevertheless, undefined as it was, management did exist. 'All the great business builders we know of – from the Medici of Renaissance Florence and the founders of the Bank of England in the late seventeenth century down to IBM's Thomas Watson in our day – had a clear theory of the business which informed all their actions and decisions,' says Peter Drucker, perhaps the best known of today's management thinkers and writers, in *Management* (1977).

The early emphasis, however, was on the subject of governance or administration, the tools of statesmanship or bureaucracy. To be an effective king or governor required definable skills – among them judgement, leadership and strategy. Writers such as Niccolo Machiavelli (1491–1527) used keen observation to identify behaviours and strategies that worked in maintaining the security and prosperity of the nation state. These same techniques, albeit refined and given the gloss of academic exactitude, are still the main basis for our observations of effective and ineffective management nearly five centuries later. While the popular perception of Machiavelli's style of management comes much closer to business soap operas such as *Dynasty* or *Dallas* than to the practical realities of persuading a bunch of manual employees to produce better automobiles, there are many useful lessons for modern chief executives in the writings of the sixteenth-century Italian historian and politician.

It was Machiavelli who identified the intriguingly individual-istic nature of management. In *The Prince* he wrote:

I believe also that he will be successful who directs his actions according to the spirit of the times, and that he whose actions do not accord with the times will not be successful. Because men are seen, in affairs that lead to the end which every man has before him, namely, glory and riches, to get there by various methods; one with caution, another with haste; one by force, another by skill; one by patience, another by its opposite; and each one succeeds in reaching the goal by a different method.

Yet it was only once the subject of management had been firmly established as an academic discipline that writers began to view Machiavelli seriously as an observer of management. It was Anthony Jay who first (and not entirely seriously) pointed out in *Management and Machiavelli* (1970) that the Italian prince's sixteenth-century method of observing what worked in terms of statesmanship pre-dated very similar conclusions about success-ful behaviour by large corporations in the twentieth century. The similarities between Machiavelli's city state and the modern corporation, in terms of their preoccupations (keeping a reason-ably contented staff who will not join the opposition, defending market share, creating a sense of united goals, deciding whether to centralise or decentralise, and so on) can be seen in much of the language we use. Sales reps have territories; autonomous executives in the regions are often referred to as barons; new-comers to the firm are recruits.

Machiavelli was pre-dated by a long line of thinking adminis-trators. Two books in particular, *The History of Management Thought* by C. S. George and *The Evolution of Management Thought* by Daniel Wren, have attempted to trace back the origins of management ideas and principles. The first of these, long out of print and difficult to find, contains a lengthy family tree – a kind of management thinkers' pedigree up to 1968, when the book was published. It awards the first honours to the Sumerians, who developed record-keeping about 5000 years BC. The Egyptians followed, introducing concepts of planning and organisation controls.

Among the Greeks and Romans, Mencius provided the first known advice on systems and standards, and Cato, who was given the job of organising the provincial administration of Spain for Rome, wrote job descriptions to ensure that people understood exactly what was expected of them in managerial or administrative roles. Of course Socrates had his bit to add. He discussed job specialisation, saying that 'every work is better done, which receives the sole and not the divided attention of the worker' and raised the issue of whether to organise departments around the work they did or the people they dealt with. Many companies today are still asking the same question and are no nearer finding an acceptable answer.

The concept of competitiveness is also one which has occupied human minds for centuries, usually in a warfaring sense, though only now is it being examined as a separate entity in the business world. From China in the fourth century BC, came Sun Tzu, a general who argued: 'The supreme act of war is to subdue the enemy without fighting.' Four hundred years previously, Hesiod observed: 'Potter is potter's enemy, and craftsman is craftsman's rival; tramp is jealous of tramp, and singer of singer.'

In the Middle Ages, discussion of the concepts we now lump together under the general heading of business management began to develop along two main branches. The first was the emergence of more efficient forms of bookkeeping and accounting, largely among the Italian merchants. Luca Pacioli, a Franciscan friar from Venice, is credited with introducing double-entry bookkeeping in the fifteenth century. Francisco di Marco developed the basics of cost accounting and the Soranzo brothers spread the idea of journal entries and ledgers.

The second branch was at the statesman level. While Machiavelli was writing *The Prince* in Italy, in England Sir Thomas More (1478–1535) was questioning why enterprises so often failed to operate efficiently and concluding that poor management was the cause. Among his solutions, like Socrates, was greater specialisation of task.

This was a theme picked up 250 years later by Adam Smith (1723–90), whose concepts of how to control organisations of manual workers were absorbed in turn by Eli Whitney a mere thirty years after. Smith, a close friend of the inventor James Watt, was a professor at Glasgow University. Better known for his economic theories (he was a staunch proponent of free trade and market forces, arguing that although businessmen, for whom he had little regard, were usually acting out of self-interest, 'an invisible hand' ensures that their efforts *en masse* result in the creation of greater wealth for society as a whole), he also speculated on the best way to manage an enterprise.

Smith, though regarded by many as the champion of capitalistic enterprise, had little faith in managers. He argued against joint-stock companies: 'The directors of such companies, being the managers rather of other people's money than of their own, it cannot well be expected that they should watch over it with the same anxious vigilance with which the partners in a private co-partnery frequently watch over their own,' wrote Smith. 'Negligence and profusion . . . must always prevail more or less, in the management of the affairs of such a company. . . . The only trades which it seems possible for a joint stock company to carry on successfully, without an exclusive privilege, are those, of which all the operations are capable of being reduced to what is called a routine, or to such a uniformity of method as admits of little or no variation.' In one passage, therefore, Smith criticised what is now the conventional form of industrial ownership and laid the foundations of what was to be called 'scientific management'.

In the United States Eli Whitney (1765–1825) pioneered the practical implementation of mass production in the late 1790s. Whitney and his partner, Simeon North, a Connecticut clockmaker, were inspired by the example of Oliver Evans of Philadelphia who had experimented with techniques of mass production at his cotton mills. Whitney and North applied these techniques to the manufacture of guns and developed the concept of interchangeable parts.

Whitney, a trained lawyer, had gained fame earlier by inventing the cotton gin, a machine for removing cotton fibres from the seeds on which they grow. Arguments over the patent of his invention forced him to look elsewhere for income. He secured a contract to supply 10,000 guns to the government in 1798. Though it took him eight years to fulfil a two-year contract, it was renewed in 1812.

Whitney taught employees to make identical parts from metal moulds, known as 'gigs'. As a result, guns could be assembled far more quickly than before. Legend has it that Whitney once threw a number of unassembled rifles at a government official and challenged him to create a usable gun.

Not only did Whitney innovate in manufacturing methods, he also experimented with different spans of control, to see how many people a supervisor could manage effectively. The concept of work analysis in the cause of improving efficiency can be largely traced to him.

At the same time in England, James Watt (1769–1848) and Matthew Robinson Boulton (1770–1842) were developing new management techniques to take full advantage of the pioneering work of their more acclaimed fathers. A historian of the duo's Soho Foundry observed: 'Combining a thorough education in the gentlemanly pursuits of the time with an early training as practical engineers in all stages of production, they brought to the task of organisation an entirely new outlook.'

They planned materials and components requirements and production flows, drew up detailed specifications for internal and external use and developed standard operating procedures, to ensure manual staff produced work of consistent quality. Their control techniques included keeping twenty-two accounting books so the exact profit on each machine produced could be calculated. They also used incentive payments and originated what may well have been the first executive development programme.

In the same era in France, the economist Jean Baptiste Say (1767–1832) began to look at entrepreneurship. He concluded that the innovator/manager brought to an enterprise an extra dimension. The key ingredients in a successful enterprise were now labour, capital and *management*. For the first time management was seen as a valuable discipline in its own right.

Before the Industrial Revolution, there had been little need to employ someone specifically as a manager, except in the case of running far-flung estates, where there was an established pattern for absentee landlords to appoint a minder to look after their interests. (In practice, this was more akin to the current practice of appointing an estate agent to let out property while the owners are abroad.) Although the ancient guilds had largely died out or lost influence, the organisation of work was still largely craft based. Take the building of a cathedral. The clerk of the works (the equivalent of today's architect) designed the building and hired a master mason, who carried out the work by hiring his own team of craftsmen and labourers. The master mason saw his role as a craftsman, rather than as a manager. In a more domestic role, the degrees of pecking order within a grand household were based upon seniority and status. The head housemaid carried out many of the functions of a manager, but she also carried out work of much the same sort as the more junior servants. There were exceptions to the rule. The captain of the ship might well be an employee, rather than an owner and, in either case, he would normally be trained in elementary bookkeeping and record-keeping. However, like the head housemaid he would not have seen himself as a manager.

The nineteenth-century trading companies bred traders and then, as they established plantations, administrators. The model they used was the British Civil Service – then the greatest bureaucracy the world had known since the Roman Empire. Bureaucracy was in many ways an anti-management system. By creating rules and regulations for everything (itself an approach learned from the Army) it created a machine that could substitute for genuine management.

In *Representative Government* (1861) John Stuart Mill (1806–73) argued the case for sound management of the nation's affairs in India:

> It cannot be too often repeated, that in a country like India everything depends on the personal qualities and capacities of the agents of government. This truth is the cardinal principle of Indian administration. The day when it comes to be thought that the appointment of persons to situations of trust from motives of convenience, already so criminal in England, can be practised with impunity in India, will be the beginning of the decline and fall of our empire there. Even with a sincere intention of preferring the best candidate, it will not do to rely on chance for supplying fit persons. The system must be calculated to form them.

But the system continued to churn out administrators even when the Empire was long gone. Even now the term administration clings on. The relevant postgraduate degree for a manager is not Master of Management, but Master of Business Administration.

The principles of man management, as we know them, began to emerge in the eighteenth and nineteenth centuries, more as a result of the concern felt by philanthropic entrepreneurs than as any rational attempt to define the psychology of motivation. One of the earliest writers on the subject was Daniel Defoe (1661–1731), whose moral strictures were based firmly on the work ethic and on the principle that a firm but fair and kindly hand is the best way to obtain good work from the work-force. In Defoe's *Robinson Crusoe*, Man Friday is immediately adopted into the role of a labourer. The only difference between the black slaves and white bond-workers was that the bond-workers would eventually earn their freedom.

Robert Owen (1771–1858) put some of these developing ideas of effective management into practice at his New Lanark mills in Scotland. The idealistic Owen stood apart from his contemporaries in recognising the importance of personnel management in business. His approach countered the accepted beliefs and ideology of the employing class. When Owen first visited New Lanark in 1797 he commented: 'Of all the places I have seen, I should prefer this in which to try an experiment I have long contemplated.' At the time New Lanark was the largest cotton-spinning factory in Britain. When Owen took over the management of the mills, he found 'a very wretched society' where 'vice and immorality prevailed to a monstrous extent'. He set about dealing with the problems. His philosophy was simple: 'Man's character is made for and not by him.' He believed in the malleability of human character, especially when young, and the infinite power of society to form character.

At New Lanark, working hours were reduced and pay increased. Beating children was banned, the factory no longer brought in pauper children and raised the minimum age for employment to ten. Conditions in the factory improved, and productivity increased. Owen then began improving the community. Houses were enlarged, the streets cleaned, good food supplied and a school built.

To monitor performance, Owen awarded four types of mark for the day's work to each superintendent; they, in turn, judged all his workers. The mark was translated into the colours black, blue, yellow and white, in ascending order of merit, painted on the four sides of a piece of wood mounted over the machine and turned outward according to the worker's performance. These daily marks were entered in a book as a permanent record, to be periodically inspected by Owen. He achieved an 'orderly arrangement' of the works. Managers were carefully selected and trained so they could be relied on during his absence. Addressing the superintendents of his factories, Owen wrote: 'Many of you have long experiences in your manufacturing operations of the advantages of substantial, well-contrived and well-executed machinery. If, then, due care as to the state of your inanimate machines can produce such beneficial results, what may not be expected if you devote equal attention to your vital machines, which are far more wonderfully constructed?'

Owen's theories and practice were not emulated and, faced with opposition from his Quaker partners, he was eventually forced to abandon his experiment in 1825. He went on to attempt a comparable project at New Harmony, Indiana, in the United States, which was similarly unsuccessful. Even so, in their *The Making of Scientific Management* (1946), Lyndall Urwick and co-author E. F. L. Brech described Owen as 'the pioneer of personnel management' and wrote, 'Generations ahead of his time, he preached and practised a conception of industrial relations which is, even now, accepted in only a few of the most progressive undertakings.' Owen, they said, had an 'intuitive grasp of the principles of sound management and of the methods of applying them effectively'.

In many ways Owen's thinking and approach anticipated those of Taylor and Gilbreth nearly a hundred years later. Said Owen: 'I looked very wisely at the men in their different departments, although I really knew nothing. By intensely observing everything, I maintained order and regularity throughout the establishment, which proceeded under such circumstances much better than I had anticipated.'

In Britain, Owen's ideas were taken up by a number of enlightened Victorian entrepreneurs, of whom a high proportion were Quakers or members of other Nonconformist churches (even though Owen's own innovations had met Quaker resistance in New Lanark). Titus Salt (1803–76) took his textile mill employees out of polluted Bradford into the model community that still bears his name – Saltaire. He believed, like Owen, that placing employees in a better environment would improve punctuality, sobriety and their willingness to improve themselves. Saltaire, opened in 1853, was a massive undertaking – with three miles of machinery it was the largest mill in Europe. Salt's model village had 850 houses and an array of amenities from an institute with reading room to a rifle drill room. As Salt was a teetotaller the only thing lacking was a pub. On his death, 40,000 people attended the funeral.

Similarly George Palmer (1809–1906), co-founder of Huntley and Palmer biscuits, pioneered job security, employee self-development centres and sick pay (the sick fund was started from fines imposed on employees who broke the company's strict code of conduct). He also developed modern sales management approaches, being largely responsible for organising commercial travellers within clearly specified regions, and pioneered the concept of decorative packaging for consumer goods.

The Industrial Revolution produced managerial challenges which would previously have been unthinkable. Assessing the growth of management between 1800 and 1850 Urwick and Brech observed:

> In the first fifty years after the turn of the century, complexity of administration in the iron and steel and engineering industries must have increased enormously with every decade. The growth in canal and road transport, the expansion of markets for steam engines abroad, the coming of the railways and the rapid expansion of the network of railways systems throughout the country – all these meant a call upon the resources of these industries that inevitably gave rise to a whole series of new management situations. They created an imperative need for a technique of control that would enable manufacturers to keep track of their resources and to direct their production towards the achievement of pre-determined plans, however unsystematically evolved.

It was the engineering-oriented entrepreneurs who began to combine concepts of man management and work organisation. A remarkable number emigrated from Scotland or Ireland to the

United States, among them James Montgomery (1771–1854), who had demonstrated in Glasgow cotton mills that close attention to organising work between machines could improve both quality and productivity. He went to America to work for York Mills at Saco, Maine, and continued to expound his theories of management, which focused on achieving cost containment and problem prevention through the quality of supervision. Among his noted comments was that a supervisor must be 'just and impartial – firm and incisive – always on the alert to prevent rather than check faults after they have taken place'.

Many of these entrepreneurs forged a connection of one sort or another with the rapidly expanding railway system in the New World. Douglas Craig McCallum (1815–78) was a Scot who gave up a successful career as an architect to join the railroads. His attempts in the early 1850s to instil basic principles of effective supervision foundered on the intransigence of the labourers, who went on strike. His principles were:

1. A proper division of responsibilities
2. Sufficient power conferred to enable the same to be fully carried out, that such responsibilities may be real in their character
3. The means of knowing whether such responsibilities are faithfully executed
4. Great promptness in the report of all dereliction of duty, that evils may be at once corrected
5. Such information to be obtained through a series of daily reports and checks that will not embarrass principal officers, nor lessen their influence with their subordinates
6. The adoption of a system, as a whole, which will not only enable the General Superintendent to detect errors immediately, but will also point out the delinquent.

If the workers had heard of Big Brother, they would have undoubtedly have made the comparison. However, tactless as the language of McCallum's principles proved to be, the concept of transparency of performance and rapid correction of problems was gradually to become a fundamental part of factory management. Moreover, in his diligence to ensure that everyone knew what was expected of him, McCallum presented us with the business bureaucrat's favourite toy – the organisation chart.

McCallum quit after an extended strike by railworkers who objected to his principles. He ended up a major general, keeping Sherman supplied during the US Civil War. However, Henry Varnum Poor (1812–1905), the editor of the *American Railroad Journal*, recognised what McCallum was trying to do and built upon his experiences to foreshadow modern theories of leadership. Top management must become 'the soul of the enterprise', he declared, or, as we might now express it, must provide the guiding vision of the company. From their vantage point, managers must direct the course of events within each function so that every department works towards the same vision or purpose. Their role is one of organisation, systems management and conflict resolution.

Harrington Emerson (1853–1931) was the son of a Presbyterian minister. Educated in Bavaria, he emigrated to America and ended up working as an engineer on the Santa Fe railroads. An admirer of the Prussian army, he set about organising the railroad in a similar way, dividing management responsibilities and jobs into line and staff. He argued that the American railroads could save $1 million a day if they all organised themselves like this.

Until the growth of the railroads in the United States, the traditional forms of business organisation remained dominant with management as the responsibility of owners or their families. But by the 1890s, the railways were the largest industrial business in the world and they had outgrown conventional management techniques and attitudes. The railroad companies had to recruit large numbers of skilled and experienced managers and people were selected on their managerial ability rather than wealth or family connections. Management became a separate entity from ownership, a recognisable and attainable skill.

By the early twentieth century there were business schools at Philadelphia (Wharton) and Dartmouth (Amos Tuck) in the United States. Some European countries also had academic institutions with similar objectives. Ambitious tomes began to appear in most developed countries, full of advice on conducting business but still rather short on theory. Significantly, Britain, the birthplace of the Industrial Revolution, did not begin to teach management as a subject until 1918, when the University of Manchester College of Technology established a department of industrial administration. It was nearly fifty years later in 1965 that Britain established its first business schools at London and Manchester.

Bemoaning the inadequacies of management education has filled a large number of reports and books, particularly in Britain. Many of the same themes occur in Urwick's 'Education for Management' report in 1947 and in the Handy and Constable reports in 1987. Reg Revans, a vocal critic of management education standards and methods, did not mince his words in his 1976 book *The Theory of Practice in Management*: 'There is a virtual lack in Britain (perhaps in the world) of any serious literature of what might be called the ideology of management education as such. Our understanding of what we need to do to train managers falls far short of our technical mastery of the training of circus animals, or even of how to programme a digital computer not merely to solve problems, but to learn how to solve problems.'

Part, though by no means all, of the problem has been the all-encapsulating nature of management. This is underlined when you consider the people included in this book. Their specialisms and knowledge are dauntingly wide-ranging. The term 'management' is constantly evolving, as is the idea of what a manager actually does. As management thinking has developed, many more skills and specialisms have been absorbed into the subject from statistics to psychology. Its far-reaching nature has successfully defeated rigid definition.

Among those who had particular impact on the new management studies at the turn of the century were the husband and wife team of Frank and Lilian Gilbreth (see page 34). They systematised the idea of time and motion studies (first pioneered by Charles Babbage in the early 1830s) to improve the efficiency of individual jobs. Another active thinker was Vilfredo Pareto (1848–1923), an Italian economist and sociologist, who settled at the University of Lausanne. Pareto tried to examine how societies function. One of his prime conclusions was that a society is a system of forces which will normally be held in equilibrium. Society breaks down when the equilibrium is destroyed. The concept was explored after his death in the famous Hawthorne experiments (see page 43) and the Tavistock Institute's experiments among British coal-miners in the 1940s and 1950s. An enthusiast for mathematical puzzles, Pareto is probably better known among managers for the Pareto principle – that 20 per cent of items a company manufactures account for 80 per cent of the value.

However, the two giants of this period were undoubtedly Henri Fayol (1841–1925) and Frederick Winslow Taylor (1856–1917), both of whom are the subjects of longer biographies at the end of this section (pages 21–4 and 24–30). Fayol was the first person to define a general theory that attempted to tie together, in a rational way, the elements of management (what managers do) and the principles of management (how to manage effectively). While many of his conclusions would now be disputed, the approach has formed the basis for most attempts to provide a rational explanation for management behaviour.

Frederick Winslow Taylor, an American, has a gravestone in Germantown, Pennsylvania, which bears the inscription 'The Father of Scientific Management'. Whereas Robert Owen had worked in something of a vacuum, gallantly attempting to convince people of his system's merits, Taylor generated a movement which had far-reaching effects. Scientific management involved the systematic observation and assessment of both how people work and how managers control and use them. Taylor claimed that 'Scientific management involves a complete mental revolution on the part of the working man engaged in any industry, and it involves an equally complete revolution on the part of those on the management's side.' Unlike Owen Taylor sought to dehumanise work: 'One of the very first requirements for a man who is fit to handle pig iron as a regular occupation is that he shall be so stupid and so phlegmatic that he more nearly resembles an ox than any other type.'

The revolution Taylor envisaged was in fact largely anticipated by the work of Charles Babbage (1792–1871) in Britain fifty years before. Babbage studied factories in Britain and Europe, recording his conclusions in *On the Economy of Machinery and Manufactures* (1832) – perhaps the first management best-seller, selling over ten thousand copies. Babbage's similarity in outlook to Taylor is evident in his comment, 'It is of great importance to know the precise expenses of every process

as well as of the wear and tear of machinery which is due to it.'
However, Taylor did not read Babbage's work.

The development of scientific management was keenly followed throughout the world. Taylor's disciples included the Michelin brothers, Henry-Louis Le Chatelier, who helped introduce the ideas into France, and a host of others. In Japan, Taylor's book *Principles and Methods of Scientific Management* was translated under the title *Secrets for Eliminating Futile Work and Increasing Production*. In the next ten years a million copies of *Secrets* were sold.

The managerial implications of Taylorism were discussed by Rosabeth Moss Kanter in her best-selling book *The Change Masters* (1983). Kanter's words echo those of Robert Owen when he called on his supervisors to look after their people as well as their machines. Kanter writes: 'In turn-of-the-century organizational theory and its "scientific management" legacy, individuals constituted not assets but sources of error. The ideal organization was designed to free itself from human error or human intervention, running automatically to turn out predictable products and predictable profits. Management was there to handle the few unexpected events that could occur.'

In a similar vein, as the effects of scientific management were beginning to be felt, political scientist Mary Parker Follett (1868–1933) warned: 'We should remember that we can never wholly separate the human from the mechanical side. The study of human relations in business and the study of the technique of operating are bound up together.'

While Taylorism raised controversy, with managers complaining about tight controls and workers about exploitation, concern switched in the next twenty years away from the complexities of the task of work to human relations. The psychological and social needs of employees were back on the agenda, really for the first time since Owen.

Between and during the two world wars, the most influential management thinkers were Chester Barnard (1886–1961), Max Weber (1864–1920), Elton Mayo (1880–1949), Mary Parker Follett and Lyndall Urwick (1891–1983). The latter three have chapters of their own later on in this book, but Barnard and Weber demand special mention.

Chester Barnard was a disciple of Pareto, Weber and Kurt

Lewin. Born on a farm in Malden, Massachusetts, he won an economics scholarship to Harvard, but left before completing his degree, to join the statistical department of American Telephone and Telegraph. Barnard was one of the few major management thinkers of the twentieth century to hold a senior line management position, eventually becoming president of the New Jersey Bell company. Active in numerous good causes, he saw business organisations as the most effective means of achieving widespread social advancement. The lessons of history, he explained in the series of lectures that were eventually published under the title *The Functions of the Executive* (1938), showed that both the state and the Church had failed to steer beneficial social change because they were concerned primarily with authority rather than co-operation.

Lyndall Urwick said of *The Functions of the Executive*: 'It is doubtful if any other book since Taylor's *Scientific Management* has had a deeper influence on the thinking of serious business leaders about the nature of their work.'

As part of his belief in the broader implications of organisation, Barnard argued that corporations required involvement from executives, employees, investors, suppliers and customers. 'I rejected the concept of organization as compromising a rather definite group of people whose behavior is coordinated with reference to some explicit goal or goals,' said Barnard. 'In a community all acts of individuals and of organizations are directly or indirectly interconnected and interdependent.'

Barnard's theory of organisation starts with the assumption that people have individual motivations. When they agree to co-operate with other people for common goals, they become an organisation. Implicit in the notion of co-operation is communication between them. Willingness to co-operate is not an absolute – it will vary from person to person and with time, as people's attitudes, moods and circumstances change. The organisation has to stimulate willingness through incentives such as pay and working conditions, and by stimulating positive attitudes (that is, by motivating them). The common goals, which Barnard calls *purpose*, will frequently differ from the goals of the individual members. What is important is that people accept that helping the organisation achieve its goals will help them achieve theirs.

The third element, communications, is what ties people and organisations together. Barnard enunciated three basic principles of communications, which can be expressed simply as:

- Make sure everyone knows what the channels of communication are
- Make sure there is a formal channel of communication to tie in every member
- Make the line of communication as direct or short as possible.

These principles, which Barnard energetically applied to New Jersey Bell, applied to all sizes of organisation, he claimed. Large organisations were simply made up of lots of small organisations; these, too, had their own goals but needed to co-operate and communicate with the larger organisation in order to survive. Small groups could operate informally, but as they grew they had to establish formal systems to make goals explicit and to ensure that everyone understood and endorsed them as valid. To Barnard, all organisations were systems which were subordinate to larger systems, such as society. 'At root, the cause of the instability and limited duration of formal organizations lies in the forces outside. These forces both furnish the materials which are used by organizations and limit their action.'

Within this definition of organisations, Barnard believed the functions that managers should perform became explicit. The three most critical functions were:

- To establish and manage the communications systems
- To motivate individuals to exert themselves in support of the organisation's purpose
- To formulate the organisation's purpose in a communicable way.

Barnard also contributed to the debate on the nature of managerial authority. Whereas Follett and others had tried to define authority in terms of position and role, Barnard maintained that authority only existed if people could accept it. There were, he explained, both objective and subjective types of authority. Objective authority came from the individual's willingness to respect either the boss himself or his position. Subjective authority depended on how people interpreted an order. They would only comply if they:

- understood it
- saw it as consistent with the goals of the organisation at that time
- saw it as consistent with their own goals at that time
- had the mental and physical capability to do so.

Barnard's other valuable contribution to management thinking was to highlight the difference between effectiveness and efficiency. Although he used the terms in a specialised manner, the distinction has proven to be one of the most useful insights into whether the effort and goals of an individual department or employee are aligned or misaligned with those of the organisation as a whole.

Sadly, Barnard's work remains neglected. Perhaps this is explained by his claim that *The Functions of the Executive* took five to ten readings to understand. For Barnard there were no simple answers: 'However desirable clarity and simplicity of statement, it is not desirable to underestimate either the difficulties of observation and experiment or those of constructing hypotheses that may prove helpful,' he wrote. Such was Barnard's intellect that a Harvard professor said he had 'a power of analysis and synthesis so sweeping that I class his gift with that of St Thomas and da Vinci'. *Fortune* magazine was similarly enthusiastic, claiming in 1948 that Barnard 'possibly' has 'the most capacious intellect of any business executive in the US'. A portrait of the time described him in more standardised terms as 'a tall, well-built man who looks the part of the capable business executive'.

It was at the 'capable business executive' that Barnard's work was aimed and his ideas remain relevant today. A reviewer in *New Management* magazine (vol. 2, no. 3 (1985), p. 60), for example, wrote: 'Barnard's theories – based as they were on both intellect and experience – seem as valid in 1984 as they did in 1938. . . . It is easy to forget that Barnard was writing in the 1930s. Such ideas as the importance of the informal organisation, the limitations of superior authority and financial rewards, the systematic nature of an organisation, the need for clear communication of purpose, and the need to go beyond purely rational processes would make a national best-seller in the 1980s.'

The German social scientist Max Weber took a different tack as a professor of law at the University of Freiburg and the University of Heidelberg. His main concern was with the nature of bureaucracies, which he saw as the most significant form of organisation, and with the impact of the Protestant work ethic on society. However, Weber's most significant publication was *The Theory of Social and Economic Organization* (1947). One of the first people to try to define different *types* of organisation, he distinguishes between them on the basis of how they use authority (where people behave in the required manner voluntarily) and power (where people are forced to do what they are told). This emphasis on behaviour was very different from previous attempts at categorisation, which relied on describing different types of hierarchy – in other words, they looked at formal organisation structure, rather than what actually happened inside the organisation.

Observation of power behaviours and authority behaviours by managers led Weber to depict three types of organisation. These are not mutually exclusive – you might find all three in various parts of the same organisation, depending on the style of the individual managers, but, argued Weber, they depict how managers get things done. To some extent these three types represent the stages of development of any enterprise. In the early years it may be led by a charismatic leader, someone whose ideas and enthusiasm inspire his colleagues. Other people in a *charismatic* organisation accept the leader's vision and rules, often without question. Religious movements are perhaps the purest form of this kind of organisation.

Then the founder dies, retires or simply loses his touch. A number of options then present themselves. Unless another leader of similar stature is waiting in the wings, the organisation will either disintegrate with in-fighting or lapse by default into one of the other types.

In the second form of organisation, the competing interests have achieved a measure of stability, as predicted by Pareto. *Traditional organisations* emphasise precedent and custom. Rules are established more as a form of ritual, than as a rational response to external change. In *rational-legal* organisations, the bureaucracy comes into its own. In these organisations, every function and job is designed to fulfil a specific purpose. Legality – and hence authority – comes from the rules, which are documented in detail and provide the touchstone for decisions. The military, with its multitudinous regulations, is an arch example of this. Rationality comes from the ordered nature of the hierarchy, where everyone knows his place and his role.

Although we now use the term bureaucracy to mean codified inefficiency, to Weber, bureaucracy was exactly the opposite – the nearest to machine-like efficiency that a human organisation could come. The elements of the purest form of bureaucracy, as described by Weber, remain strikingly familiar, even today: specialised tasks; formal rules and procedures; hierarchy; advancement through merit rather than indiscriminate personal choice; standard rewards and punishments; job security as a reward for commitment to the company; and work and leisure clearly separated.

While Weber expected the impersonal bureaucracy eventually to become the most common type of organisation, he was acutely conscious of the social impact that might have. He wrote at one stage: 'It is horrible to think that the world could one day be filled with nothing but those little cogs, little men clinging to little jobs and striving towards bigger ones. . . . This passion for bureaucracy . . . is enough to drive me to despair.'

The Second World War provided a watershed for management thinking. Until the late 1940s, the investigators of employee and managerial behaviour, of how organisations function and how they achieve complex goals had largely been isolated voices. To the practising businessman, the mixed bag of sociologists and philosophers, who had produced so many intellectually interesting theories, was largely irrelevant to the practical job of running a business. The engineers who were attempting to systematise shop floor operations and behaviour received a kinder audience, but it was relatively easy for managers to reassure themselves that none of this affected the way they did *their* jobs.

In the opening chapter of his book *Managing* (1984), former ITT chief executive Harold Geneen warns: 'You cannot run a business, or anything else, on a theory.' From his experience he writes: 'I have never come across a chief executive who tried, much less succeeded, running his company according to any set formula, chart or business theory.' Management is often intuitive and highly individualised. The section on Henry Ford I (page 30) gives a perfect example of how successful, and vulnerable, intuitive management can be. The perennial question remains – can good management practices be learned?

Many seem to think so. A healthy ration of new ideas, or repackaged old ideas, is produced every year. Ralph Kilmann of the University of Pittsburgh, and author of the aptly titled *Beyond the Quick Fix* (1984), observes: 'Every few years, a new approach is offered for unleashing the full potential of organized efforts. But this is like the search for the Holy Grail: each new approach looks for the one single answer.' Yet the search for answers has meant that a good deal of managerial complacency has been shaken since 1945. Management studies began to attract a surge of brilliant minds, whose assault on fundamental issues gradually raised the credibility of the subject both in academia and in business itself. The areas they chose to study – in particular, strategic planning – were at the heart of what managers considered to be their jobs.

Peter Drucker has identified seven conceptual foundations to the post-war management boom:

(1) scientific management of work as the key to productivity;
(2) decentralization as a basic principle of organization;
(3) personnel management as the orderly way of fitting people into organization structures (which included such things as job descriptions, appraisals, wage and salary administration, but also human relations); (4) manager development to provide today for the management needs of tomorrow; (5) managerial accounting, that is, the use of analysis and information as the foundation for managerial decision making; (6) marketing; (7) finally, there was long-range planning.

The plethora of trends and new ideas since 1945 demonstrates that management thinking has in itself become big business. Consultancies proliferate and the management book market is booming. In the United States sales can be in millions, while in the United Kingdom several management books have exceeded sales of 100,000 in the past five years. Most of these books are now aimed at a far wider and less specialised audience. With managers such as John Harvey Jones and Lee Iacocca taking a higher profile, individual management styles are far more accessible than ever before. Management is increasingly recognised for what it is: a fundamental and indispensable human activity.

Henri Fayol

Born France, 1841
Died 1925
Manager

In his book *Corporate Strategy*, Igor Ansoff wrote: 'A talented and prophetic Frenchman, Henri Fayol, anticipated imaginatively and soundly most of the more recent analyses of modern business practice.'

Henri Fayol's inspiration for his theories on management came in the unlikely setting of the French mining industry. At the age of seventeen Fayol went to the School of Mines at St Étienne, and at nineteen he took his first job as an engineer at the French mining company Commentry-Fourchamboult-Decazeville (commonly called Comamboult). He was to spend the rest of his career with the company, rising through the ranks to become managing director in 1888, a post he held until 1918.

When Fayol took charge of the company it 'was declining and on the road to bankruptcy', as he later recalled. From 1885 until 1888 it had paid no dividends. Putting his theories into practice Fayol turned the company round. Lyndall Urwick wrote: 'From the day he took charge the tide turned. . . . When Fayol retired Comamboult's financial situation was unassailable and its staff of exceptional quality.' Comamboult later became part of Le Creusot Loire, one of France's largest metallurgical groups.

The turn-round was achieved despite increased competition and Fayol's lack of metallurgical knowledge. His success was based on what became known as the 'functional principle'. In practice, Fayol said this involved:

A programme of action prepared by means of annual and ten-year forecasts.

An organisation chart to guarantee order and assure each man a definite place; careful recruiting and technical, intellectual, moral, administrative training of the personnel in all ranks in order to find the right man for each place.

Observation of the necessary principles in the execution of command (i.e. direction).

Meetings of the departmental heads of every division; conferences of the division heads presided over by the managing director to insure coordination.

Universal control, based on clear accounting data rapidly made available.

In developing the functional principle, Fayol created the first rational approach to the organisation of enterprise. What distinguished Fayol from the likes of Taylor and, later, Mayo, was his interest in management and top management in particular. Though both Taylor and Fayol accepted the idea of the division of work they differed on where the changes should start. Fayol started at the top; Taylor at the bottom.

Fayol's seminal publication *Administration Industrielle et Générale* came in 1916, late in his life, and it was only in 1949 that the English version was published. It was preceded by a number of technical articles on mining engineering and administration. In his preface Fayol wrote: 'Management plays a very important part in the government of undertakings; of all undertakings, large or small, industrial, commercial, political, religious or any other.'

As a champion of management, Fayol argued that management theory should be taught at schools in the same way as other subjects. Later in his life, Fayol lectured at the École Supérieure de la Guerre.

The main task of the organisational head, Fayol reasoned, was 'prevoyance' – forecasting and planning: 'Thinking out a plan and ensuring its success is one of the keenest satisfactions for an intelligent man to experience.'

Administration, Fayol argued, was an important factor, but there were many more in management:

The administrative ability of the personnel is one of the elements in the prosperity of the enterprise, but there are so many others that vary simultaneously that it would be a gross error to conclude that success is always a sign of good administration. The contrary is often seen: prodigies of administration may be accomplished in the liquidation of some unhappy business; the constituents of prosperity are so numerous and so diverse that it is generally difficult to disentangle the effects of administrative action therefrom.

During his lengthy career, Fayol developed fourteen basic principles of management, which every organisation needed to address. These were: division of work, authority, discipline, unity of command, unity of direction, subordination of individual interest to the common interest, remuneration, centralisation, the chain of authority, order, equity, stability of tenure of employees, initiative and morale. But he made it clear that there could be many more rules and management had to be flexible. 'There is nothing . . . absolute in management affairs. Seldom do we have to apply the same principle twice in identical conditions; allowance must be made for different changing circumstances.'

The application of Fayol's theories in today's business world is inevitably limited yet some of his theories are still widely used. It is commonplace to have, for example, 'unity of direction' (one head and one plan for each business activity) and 'unity of command' (each person only having one boss) as is the idea that responsibility should be equivalent to authority. However, Peter Drucker illustrated the defects in Fayol's theories in *Management*:

Functionalism works very well in the kind of business for which it was designed. The model for Henri Fayol's functional design early in this century was the coal-mining company he ran. It was a fairly large business at that time but would have been considered rather small today. Except for a few engineers, it employed only manual workers who all did one kind of work. A coal mine has only one product, and it varies only in size. Coal requires no treatment beyond simple washing and sorting. Coal had, at least at that time, only a few markets – steel mills, railroads and steamships, power plants, and homeowners. But in these markets it had practically a monopoly, and while the machinery and tools for mining coal were changing rapidly in Fayol's day, the process itself did not change at all. There was not much scope for innovation.

Fayol's company is the kind of business that the functional design principle organizes well. Anything more complex, more dynamic, or more innovative demands performance capacities that the functional principle does not possess. If used beyond the limits of Fayol's model, functional structure rapidly becomes costly in terms of time and effort. It also runs a high risk of directing the energies of the organization away from performance and towards mere busyness. In businesses that exceed Fayol's model, in size, in complexity, or in innovative scope, functional design should be used only as one principle and never as the principle. And even in businesses that fit Fayol's model, top-management design and structure require a different design principle.

Fayol's theories were most notably put into practice by Alfred Sloan at General Motors.

Frederick Winslow Taylor

Born Germantown, Pennsylvania, 1856
Died 1917
Engineer and consultant

In *Shop Management*, Frederick Taylor wrote that 'Good manners, education and even special training and skill count for less in an executive position than the grit, determination and bulldog endurance that knows no defeat.' Taylorism, the movement he gave his name to, was perhaps the first true management movement. Among prominent industrialists its enthusiastic supporters included the Michelin brothers, and even Lenin observed in *Pravda*: 'We should try out every scientific and progressive suggestion of the Taylor system.'

Frederick Winslow Taylor was born into an affluent Philadelphia family and was distinguished early on in life by his interest in mechanics and engineering. He identified problems and attempted to create machines to solve them, developing apparatus to allow him to sleep properly and even examining the science of playing croquet. Later in life, Taylor developed an interest in tennis; he won the US doubles championship in 1881 and along the way invented an improved tennis net and a racket shaped like a spoon. Over a hundred patents were eventually taken out by him for his various inventions.

By 1873, Taylor was talking of becoming an engineer and in the following year joined the Enterprise Hydraulic Works in Philadelphia as an apprentice – a peculiar career move, considering his well-heeled background. Later he was to reflect that this period was an awakening 'to the reality and seriousness of life'.

In 1878, Taylor completed his apprenticeship and joined the Midvale Steel Works, which was to provide the first opportunity for him to try out his theories. At Midvale, Taylor started as a labourer before becoming a clerk, machinist and then a sub-foreman, his managerial baptism. In the 1880s, he continued to progress up the scale to become chief engineer, a position that allowed him to indulge his interest in inventions. He developed a series of implements to help in cutting metal and came to the conclusion that scientific advancement has to go hand in hand with organisational development. Taylor saw that if he could improve the way the machinery worked, he could also analyse and improve the operation and management of the machines.

Taylor set about implementing change. The jobs of foremen were redefined and a set of procedures was introduced for some of the machine jobs. Stop watches were distributed to the foremen, as Taylor attempted to divide jobs into separate elements. The examination of times taken for each job meant Taylor was able to change piece rates. He was able to prove scientifically that a machinist could produce a specific quantity of output in a given time. Taylor restructured the pay system around his calculations of what people should be able to achieve, creating a 'differential piece rate' for each job.

The machinists, as skilled workers, posed a few problems for Taylor and his attentions switched to labourers. In *Principles of Scientific Management* (1911) Taylor explained: 'What we hoped to ultimately determine was . . . how many foot-pounds of work a man could do in a day.' Getting the best from each employee required robotic obedience to Taylor's interpretation of what a job involved. Taylor believed that people worked solely for money (ironically, he probably had no financial need to work himself). Nothing else mattered except that they did their work in the most efficient, scientific way possible. In a lecture at Harvard Business School, Taylor argued: 'The most serious of the delusions and fallacies under which workmen, and particularly those in many of the unions, are suffering is that it is in their interest to limit the amount of work which a man should do in a day.'

Taylor caught the spirit of the time. In Europe similar conclusions were being drawn, and in Britain Joseph Slater Lewis's book *The Commercial Organisation of Factories* (1896) advised: 'Each manufacturing operation, or each set of operations, should, when an estimate is being prepared, be carefully dissected.' Lewis's (1852–1901) ideas ran parallel to Taylor's, even though neither knew it.

To achieve the utmost efficiency, Taylor proposed that managers should follow a five-step process:

First. Find, say, ten or fifteen different men (preferably in as many separate establishments and different parts of the country), who are especially skilful in doing the particular work to be analysed.

Second. Study the exact series of elementary operations or motions, which each of these men uses in doing the work which is being investigated, as well as the implements each man uses.

Third. Study with a stop watch the time required to make each of these elementary movements and then select the quickest way of doing each element of the work.

Fourth. Eliminate all false movements, slow movements, and useless movements.

Fifth. After doing away with all unnecessary movements, collect into one series the quickest and best movements as well as the best implements.

The rudiments of what was to become known as 'scientific management' were in place by the time Taylor left Midvale in 1889. His new venture, in which he invested $45,000 of his fortune, was with the Manufacturing Investment Company and called for a completely different approach. The stockholders wanted short-term profits and as manager Taylor had to provide them. True to his theories, he introduced differential piece rates though this time without the complex time studies he had undertaken at Midvale. The results were quick and impressive – labour costs plummeted, and the workers were paid more while producing three times as much. However, Taylor continued to face pressure from investors in the company who were critical of him. In 1893 he left, convinced, despite the disappointments he had experienced, that his ideas were marketable.

Initially, few companies came forward to use Taylor as a consultant, but the publication of *A Piece Rate System* (1895) created enough of a stir to keep Taylor at work. He recruited a former colleague to help him establish 'what constitutes a day's work' and noted 'we are almost pioneers'. His prestige spreading slowly, Taylor was brought in by the Johnson Company in Pennsylvania in 1896 to apply his theories fully. The differential piece rate system was introduced as well as new accounting procedures and systematic purchasing and supply methods. Though successful, Taylor's largest experiment with scientific management was to be hindered by lack of resources. He achieved, in some instances, drastic cost reductions, but in the depression of the 1890s the company did not have enough money to fully fund Taylor's ideas.

Taylor's next move was to an ailing ball-bearing company, where he applied his methods rigorously. 'The work of each of the forty grinders was inspected for quality every fifteen minutes at least, so that no workman could produce a bad quality of work for more than this length of time without having the attention of the foreman called to this fact,' he wrote. The inspectors themselves were kept hard at work by 'assistants' who recorded their work every hour to make sure they were progressing at the correct rate. In such companies, struggling for survival and anxious for any solution Taylor could provide, the onus of scientific management fell on the employees. The truth was that as they became more productive fewer were hired.

These first experiments in scientific management were undertaken in times of depression. When Taylor joined the Bethlehem Iron Company in Pennsylvania things were quite different. The company was a large successful military contractor handicapped by bottle-necks in its production processes. Taylor set about revitalising the company with gusto. By 1901 he had converted some of the plant into the most modern in the world.

His organisational work had been supplemented by his discovery of high-speed tool steel (the hotter the metal the more efficient it is), an invention that netted Taylor and his co-inventor $50,000.

At Bethlehem, Taylor concentrated on the work of the labourers. Few could keep up with his timed rate for doing the work. But large cost savings were made quickly nevertheless. Taylor's assistant C. H. Buckley explained: 'When he [the worker] receives his instruction card he glances at the time allowed for each operation and the total time to finish the piece. He then begins a mental calculation based on his work experience with similar work, the result of which is, "Impossible!". A very stupid observer can readily see this stamped on his countenance.' Faced with this, Taylor would confront the man with a stop-watch on the next morning after he had already spent a day trying to meet his instructions. The stop-watch revealed the operations could be completed. Goaded on by the thought of a bonus, the worker would deem his instructions reasonable and achievable.

In Taylor's system there was a strong element of dehumanising the work-force. This, Lyndall Urwick later realised, prevented Taylorism being fully implemented in Britain, where labour was better organised. It was an element which had been recognised long before by Adam Smith, who wrote: 'A man who spends his life carrying out a small number of very simple operations with perhaps the same effects has no room to develop his intelligence or to stretch his imagination so as to look for ways of overcoming difficulties which never occur. He thereby loses quite naturally the habit of using these faculties and, in general, he becomes as stupid and as ignorant as it is possible for a human being to become.' Labour organisations were vitriolic in their condemnation of Taylor's methods. One American union said: 'No tyrant or slave-driver in the ecstasy of his most delirious dream ever sought to place upon abject slaves a condition more repugnant.'

In 1901, Taylor was ousted from Bethlehem and he set his mind to spreading his ideas. As a consultant in the 1890s he was charging $35 a day plus expenses and had amassed a considerable fortune. The most successful spring to his career in the past had been the publication of *A Piece Rate System*. The emergence of *Shop Management* in 1903 was also greeted with enthusiasm (although it regurgitated some of what was in his earlier book).

Taylor's work at Midvale and Bethlehem had introduced a species of scientific management. Though his ideas were not tried in their entirety at either, much of what Taylor introduced was retained in the future. Increasingly, he became a source of information while his many disciples did the work. To put his ideas into a more accessible form, Taylor produced *The Principles of Scientific Management* (1911). In this more popular form, Taylor argued that scientific methods should replace indiscriminate means of measurement and working, people should be scientifically selected and trained, and work should be equally divided between managers and workers. The flaw in this simplistic and populist approach was that it focused the argument on the personnel issue, rather than engineering or mechanics where Taylor excelled. The book was serialised in *The American Magazine* and Taylor's popularity expanded rapidly. He later travelled to Europe, where his teachings had some effect, and lectured widely in the United States.

Assessing Taylor's contribution to management thinking, Peter Drucker writes in *Management*:

> It is fashionable today to look down on Taylor for his outdated psychology, but Taylor was the first man in history who did not take work for granted, but looked at it and studied it. His approach to work is still the basic foundation. And, although Taylor in his approach to the worker was clearly a man of the nineteenth century, he started out with social rather than engineering or profit objectives. What led Taylor to his work and provided his motivation throughout was first the desire to free the worker from the burden of heavy toil, destructive of body and soul. And then it was the hope to make it possible to give the labourer a decent livelihood through increasing the productivity of work.

Taylor's legacy still lives on to some extent. As recently as 1975, a book was written on applying Taylor's methods to increase productivity in government departments and service industry. It was also published by the Japanese, as was Taylor's original work.

With commendable simplicity, Taylor provided a short statement of management's objectives: 'The principal object of management should be to secure the maximum prosperity for the employer, coupled with the maximum prosperity of each employee.' He promised a 'mental revolution'. Though he failed to achieve all his aims, he certainly explored previously uncharted territory.

Henry Ford I

Born Michigan, 1863
Died 1947
Automobile manufacturer

The achievements of Henry Ford I are much discussed but rarely agreed on. Theodore Levitt, in his book *The Marketing Imagination*, casts aside one common assessment of Ford's work and proffers another:

> Henry Ford's singular contribution was not that he invented, or even reinvented, the assembly line. He didn't. He merely rediscovered it while witnessing the operation of Julius Rosenwald's Sears, Roebuck mail-order warehouse in Chicago, where roving clerks assembled orders by picking items off the shelves. Ford's unique insight was that the potential buyer's real problem was getting enough money to buy a car, and he set out to solve that problem by finding a way to make cars more cheaply.

In his autobiography, former Ford President Lee Iacocca provides another view of Ford's greatest achievement:

> Where the old man was truly innovative was in coming up with the $5 day in 1914. Five bucks was more than double what workers had been making, and the publicity from this announcement was overwhelming.
>
> What the public hasn't always realised was that Ford didn't make his offer to the workers out of any great generosity or compassion. It wasn't their standard of living he cared about. Henry Ford never hid his real reason for the $5 day: he wanted his workers to earn enough so that they could eventually buy their own cars. In other words, Henry Ford was creating a middle class.

Alfred P. Sloan, later to be Ford's great competitor at General Motors, wrote in *My Years with General Motors*:

> Mr Ford's assembly-line automobile production, high minimum wage, and low-priced car were revolutionary and stand among the greatest contributions to our industrial culture. His basic conception of one car in one utility model at an ever lower price was what the market, especially the farm market, mainly needed at the time.

What can be said with some certainty is Ford started with next to nothing in 1905. By 1920 he controlled the world's largest and most profitable manufacturing enterprise. The Ford Motor Company almost held a monopoly in the American automobile market and led in most of the other important automobile markets of the world. It had cash reserves of about a billion dollars.

This success was not built on enlightened management. Indeed, Henry Ford I had little to say on the subject. Managing was left, for the most part, to his assistant James Couzens while Ford concentrated his mind on cars and selling as many of them as possible. His success he put down to 'hunches'.

His most celebrated 'hunch' was the Model T, the first car to be made using production-line techniques. The Model T was a remarkable marketing feat. As Theodore Levitt points out in *Innovation in Marketing* (1962):

> We habitually celebrate [Ford] for the wrong reason, his production genius. His real genius was marketing. We think he was able to cut his selling price and therefore sell millions of $500 cars because his invention of the assembly line had reduced the costs. Actually he invented the assembly line because he had concluded that at $500 he could sell millions of cars. Mass production was the result, not the cause of his low prices.

Ford's initial interest had been with fast cars. A successful racer himself, he was described as being in the 'front rank of American chauffeurs'. Later he developed the 999, a large red car characterised, rather worryingly, by flames coming out of its engine. Ford did not want to risk his life driving the 999 and hired a bicycle racing champion to do so for him, with considerable success. In 1904 Ford drove the car himself and set a new mile record on the ice of Lake St Clair.

The Ford company began by following the trend for fast and luxurious cars. During the first five years it had eight models, each with a different letter of the alphabet. In the 1905–6 season it made a concerted effort in the luxury market with the cheapest Ford selling at $1,000, the most expensive at $2,000. Profits fell by two-thirds. Ford responded by lowering prices and sales boomed.

Ford's dream, however, was to create a 'universal car'. He had little time for the experiment in luxury cars and is reported to have commented: 'I've got no use for a motor that has more spark plugs than a cow has teats.' He envisaged a car that could be used by farmers to go to market and, on returning, to saw wood, pump water and run machinery. He anticipated this 'universal car' would be made as much alike as 'pins or matches'.

Mass production, Ford rightly perceived, was the key to achieving uniform products. He believed in providing the market with what it wanted – an affordable practical car. The Model T, designed by Ford and C. H. Wills was initially priced at $850, though its lowest cost was $260. Its advertisements boasted the Model T was 'The most reliable machine in the world. A two-cylinder car of ample power for the steepest hills and the muddiest roads, built to stand the severest strains. The same genius which conceived the world's record maker – the 999 – has made possible the production of a thoroughly practical car at a moderate price'.

Ford's sales manager called the Model T 'practically a farmer's car' and Ford's dream of putting it to use on the farm proved truer than he may have anticipated – a 'Ford attachment' was later sold which could be hooked up to the Model T to operate belt-driven farm machinery.

Ford's idealism was, to a large extent, eventually transformed into reality. His policy was optimistically to keep repeating what was considered impossible and then try to achieve it. When cars cost more than houses, Ford walked round his plant telling workers they'd soon be able to afford one. When it took days to make a car, Ford was talking about producing one per minute (a feat he achieved in 1920).

An insight into Ford's outlook was given in a court case. When questioned, Ford said making money was incidental to building factories, creating employment and selling cars. Asked to explain he said: 'Business is a service, not a bonanza.'

But on some occasions, supplying service meant a bonanza for Ford customers. In 1914 Ford promised that if people bought more than 300,000 Model Ts he'd return $50 to every purchaser. Sales hit 308,000 and Ford distributed $15 million. There was also an international dimension to his marketing. There was a Ford car in Britain as early as 1903 and Ford was the first company to sell cars in many other countries.

In his book *My Life and Work*, published in 1923, Ford explained:

> Our policy is to reduce the price, extend the operations, and improve the article. You will notice that the reduction of price comes first. We have never considered any costs as fixed. Therefore we first reduce the price to the point where we believe more sales will result. Then we go ahead and try to make the prices. We do not bother about the costs. The new price forces the costs down. The more usual way is to take the costs and then determine the price, and although that method may be scientific in the narrow sense, it is not scientific in the broad sense, because what earthly use is it to know the cost if it tells you that you cannot manufacture at a price at which the article can be sold? But more to the point is the fact that, although one may calculate what a cost is, and of course all of our costs are carefully calculated, no one knows what a cost ought to be. One of the ways of discovering . . . is to name a price so low as to force everybody in the place to the highest point of efficiency. The low price makes everybody dig for profits. We make more discoveries concerning manufacturing and selling under this forced method than by any method of leisurely investigation.

Ford's lack of faith in management was almost as legendary as his success. On the question of internal communications, for example, Ford said: 'It is not necessary for any one department to know what any other department is doing. . . . It is the business of those who plan the entire work to see that all of the departments are working . . . towards the same end.'

By the late 1920s Ford's empire was falling about him. It was relegated to third place among US car makers and was losing huge amounts of money. It was only in 1944, when Henry Ford II was brought in, that the company was resurrected. In analysing what went wrong at Ford, Peter Drucker calls it a 'controlled experiment in mismanagement' and in *Management* goes on to say:

> The first Ford failed because of his firm belief that a business did not need managers and management. All it needed, he believed, was the owner-entrepreneur with his 'helpers.' The only difference between Ford and most of his contemporaries in business was that, as in everything he did, Henry Ford stuck uncompromisingly to his convictions. He applied them strictly, firing or sidelining any one of his 'helpers,' no matter how able, who dared act as a 'manager,' make a decision or take action without orders from Ford. The way he applied his theory can only be described as a test, one that ended up by fully disproving Ford's theory.

Frank Gilbreth

Born Fairfield, Maine, 1868
Died 1924
Building contractor and consultant

Lilian Gilbreth

Born Oakland, California, 1878
Died 1972
Industrial psychologist

Frank and Lilian Gilbreth were a formidable husband and wife team. Frank was a successful businessman, Lilian an eminent industrial psychologist, referred to by some as the 'mother of management'.

Though qualified to go to the Massachusetts Institute of Technology, Frank Gilbreth decided to become an apprentice in the building trade. After serving his apprenticeship he set up his own contracting business in Boston. During his business career he, like Frederick Taylor, patented many inventions including a new design for scaffolding, as well as new methods of waterproofing cellars and of concrete construction. His business was so successful that it later expanded to open New York and London offices.

In 1912, at the age of forty-four, Gilbreth became a consultant. For a man of his age, with a thriving business already established, it was a risky venture but Gilbreth had been converted to scientific management and was keen to develop his fledgling theories on what he labelled 'motion study'. Together with Lilian, Gilbreth set about advancing Taylor's theories on scientific management. Put simply, Gilbreth believed in discovering the best means of performing each part of a job so it would be more effectively carried out. This required thorough analysis of each element and Gilbreth pioneered the use of cameras in examining how people went about their work.

'A general rule of motion economy is to make the shortest motions possible,' Gilbreth wrote in *Motion Study* (published in 1911). 'Eliminating unnecessary distances that workers' hands and arms must travel will eliminate miles of motions per man in a working day as compared with usual practice.' In his work, Gilbreth studied acceleration, to what degree motions were automatic, how motions combined in sequence, and the costs of a motion. 'Each motion should be made so as to be most economically combined with the next motion, like the billiard player who plays for position.'

In fact, the Gilbreths were taking advantage of the phenomenon described by Charles Babbage: 'If the observer stands with his watch in his hand before a person heading a pin, the workman will almost certainly increase his speed, and the estimate will be too large. A much better average will result from inquiring what quantity is considered a fair day's work.'

Gilbreth's experience in the building trade encouraged him to use his methods in bricklaying and – during the First World War – for training soldiers and rehabilitating the disabled. With bricklayers Gilbreth was able to raise individual output from 1,000 to 2,700 bricks per day. Lengthy research allowed him to classify the elements of human motions, labelling them 'therbligs' – Gilbreth (almost) spelt backwards. He recorded seventeen basic elements and developed a therblig chart which recorded a series of elements involved in a complex activity such as working a machine tool.

The Gilbreths took a broader view than Taylor, arguing 'no organisation can hope to hold its members that does not consider not only the welfare of the organisation as a whole, but also the welfare of the individuals composing that organisation'. At the New England Butt Company in Providence, Gilbreth put Taylor's principles into wholesale practice, but the difference was that employees were not depersonalised automatons. To achieve the greatest level of efficiency demanded the attention of a wide variety of specialists. Gilbreth wrote:

> The determination of the path which will result in the greatest economy of motion and the greatest increase of output is a subject for the closest investigation and the most scientific determination. Not until data are accumulated by trained observers can standard paths be adopted. The laws underlying physics, physiology, and psychology must be considered and followed. In the meantime, merely applying the results of observation will reduce motions and costs and increase output to an amazing degree.

On Frank Gilbreth's death in 1924, Lilian, a teacher as well as psychologist, became President of Gilbreth Inc. which had clients in Germany and Holland as well as among the United States' biggest companies, including Lever and Eastman Kodak. At first, Lilian had been relegated to a minor role. When their *Primer of Scientific Management* was published her name was not included, as the publisher didn't think a woman author was appropriate. However, Lilian Gilbreth's commitment was such that she went to Europe two days after her husband's death to read out a paper he had planned to give. Explaining her actions she said: 'I am only adhering to my husband's principles – the elimination of waste motion.'

Explaining the genesis of her and her husband's work, Lilian Gilbreth wrote:

> Mr Gilbreth felt that the least developed field in industry lay along the lines of discovering and using better methods, and

he formulated very early in his life the idea of finding 'the one best way to do work.' This necessitated finding the best available worker, the best surroundings, equipment and tools, and the best method. The work then developed along two lines. First, an investigation of the worker from every standpoint possible, the physiological, and so on, finding out his capabilities, his aptitudes, his aspirations, and his desire for any special type of work. As you can imagine, this led us into all the human sciences with a special stress on advances in education, the new psychology and psychiatry in its various departments.

While bringing up a family of twelve, Lilian Gilbreth toured the world promoting her and her husband's theories. Their collective achievement has generally been passed by, but it was the Gilbreths who produced the first inkling of what was to become management development. Their 'master promotion chart', based on the idea that 'no worker who is constitutionally able to become a permanent member of an organization will wish to change if he or she is receiving adequate pay and has ample opportunity for advancement', paved the way for a great deal of the motivation and development theories which were to follow.

The Gilbreths also applied their theories in the home. The household was divided into work surfaces, centres and motions with charts and a follow-up system. One child was assigned to buy all birthday presents for the family to save time. Later, two of their children wrote a best-seller, *Cheaper by the Dozen*, a reference to the family's twelve children and organisation.

Mary Parker Follett

Born Quincy, Massachusetts, 1868
Died 1933
Political scientist

'Before Mary Parker Follett applied her broad mind to it, management had been the intellectual property of efficiency-minded men,' writes Sir Peter Parker in his foreword to a recent book on Follett's management theories. Tom Horton of the

American Management Association adds simply: 'She had this keen power of observation and did her homework.'

Bostonian Follett remains, to a large extent, undiscovered in the Western world of management and business. In Japan, however, there is a Follett Society which propagates her views, believing they are as relevant in the late twentieth century as ever before. Follett's theories and writings do, to a large extent, transcend the preoccupations of their time. The narrow field of thinking and research by people such as Taylor was not for Follett (even though she was a member of the Taylor Society at one time). Her interests and opinions were broad-ranging and concerned with far more than the actual task of work.

In her 1987 study of Follett (*Dynamic Managing – the Follett Way*), Pauline Graham points out that Follett addressed herself to five fundamental questions which she identifies as:

- How can we organise, manage ourselves as individuals to achieve a fuller, richer life?
- What do we want people to do?
- How can we control and guide people's conduct at work and in social relations?
- How can we contribute to the success of the groups in which we operate?
- How can we create unity of action out of the diversity of our interests and institutions to lead us to a better-ordered and more productive society?

Follett began providing answers with her first book, *The Speaker of the House of Representatives*, published in 1896. Theodore Roosevelt declared it indispensable reading. The book meticulously revealed the methods used by strong Speakers in the House of Representatives to exert their influence and power. Such knowledge of the legislative process, especially in a woman, won widespread admiration and was the start of a career, which was soon to outgrow political science.

In a much quoted phrase, Follett once said: 'Idealism and realism meet in the actual.' Her interest in how the two combined provides a thread throughout her career. In particular, she became immersed in human relations. Unlike Elton Mayo and the Hawthorne experimenters, Follett's work was based not on years of expensive research, but on an understanding of humanity developed in a period doing social work and nurtured throughout her life. Lyndall Urwick, a champion of Follett, observed: 'Her intense interest in human beings, coupled with what amounted to a genius for relating individual experience, however humble and obscure, to general principles, made her an altogether exceptional research worker.'

Follett argued her case under the banner of humanity. 'I think we should undepartmentalise our thinking in regard to every problem that comes to us. I do not think that we have psychological and ethical and economic problems. We have *human* problems, with psychological, ethical and economic aspects, and as many others as you like,' she wrote in *Dynamic Administration*. This belief firmly separated her from the followers of Taylor and scientific management. Her warnings about the perils of scientific management were frequent. 'We should remember that we can never wholly separate the human from the mechanical side,' she wrote. 'The study of human relations in business and the study of the technique of operating are bound up together. . . . If the industrial manager is to get the fruits of Scientific Management, he must understand first the intricate workings of a group.'

Follett developed a profound interest in group relations and the dynamics of the group. Although her work followed on, to some extent, from the pioneering work of Robert Owen in the nineteenth century, she was among the first to realise the importance of groups and their workings. 'Responsibility is the great developer of men,' wrote Follett – a comment in stark contrast to the diminution of responsibility inherent in scientific management theories. Group working was, to Follett, an essential starting point for any organisation in developing such a sense of responsibility. 'It seems to me that the first test of business administration, of business organisation should be whether you have a business which has all its parts so coordinated, so moving together in their closely adjusting activities, so linking, interlocking, interrelating that they make a working unit, a functional whole. This principle applies to the relation of men, the relation of services, the relation of departments.'

She turned the terminology of science on its head, arguing, 'What we want is coordination from the bottom up and all along the line. This is successful organisation engineering.' Individuals were not to be left in isolation concentrating on a single task, but integrated into an overall organisation. (The belief in integration was later developed by people like Russ Ackoff.)

Follett saw through the myth, propagated to a large extent by scientific management, that managers and workers are fundamentally different. She did not accept the differentiation between people who use their bodies to earn a living and people who use their brains. Managers, said Follett, need a knowledge of physical work in order to carry out their jobs properly.

The belief in integration, taken to its logical conclusions, was clearly a challenging one for early twentieth-century managers. Her ideas were synthesised in *The New State: Group Organization – the Solution of Popular Government* (1918). It proffered theories on politics and government, which were revolutionary. The institutions of government bureaucracy, Follett suggested, should be replaced by local groups working together to solve their problems. This was, and still is, a direct challenge to the prevailing sense of hierarchy. 'Authority should go with knowledge and experience; that is where obedience is due, no matter whether it is up the line or down the line,' wrote Follett.

Instead of regarding conflict as an entirely negative force in the workplace, Follett saw its positive side as 'a normal process by which socially valuable differences register themselves for the enrichment of all'. Sir Peter Parker writes: 'Her view from outside-in kept her from grandiose theories. She insisted on the logic of the situation. Problems were inevitable but still an opportunity: their resolution was likely to be more secure if neither side dominated, nor meshed into muddled compromise. A problem could be constructive if it made more explicit the logic of the situation and developed an integrated, new approach.'

This logic and concept of integration was also brought to bear on the now voguish subject of leadership. In *Freedom and Coordination* (1949) she wrote: 'The essentials of leadership: the ability to grasp a total situation: facts, present and potential, aims and purposes, and men. The leader must see a whole. He must see the relation between all the different factors in a situation.' In fact, Follett fully recognised the need for a leader to possess, in modern terminology, vision. In *Dynamic Administration* she wrote: 'The most successful leader of all is one who sees another picture not yet actualised. He sees the things which belong in his present picture but which are not yet there. . . . Above all, he should make his co-workers see that it is not his purpose which is to be achieved, but a common purpose, born of the desires and the activities of the group.' She had, even so, little time for the cult of personality among leaders.

Follett's biographer, Pauline Graham, provides this appreciation of Follett's contribution:

> Her achievement was that she created a philosophy of management embedded in the full complexity of human nature. She certainly dissected the function of management and the managing process but her purpose in doing this was not to extract one supposedly main element and use it to erect the simplistic and mechanistic theory; it was to understand all of them in their intricate dynamic interactions, the better to integrate and unify them into the more effective working whole. So many others, from Taylor onwards, saw and still see management as a series of separate functions, with one more important than the others to which the others have to be subservient. Follett saw things differently.

'Nobody did more to bring work back into human proportions than this gaunt, plain Bostonian lady,' Sir Peter Parker has said. Urwick and Brech came to similarly enthusiastic conclusions. 'She was concerned solely with expounding the basic human emotions and forces that underlie the process of organization – the dynamic as opposed to the static or structural aspect of the subject. But in the course of that exposition she analysed the foundations of the whole science, of administration and management.' Perhaps her most conspicuous achievement was to be aware that management was, in itself, as vibrant a subject to study as any other. 'I like to do my thinking where it is most alive. Management, not bankers nor stockholders, is the fundamental element in industry. It is good management that draws credit, that draws workers, that draws customers. Whatever changes should come, whether industry is owned by capitalists, or by the state, or by the workers, it will always have to be managed. Management is the permanent function of business.'

Elton Mayo

Born Adelaide, Australia, 1880
Died 1949
Social psychologist

Elton Mayo is the only Australian to feature in the canon of great management thinkers and writers. Yet his most important work was carried out in the United States at Harvard.

A graduate of Adelaide University, Mayo also studied medicine in Edinburgh and London where he carried out work on psychopathology. In 1903 he went to Africa and then returned to write and teach in London until his career took another twist when he joined an Adelaide printing company as a partner in 1905. After taking another degree, in 1911, he became a lecturer in mental and moral philosophy at the new University of Queensland. He stayed there, becoming a professor in 1919, until departing for the United States in 1923. He spent three years at the University of Pennsylvania, examining labour turnover at a textile mill, before joining Harvard as associate professor of industrial research in 1926. Between 1929 and 1947 Mayo worked as a full professor at Harvard.

The foundations of much of Mayo's later work were set in Australia. He lectured for the Workers' Education Association and studied the nature of nervous breakdowns during the First World War. Under the influence of Freud, Jung and Pierre Janet, Mayo and a Brisbane physician pioneered the psychoanalytic treatment of shell-shock. While in Australia, Mayo published his first book *Democracy and Freedom*. The book was not a radical departure, as the title perhaps suggests, from the work he was then involved in. Instead, Mayo applied his work on wartime nervous problems to industrial strife. He argued that the morale and mental health of working people was related to the social aspects of their work. It was not a political treatise, but a call for increased sociological awareness on the part of management.

Mayo's significance lies in his research into the importance of non-economic satisfaction in employee productivity (a theme which was to be developed in the 1950s by Argyris, Herzberg and Maslow). Financial motivation, so beloved of Taylor, was relegated to a position of relative unimportance in Mayo's outlook. Explaining his views on Taylor, he wrote: 'As a system, Taylorism effects much in the way of economy of labour; its chief defect is that workmen are not asked to collaborate in effecting such economies; a method is devised without their knowledge and then imposed on them. What wonder if workers are suspicious of such innovations. So long as commerce specialises in business methods which take no account of human nature and social motives, so long may we expect strikes and sabotage to be the ordinary accompaniment of industry.'

Mayo argued that the massive industrial and technological strides forward in the nineteenth century had not been matched by comparative changes in working patterns or methods. This faith in communicating the nature of change to the work-force was to be picked up over fifty years later by Peters and Waterman. Mayo's observation that 'we live in a constant flux of personal associations, as of technical procedures' also echoes more recent work on adapting to change (Mayo also made use of the now fashionable word 'adaptive' to describe his ideal society).

Mayo used scientific investigation to prove that taking workers' attitudes into consideration paid off in commercial terms. He studied the relationship between people working together, but unlike Taylor paid relatively little attention to the work itself.

The lengthy research project he joined, and then led, was labelled the Hawthorne Investigations. It was a ten-year research project at the Western Electric Company's Hawthorne Works in Chicago. Starting in 1927, it involved a mixed team of Harvard biological and social scientists. The investigations covered around twenty thousand people at the Hawthorne works and between seventy-five and a hundred investigators.

The company itself was, in the opinion of Mayo, an exceptional example. It was 'definitely committed to justice and humanity in its dealings with workers, and with general morale high'. Prominent in the team was Fritz Roethlisberger (1898–1974) who had joined Harvard (where he was to spend all his career) in 1927 when the Hawthorne Investigations began. He had previously been working as a counsellor for students with psychological problems.

The research involved direct studies of the actual behaviour of small working groups. Roethlisberger revealingly observed: 'The manager is neither managing men nor managing work . . . he is administering a social system.' As the research developed, the group became increasingly interested by this social system. Roethlisberger, for example, wrote:

> The Hawthorne researchers became more and more interested in the informal employee groups, which tend to form within the formal organisation of the company, and which are not likely to be represented in the organisation chart. They became interested in the beliefs and creeds which have the effect of making each individual feel an integral part of the group and which make the group appear as a single unit, in the social codes and norms of behaviour, by means of which employees automatically work together in a group without any conscious choice as to whether they will or will not co-operate. They studied the important social functions these groups perform for their members, the histories of these informal work groups, how they spontaneously appear, how they tend to perpetuate themselves, multiply, and disappear, how they are in constant jeopardy from technical change, and hence how they tend to resist innovation.

Mayo provided a similar insight:

> It is at least evident that the economists' presupposition of individual self-preservation as motive and logic as instrument is not characteristic of the industrial facts ordinarily encountered. The desire to stand well with one's fellows, the so-called human instinct of association, easily outweighs the merely individual interest and the logic of reasoning upon which so many spurious principles of management are based.

To Mayo, therefore, the worker's individuality was subjugated to group effort controlled by management. The worker, to work to full potential, needs to be aware of the broader implications of his work for society – it is not the task itself which is important but the interaction between task, worker, manager and society.

In *The Social Problems of an Industrial Civilization* Mayo mapped out the constant challenges to society:

Every social group, at whatever level of culture, must face and clearly state two perpetual and recurrent problems of administration. It must secure for its individual and group membership:

1. The satisfaction of material and economic needs.
2. The maintenance of spontaneous cooperation throughout the organisation.

Lyndall Urwick commented on the Hawthorne Investigations: 'They emphasised as never before the predominating influence of the climate of social opinion and emotion in the group as determinants of economic performance.' To Mayo, logical thinking and self-interest were the last resort 'when social association has failed'. The major objective of management, he argued, should be to encourage co-operation and team work among employees.

However, Mayo, like Taylor, believed management needed to be scientifically based. His research was exhaustive and supported by a faith in knowledge based on experience (a topic later developed by Reg Revans). In *The Social Problems of Industrial Civilization*, Mayo wrote: 'Observation – skill – experiment and logic – these must be regarded as the three stages of advancement.'

In a 1962 lecture reviewing his work with the Hawthorne Investigations, Roethlisberger pointed to another important element in the work – the idea of the organisation and its relationship with society as a whole.

Organizations were to be conceived fundamentally as natural social units, but they differed in one important respect from other kinds of social groupings and social organizations that emerge whenever men are living together and that sociologists generally try to explain. They were different in the sense that they were social units that had been established for the explicit purpose of achieving certain goals. Built into them by the goals to be achieved and the means by which they were to be achieved were certain prescribed and planned relations not spontaneously emerged in the course of social interaction.

The corporate organisation was identified as an individual entity, linked to society, but with its own *modus operandi*.

The social system was later much criticised. Daniel Bell wrote that Mayo and his associates 'uncritically adopt industry's own conception of workers as means to be manipulated or adjusted to impersonal ends. The belief in man as an end in himself has been ground under by the machine, and the social science of the factory researchers is not a science of man, but a cow-sociology.' Another critic commented: 'The industrialist is likely to believe that Mayo's conclusions are true but irrelevant; the social psychologist that they are true but obvious; the sociologist that they are true but that they do not go far enough.'

Mayo, described by one writer as 'a short man, who smoked excessively, and suffered from chronic hypertension', died in England. A school of management in Adelaide was later named after him.

Lyndall F. Urwick

Born Malvern, England, 1891
Died 1983
Consultant

Following Urwick's death in December 1983, *Management Today* printed lengthy extracts from his work pointing out that his thinking was as relevant in the 1980s as it was forty years previously. It labelled him 'the only Englishman to rank beside the great management pioneers'.

Urwick's management thinking was founded on his early experience with his family firm of glove-makers and military service. Having graduated in history from Oxford in 1913, Urwick's work was interrupted by the First World War. Two wartime experiences proved essential in the development of his theories. He read Frederick Taylor's *Scientific Management* while in the trenches in Belgium. As a result, he began a lifetime's commitment to the principles of scientific management, although he believed that Taylor's principles were unsuited to the British industrial relations situation. The organisation of the army also provided Urwick with inspiration. As an administrative staff officer, Urwick became aware of the military idea of 'staff and line', which he was later to adapt to business organisation.

In the post-war years Urwick worked for Rowntree in York whilst finding the time to lecture at Oxford management conferences, a forum for progressive management thinkers. In 1928, he became director of the International Management Institute in Geneva. It was the first international management body with the aim of providing information on scientific management. Urwick travelled widely, exchanging opinions with leading management thinkers such as Mary Parker Follett and Elton Mayo.

On returning to London in 1934, Urwick established a management consultancy business, Urwick, Orr and Partners, floated on less than £1,000. By 1939 it had over thirty consultants. Orr, a Scottish engineer, remained until 1945; Urwick was managing partner from 1945 to 1951 and chairman until 1961. His prophetic thinking lay behind the creation of one of the world's most prominent management consultancy companies. 'Just as Shelley was the poet's poet, he seems to me to be the consultant's consultant,' said Lilian Gilbreth.

Urwick was a founder member of the British Institute of Management and argued that the government needed to put 'good management' at the forefront of its agenda. His message was forcefully direct: 'Unless it is prepared to place good management within the machinery of government in the forefront of its agenda and to stimulate its servants to place greater emphasis on the executive as opposed to the political virtues, it will find that the best intentions are negatived by its inability to drive faster a machine designed for a far more leisurely age.'

The 1947 Urwick Report on Education for Management marked one of the first real investigations into British management education. In it Urwick argued: 'Theoretical study alone cannot make a manager', and he defined management as 'all those activities involving responsibility for the work of others. These cover a very wide range. The educational requirements for the different levels of responsibility vary greatly. But we believe there are certain common principles of management whatever the degree of responsibility involved.'

He anticipated the demands for improved management training which, even now, continue to be regularly issued. 'Nothing in managing touches more closely on the prospects of industrial society than the problem of the training and the selection of those who will administer business. Upon its solution depend not only co-operation in the present, but the ultimate acceptance by mankind of the machine technology as a way of life,' wrote Urwick.

Together with E. F. L. Brech, he produced the three-volume *The Making of Scientific Management* (1946) which provided a detailed introduction to the work of some of the earliest management thinkers.

Analysing Urwick's work, Philip Sadler of Ashridge Management College writes: 'The principles which Urwick gathered together . . . have come to be known as the "classical" principles of management. They are based on a combination of experience and philosophy rather than rigorous research and have been widely criticised for this. They have attracted criticism on other grounds also. First, the underlying assumption of their work – that there exists a common set of principles applicable to management in all types of situation – has been frequently challenged. Second, their work is criticised (perhaps unfairly) on the grounds that the world in which they had their experience no longer exists and that the principles they derived from that experience have little or no validity for the contemporary organisation operating in the modern business environment.'

Even so, Urwick's work remains of significance – he was one of the first in Britain to realise the importance of management and the need for extensive management education.

CHAPTER 2

The Organisation and Systems Men

The idea that the way organisations were structured could make a significant difference in their efficiency took a long time to dawn. There were only two rational models – the military or the bureaucratic – and in practice the differences between them were relatively minor. The thought of paying a consultant millions of dollars to advise on how to restructure a company's divisions seemed ludicrous until recent decades. In practice, however, it gradually became clear that all companies were not organised and run in the same manner. Could, then, the way in which companies structured themselves affect their long-term profitability?

The organisation and systems men set out to measure how organisations were put together, what held them together thereafter and what mechanisms were needed to get things done. Max Weber, whose ideas we discussed in the previous chapter, defined types of organisations according to their power or authority structure. He was followed by a host of other academics, taking a variety of approaches. In this chapter we look at some of those people and how their ideas developed.

Luther Gulick (born 1892) was concerned primarily with how managers get things done. Gulick held a variety of governmental and educational posts and was highly influential as a member of President Roosevelt's Committee on Administrative Management (1936–8). Alongside Louis Brownlow and Charles Marriam, Gulick's plans formed the basis of Roosevelt's reorganisation of federal government. Gulick argued: 'Real efficiency must be built into the structure of a government just as it is built into a piece of machinery.' Indeed from the early 1930s he had been advocating a reassessment of governmental organisation. 'The Government is becoming and is apparently destined to remain, at least to a degree, the super-holding company of the economic life of the Nation. The fundamental new function which government assumes in this process is that of devising and imposing a consistent master plan of national life. This will require a new division of actual work and therefore a new theory of the division of powers.'

The presidential committee argued the case for sound management practices in all areas of society and government in particular. 'A government without good management is a house builded on sand,' Roosevelt observed. The report placed management as a matter of prime national importance. 'The forward march of American democracy at this point of our history depends more upon effective management than upon any other single factor,' they concluded. In fact such ideas were more readily embraced by the Japanese than the Americans (ironically Gulick was born in Japan).

Gulick built on Fayol's theories in trying to analyse executive tasks and came up with the now famous acronym PODSCORB, which stands for:

- Planning: establishing broadly what needs to be done and how to achieve it
- Organising: creating formal management structures
- Directing: carrying out the role of leader – making decisions, giving orders and making sure they are carried out
- Staffing: recruiting, selecting and training people to do the work
- Co-ordinating: pulling together disparate elements of the work, so that they all support the same overall objectives
- Reporting: through records, measurement and monitoring, keeping track of progress and providing relevant feedback to himself, his superiors and subordinates
- Budgeting: the process of control, particularly financial control.

These, Gulick identified as the functional elements of administration. They were developed in his most influential book *Papers on the Science of Administration* (edited with Lyndall Urwick and republished in 1987).

In many ways, Gulick was one of the last of the old guard of management thinkers. The idea that there was a single, general prescription for successful management was fast being undermined by more deeply researched studies that suggested management simply wasn't that simple. However, the influence Gulick had should not be underestimated.

In the United Kingdom during the same era more research-based work was being done by Joan Woodward (1916–71). Most of her research into organisations was carried out at the South-east Sussex Technical College and subsequently at Imperial College, London. The key studies took place between 1953 and 1957 with a hundred British manufacturing companies, of various sizes from medium to large. She and her researchers found that there were wide differences between firms in characteristics such as the number of levels in the management hierarchy, how people's authority and responsibility were defined, how far the work was divided among specialists, and how many people reported to each supervisor.

After a great deal of analysis, it appeared that the critical factor was the kind of production technology the company used. That, in turn, depended on the products it made and the markets it served. Woodward identified three main categories of technology, of increasing complexity – unit or small batch production; mass or large batch production; and process production. Each of these had its own sub-categories. Each also had its own typical structure and methods of getting things done. The unit or small batch manufacturers tended to have relatively few layers in their hierarchies; the process manufacturers tended to have far more layers. Both types of organisation typically have small 'spans of control' (numbers of people reporting to one supervisor) – in the first case because the technology requires greater 'hands on' supervision; in the latter because the work-force tends to be of a higher ability level and because the technology requires fewer people at each location within the production process. But mass production organisations typically had very large spans of control (sometimes up to eighty people reporting to one supervisor), because the technology required every job to be very closely defined and specialised.

Later work by Woodward and her colleagues explored how companies exerted control over their operations. They found that control systems grew up around two dimensions: personal–impersonal and fragmented–cohesive. The personal–impersonal dimension ranges from the perhaps idiosyncratic supervision of an entrepreneur on the premises, who sets the rules and arbitrates away any conflicts (typical of many small companies); through impersonal systems that rely on administrative procedures (typical of larger companies and bureaucracies); to automatic controls. The nearer to this end of the spectrum that a company comes, the greater the separation between planning and doing.

The second control dimension ranges from companies where every unit has its own methods of control, to companies where all control systems are integrated and reconciled centrally. The former tends to lead to conflict of objectives and duplicated effort; the latter, if taken to extremes, to an unhealthy rigidity of operations. Where companies sit on these dimensions will vary at least in part according to the type of production, says Woodward.

Assessing Woodward's contribution to management theory, *Writers on Organizations* (1981) concludes:

Woodward's study pioneered both in empirical investigation and in setting a fresh framework of thought. Prior to it, thinking about organization depended on the apt but over-generalized statements of experienced managers, and on isolated case studies of particular firms. Woodward showed the possibilities of comparisons of large numbers of firms so that generalizations might be securely based and their limits seen.

Of course, Woodward's work was based firmly in manufacturing. Applying her conclusions to service organisations is difficult.

During this period one of the first impacts of what we now call computer science was on management thinking. In order to develop computer systems, it was necessary to understand how systems worked in the real world. Mathematicians and sociologists found common cause in investigating how business organisations functioned as systems. Ludwig von Bertalanffy (1901–72) had introduced the phrase 'general systems theory' to describe the main characteristics of organisations as systems shortly before the Second World War. Most important among these characteristics were that:

- organisms (or organisations) were made up of systems
- all systems tend towards achieving equilibrium
- and that organisations are 'open' systems in that they affect and are affected by their environment.

The first major figure to develop these ideas was Norbert Wiener (1894–1964). Wiener, a mathematician and a member of the Massachusetts Institute of Technology faculty for over forty years, was the author of *Cybernetics*, published in 1949. The term 'cybernetics' comes from the Greek for steersman and Wiener's book studies 'control and communication in the animal and the machine'. 'The typical example is the governor of a steam engine, which senses mechanically when the engine is going too fast and reduces the supply of steam.'

Wiener was heavily influenced by his wartime research at MIT where he worked on guided missiles. From this he developed an interest in the 'handling of information'. Dealing with complex computers and radar, Wiener detected a similarity between these machines and the human brain and nervous system.

Wiener received relatively little notice. It was left to an eccentric Englishman, Anthony Stafford Beer (born 1926), to make cybernetics a practical management tool. Beer spent his early years in India as a soldier, then pursued a varied career as research scientist, publishing director and eventually became visiting professor of cybernetics at the University of Manchester and adjunct professor of statistics at the Wharton School in Pennsylvania. He established his own consultancy SIGMA (Science In General Management), which friends immediately decided was an acronym for Stafford Is Going Mad Again, and put many of his ideas into practice in Chile under the ill-fated Allende government in the early 1970s.

Beer defines cybernetics as the science of effective organisation and his basic thesis, as explained in *Brain of the Firm* (1972), is that organisations are like people. They have, for example, a brain and a central nervous system. He ascribes many of the problems that companies (and countries) experience to straight-forward misunderstanding of the way systems work. He says: 'Our institutions are failing because they disobey fundamental laws of effective organization which their administrators do not know about.' For example, 'When a government acts, it is perforce reacting to a situation where the statistical delay often happens to be half a cycle in the economic rise and fall of prosperity, so that the government may find itself doing exactly the wrong thing most of the time.'

The root of the problem lies in the way systems develop within organisations. Their main function, he believes, is frequently to support the edifice rather than to help achieve specific goals. The best way of understanding how an organisation works, he maintains, is to ignore the formal organisation chart – which simply tells you theoretically what ought to happen – and to chart how each part of the organisation really reacts with the others. In this way, the effects of any changes made in the system can be predicted in advance.

The uniqueness and deficiencies of Beer's approach have been summarised by Philip Sadler, principal of Ashridge Management College: 'The management world described by Beer and others writing in the same vein is one with a strange language of its own – familiar perhaps to specialists in control engineering or to consultant neurologists, but foreign to generalists, and marketing and personnel specialists to whom terms such as "heuristic", "negentropy" and "reticulum" convey little or nothing. At the same time it is a world in which problems of labour relations, emotions, attitudes, irrational conflicts and organizational politics have no place.'

In the United States, the area of systems dynamics was developed by Jay Forrester (born 1918), a professor at MIT's Sloan School of Management. 'Everyone speaks of systems: computer systems, air traffic control systems, economic systems, and social systems. But few realise how pervasive are systems in creating more of the puzzling difficulties that confront us,' says Forrester. 'For the last thirty years I have been developing a field known as system dynamics. System dynamics combines the theory, methods and philosophy needed to analyse the behaviour of systems not only in management, but also in environmental change, politics, economic behaviour, medicine, engineering, and other fields. System dynamics provides a common foundation that can be applied wherever we want to understand and influence how things change through time.

'The system dynamics process starts from a problem to be solved – an undesirable behaviour that is to be corrected or avoided. The first step is to tap the wealth of information that people possess in their heads. The mental data base is a rich source of information about the parts of a system, about the information available at different points in a system, and about the policies being followed in decision making. The management and social sciences have in the past unduly restricted themselves to measured data and have neglected the far richer and more informative body of information that exists in the knowledge and experience of those in the active, working world.'

A more historical approach to organisations and systems has been taken by Alfred Chandler (born 1918). Chandler, a business historian and Pulitzer prize-winner, has been an influential figure in both strategy (which we will discuss in Chapter 4) and business structure. He has been Straus Professor of Business History at Harvard since 1971.

Chandler draws his conclusions about the most efficient way to organise a large company from history, in particular from what he calls 'the formative years of modern capitalism' – the mid nineteenth century to the end of the First World War. During this period, the typical entrepreneurial or family firm gave way to larger organisations containing multiple units. A new form of management was needed because the owner-manager could not be everywhere at once. In addition, a new breed of manager was needed to operate in this environment – the salaried professional.

In Chandler's analysis, the effective organisation now separates strategy and day-to-day operations. Strategy becomes the responsibility of managers at headquarters, leaving the unit managers to concentrate on the here and now in decentralised units. In effect, he was advising creating a line management who would carry out plans developed by a more senior staff function elsewhere.

Another approach comes from Harvard Business School's Paul Lawrence and Jay Lorsch, disciples of Chester Barnard. They argue that every organisation is composed of multiple paradoxes. On the one hand, each department or unit has its own objectives and environment. It responds to those in its own way, both in terms of how it is structured, the time horizons people assume, the formality or informality of how it goes about its tasks and so on. All these factors contribute towards what they call *differentiation*. At the same time, each unit needs to work with others in pursuit of common goals. That requires a certain amount of *integration*, to ensure that they are all working with, rather than against each other. In their studies of US firms in a variety of manufacturing industries, they found that companies with a high level of differentiation could also have a high level of integration. The reason was simple: the greater the differentiation, the more potential for conflict between departments and therefore the greater the need for mechanisms to help them work together.

Lawrence initially acted as Lorsch's thesis adviser before they co-wrote *Organization and the Environment* (1967). Lorsch's fascination with organisational behaviour has its roots in his army service. There he became interested in the reasons why people did not do what they were supposed to do. This interest was furthered when Lorsch studied under Fritz Roethlisberger at Harvard. Since then Lorsch has produced over a dozen books on organisation (*Developing Organizations* (1969) was the sequel to *Organization and the Environment*) and decision-making (including *Decision Making at the Top* (1983)).

Tom Burns is a disciple of Weber. Professor of sociology at Edinburgh University until his retirement in 1981, he studied how organisations react to and deal with change. Working with Scottish electronics companies in the 1960s, he concluded that ability to handle change depends to a large extent on where a company lies on a continuum whose extremes are virtual mirror images of each other in the way they are managed.

At one end is a type of organisation, which he calls mechanistic. Very similar to Weber's rational-legal organisation, it has clearly defined levels of responsibility and allocation of tasks. Control and co-ordination are exercised firmly from the top; communication is primarily vertical, with horizontal communication rarely encouraged (if you want something from another department you pass the message up, not across, and wait for it to reach the appropriate level, then make its way down again); rules are strictly enforced and a high degree of conformity is expected.

At the other end is the organic organisation, where responsibilities may change rapidly and where the boxes on the organisation chart (if there is one) are not fixed. Communication occurs in all directions and involvement across departmental barriers is encouraged. The structure and the way people behave within it are designed for maximum flexibility. Interestingly, this description is very similar to that in Tom Peters's depiction of the ideally adapted organisation in *Thriving on Chaos* (1987) nearly twenty years later.

Most organisations fall somewhere between these two extremes, which are, if you like, the difference between the dinosaur and the chameleon. Burns's interest focuses on organisations nearer the dinosaur end of the continuum (if only because organisations at the other end were thin on the ground). In assessing how they dealt with change in the outside world, he discovered that there was not one set of systems, but three or more. The most obvious was the formal hierarchy, the written procedures and prescribed ways of doing things. But there were also two other sets of systems – career systems and political systems. When a potential change appears on the horizon, people do not evaluate it solely according to organisational goals; they also look at the impact it might have on their own career. If they think it will have a negative effect, they do all they can to block the change, even if they are making supportive noises in the discussion meetings of the formal system. (Rosabeth Moss Kanter develops this theme magnificently in her 1983 book *The Change Masters*.) Political systems are about power. Even if the change will not directly affect an executive's career prospects, it may alter the balance of power *vis-à-vis* his colleagues. Again, he will use informal networks and blocking techniques either to stop the change or adapt it to support his position.

Alvin Gouldner (1920–80) was another disciple of Weber. While accepting the notion of the bureaucracy as an effective system of management, he asked the fundamental question: 'How do managers in a bureaucracy get people to do what they are told?' It wasn't a question Weber had dealt with in any depth. What he found brought into question many of Weber's conclusions, because it showed that bureaucracy frequently decreased efficiency and increased conflict.

The source of Gouldner's criticism lies in his identification of three forms of behaviour that people in bureaucracies adopt.

People in representative bureaucracies accept that knowledge and expertise are a rational basis for rules and decision-making. Because the rules tend to support values held strongly by the people in the organisation, there is relatively little conflict, so long as those people who make the rules are perceived as genuine experts. Conformity with the rules is a source of praise and esteem. People who do not stick to the rules are seen as errant children, who haven't quite grasped the values.

In punishment-centred bureaucracies, non-conformity is a sin. The 'correct' behaviour, as set out in the rules, is enforced by coercion. This coercion can come from management or from the trade union. If, as often happens, there are two or more strongly held sets of rules (for example, management's and the union's) then conflict tends to spiral. If the situation is resolved, it is by force rather than by discussion or compromise.

The third form of behaviour is the mock bureaucracy. Here everyone regards the rules as being imposed from outside (for example, from an overseas headquarters). Because the authority figures in the organisation clearly feel no ownership of the rules or commitment to them, everyone simply goes through the motions, if they take any notice at all. Indeed, they may deliberately carry out infringements, because it demonstrates their independence of the outside agency that originated them. A great deal of ingenuity goes into subverting or getting round the rules – if only because that is the only way people can get on with what they regard as the real job.

Gouldner's contribution to management thinking was to bring discussion of the 'ideal' organisation back to earth. He demonstrated that any organisation will be perverted by the people in it unless they are fully in accord with its values and goals and reminded us how complex systems that involve people can be.

Another major thinker in this area is Herbert Simon, a social scientist who won the Nobel Prize for Economics in 1978. For many years he and his colleagues at Carnegie-Mellon University, Pittsburgh, where he is professor of computer science and psychology, have been studying how people make decisions. From his work, using computers to simulate thinking processes, he defines three steps towards making a decision. The first is *intelligence* – identifying a situation which calls for a decision.

The second is *design* – conceiving and developing alternative courses of action, and assessing their implications. The third is *choice* – selecting which of the alternatives to proceed with.

Simon also distinguishes between programmed and unprogrammed decisions. Programmed decisions are those where the process to handle them is already well established, so there is relatively little thinking through or analysis to do. Usually, these will involve situations you have met before or for which there is a set of rules. Unprogrammed decisions are those where there is no pre-set way of dealing with the problem. They will often be completely new situations, or more complex combinations of otherwise familiar situations. In practice, many decisions will be a mixture of these two extremes.

The problem with Simon's neat description of the decision-making process is that, although machines may operate in that manner, it seems that executives do not. As other theorists, such as Henry Mintzberg (see page 91), have demonstrated, in real life executives move into the third phase – choice – while they are still working on conceiving and developing the solution.

Also at Carnegie-Mellon are two other major thinkers on decision-making, Richard Cyert (born 1921) and James March (born 1918). They take a much more detailed view than Burns of the systems that operate within a company and tend to support Mintzberg's view of decision-making. They see a company as a coalition of interests, with the nature of the interests defined largely by the functions the various departments and their sub-units perform. Every functional unit puts its own goals first (for example, production to maintain output, sales to maintain sales volume) and the organisation's goals second (or lower). Top management has to balance these conflicts.

Cyert and March look in greater depth at how decisions are actually made and conclude that most of the time decision-making processes are 'uncoupled' from the decisions actually made – in other words, the decisions reached are not often those that would be made in an entirely rational world. There are several reasons for this, they say. In particular:

- The way in which internal conflicts are resolved tends to prevent an overall organisational view. Under what they describe as quasi-resolution of conflict, either:

    – each little unit of the company makes its own decisions in isolation and to hell with impact on the rest of the organisation

    – the organisation imposes a compromise level of consistency that everyone can subscribe to but which doesn't really match the overall needs of the organisation

    – the organisation picks off one problem area after another and deals with each in turn.

- The way in which organisations avoid dealing with uncertainty. Either they try to buy stability with long-term contracts, or they simply focus on the predictable short term and defer decisions where they are not confident of the prevailing environment.

- The way in which organisations search for alternative solutions. Searches are not continuous and systematic but *ad hoc*, motivated by a particular event. When action is taken, the search stops – even though the action may not have produced a lasting solution – until the need for further action cannot be ignored. Moreover, the search is usually confined to solutions as close as possible to the old solutions. Because the department that 'owns' the problem is given the task of sorting it out, there will be little opportunity to take new perspectives. The problem is made worse because the people thinking about the problem will have been trained to approach it in the approved way. So it is hardly surprising that the new solution is merely an adaptation of the old one.

- The way in which failure to identify workable solutions leads not to new ways of searching but to new goals. Because people in the organisation learn which types of problem they can easily resolve and those they cannot, the organisation as a whole gradually learns to focus attention on different problems. The original problem still exists, but it is now relegated in importance.

- The fact that, in many cases, the actual decision is irrelevant to the people concerned. They have other priorities related to the process of decision-making – for example, paying off or storing up favours or stealing an edge in the power struggle.

- The fact that people never have time to participate

properly. They always have other priorities and rarely participate in all the stages of making a particular decision.

The language Cyert and March use – from 'garbage cans of choices' to 'organized anarchies' – indicates the scathing nature of their attack on simplistic decision-making theories. Their remedy is basically to allow for greater creativity in decision-making, for example by experimentation or what they call a 'technology of foolishness'. In the world of the irrational, the apparent lunatic may be the only sane person around.

Charles Lindblom, professor of economics and political science at Yale, is another decision theorist whose work made an impact in the 1960s. Like Cyert and March, he begins from the point of view that simple theories of sequential, rational steps of decision-making do not reflect reality – if only because managers cannot cope with the volume and complexity of information involved. Moreover, a rational approach would keep opening up more options and alternatives, making problems less rather than more resolvable. Instead, he argues that managers work through 'disjointed incrementalism' – multiple, small-scale comparisons that do not necessarily follow logical steps.

Lindblom calls his approach 'the science of muddling through'. In fact, it is rather more consistent than that. Effective managers tend to work by controlling exposure to risk. It is much easier to do that by proceeding in small steps, than by making major dramatic changes. The process, according to Lindblom, has four main elements, all or none of which may be under way at any one time. The first involves restricting his range of outcomes of change. He discounts those circumstances that would involve radical change, because these are usually least likely and more difficult to comprehend. Second, he reduces the alternatives to the obviously practical. Third, as Cyert and March found, as he meets difficulties he changes the ends to meet the means, rather than vice versa. And fourth, he re-evaluates, redefines and reconstructs the problem as he goes along. All this means, in effect, is that for many problems there is no solution, just an intermittent chipping away at the edges of a block that may alter shape as it is worked on.

Charles H. Kepner and Benjamin Tregoe became interested

in how managers tackled problems and made decisions when they worked together at the RAND Corporation. Kepner, a psychologist, and Tregoe, a sociologist (one of many such cross-discipline teams that produced innovative thinking in the 1950s), established the international consulting firm Kepner-Tregoe and Associates in 1958, to exploit what they had discovered and applied in RAND.

They were less concerned with the theory of problem-solving than with finding practical ways to help managers become more rational and effective in dealing with problems. Rather than encourage or accept the normal mixing up of analysis and decision-making they wanted to separate the two activities. The solution, they decided, was a step-by-step process that forced managers to think problems through in a rational way. Part of the reason that their prescription became widely used is its simplicity. It involves three basic stages: analysing the problem; deciding between alternatives; and reanalysing to ensure that the solution does not create problems of its own. Within each of these stages are sub-stages, each of which the manager has to consider before passing to the next.

Of equal and possibly greater impact than Kepner-Tregoe was the concept of Management by Objectives (MBO), first outlined by Peter Drucker. He claimed MBO was practised by major companies such as General Electric – and so it was. But he observed it and encapsulated it in a manner others could develop.

MBO was turned into a set of practical methods by John Humble (born 1925). He defined it as 'a dynamic system which seeks to integrate the company's need to clarify and achieve its profit and growth goals with the manager's need to contribute and develop himself'.

At the time, MBO was revolutionary to most companies. Humble defined it as 'a dynamic system which seeks to integrate the company's needs to clarify and achieve its profit and growth goals with the manager's need to contribute and develop himself'. Humble drew together his theories partly from observation of what British companies were doing wrong – in particular treating their management development, planning systems and control systems as separate activities – and partly from observing best practice in the United States, using a three-month study grant from the Ford Foundation. What he saw in America convinced him that the three activities could be integrated and he worked at building processes that would make it happen.

Now MBO is so much a part of everyday normal management behaviour that the term is rarely used. In the late 1960s, Humble turned his attentions to emerging issues such as the integration of information technology with business strategy (only now becoming a major topic of concern to top managers). In the 1970s, he focused on corporate social responsibility; his controversial paper, 'The Responsible Multinational', was widely credited with bringing rationality back into the debate over the role of multinational companies in Third World countries. His current interests lie in 'an obsession with the management of service'.

In the United States, George Odiorne, another disciple of Drucker, was also developing the concept of MBO. Odiorne highlighted what he called 'the activity trap'. Expounding on the concept in his book *MBO II*, published in 1979, he explained that:

- people get so wrapped up in the current activity or problem that they forget what their objectives were
- as a result, their capacity to deliver the goods decreases, even while the rate of activity increases and problems often get worse rather than better
- the source of the activity trap is always the top level affected; people at lower levels usually become de-motivated because they can no longer see clearly what they are working towards
- managers in the activity trap go to great lengths to avoid facing the reality of their situation; the work itself becomes a means of distracting their attention from unpalatable reality.

Social researcher Rensis Likert (1903–81) was another American whose work and thinking had profound effects on organisational theory. He is probably best known for his book *New Patterns of Management* (1961) which was a synthesis of much of his work. In it he argued organisational management could be categorised along a continuum from system 1 (an exploitative authoritarian system), through 2 (benevolent authoritative), 3 (consultative) to 4 (participative). System 2, said Likert, was the one most common at that time. Later he added system 0, where a company had an undeveloped management system.

In their book *The Rational Manager* (1965) Kepner and Tregoe write of Likert's *New Patterns of Management*:

> Likert makes the basic flat assumption that participative management is the best kind of management, and, therefore, the task of management is to assure participation in all respects. Group discussion, he holds, becomes the best and only valid way to a good decision. In his view, problem solving is the coordinated gathering of data and the integration of it in the group; decision making is the selection of an action by acclamation. Accordingly, there are no techniques of problem solving or decision making per se, only better ways of working as group members.

They conclude that managers 'will find it difficult and far-removed from the practical reality they must contend with every day'.

Likert gained a Ph.D. in psychology from Columbia in 1932. His work there was later published as *A Technique for the Measurement of Attitudes*. He then became director of research at the Life Insurance Sales Research Bureau in Hartford, Connecticut. It was there he began work on management practices which resulted in *Morale and Agency Management*. In 1939 he moved to become director of program surveys at the US Department of Agriculture in Washington, DC. There he developed his questionnaire techniques before joining the Institute for Social Research at University of Michigan in 1946. He ran the institute until broadening his interests to organisational management and behaviour in 1970.

It was at the institute that Likert developed situational leadership research. His objective was to find correlations with specific leadership styles (that is, behaviours and attitudes) and business performance. His approach was to ask employees in US companies to answer a series of questions about their supervisors – for example, did their supervisor trust them? He used the scores to draw up a profile of how each supervisor was viewed by the people who worked with him. From these profiles, he was able to establish four broad types of management style, which he categorised as:

- Exploitative authoritarian or system 1: these managers believe in telling people what to do and using coercion if they do not comply; they do not share decision-making at all
- Benevolent authoritarian or system 2: these managers still tell people what to do, but prefer to use the carrot rather than the stick to get things done; they make most of the major decisions, but are prepared to delegate minor decisions when it suits them
- Consultative or system 3: these managers will talk matters through with subordinates, even though they still take the important decisions; they use both reward and punishment as appropriate
- Participative or system 4: these managers support their subordinates, encourage them to make decisions together, set them challenging targets and work closely with them to make sure that they achieve.

Likert claims that companies where the last style of leadership predominates tend to be most successful long-term.

He was also responsible for the useful concept of 'linking pins'. In a successful organisation, he maintains, each work group needs to be linked to the organisation in some coherent way. The most effective linkage comes from someone who is a member of more than one group. In most cases, the linking pin, who is the primary communications chain within the organisation, will be the team leader or departmental manager, who is both part of the team and a member of the management group.

But the real giants of organisational theory have been Peter Drucker (born 1909) and Henry Mintzberg (born 1939) – both of whom merit their own chapters in this book (see pages 70 and 91). Drucker's work, though it has now embraced virtually every area of management thinking, has its roots in organisational theory. His study of the organisation of General Motors, *The Concept of the Corporation* (1946), remains one of the most penetrating analyses of organisational behaviour.

Alfred P. Sloan

Born New Haven, 1875
Died 1966
Businessman

Lee Iacocca wrote in his biography: 'I envisaged myself as the new Alfred Sloan, the man who reorganized GM between the wars – and, in my opinion, the greatest genius ever in the auto business.' Charles Forte said Sloan was 'one of the most brilliant personalities in an organization that has always been rich in personalities'.

In his best-selling autobiography *My Years with General Motors* Sloan wrote: 'Management has been my specialization.' At General Motors Sloan was able to shape many of the modern concepts of business organisation. Perhaps his most notable achievement was the creation of the multi-division company. Sloan managed the huge company he developed with calm acceptance. 'I do not regard size as a barrier. To me it is only a problem of management,' said Sloan.

Sloan thought of organisation in terms far broader than those of Ford's production line. He regarded an organisation as a system by which successfully to achieve business objectives and strategies. He was a trained engineer and studied at Massachusetts Institute of Technology (later MIT named its management school after him) before becoming the general manager of the Hyatt Roller Bearing Company at the age of twenty-four. Soon after, it merged with United Motors and Sloan became its president. In 1917, in keeping with the trend for mergers in the automobile industry, United became part of General Motors. Sloan remained with the company until his retirement, shaping it into *the* dominant force in the automobile industry. Initially a director and vice-president, Sloan became president in 1923, chairman in 1946 and honorary chairman from 1956 until his death.

Given its development into the largest car maker and one of the most successful companies in the world, it is easy to underestimate the unhealthiness of General Motors in the early 1920s. The company had come about through a series of acquisitions and mergers with companies which were usually struggling from Ford's intense competition. On acquiring these companies, GM offered little support. It had extremely limited financial strength, no leading cars and was burdened by basic mismanagement – the companies acquired were allowed to keep the same ineffective managers as before. Even so, by 1920, GM was worth at least $170 million and produced 17 per cent of cars and trucks sold in the United States.

The organisation and management style of GM was established by its founder William Durant. A creator rather than a professional manager ('Mr Durant was a great man with a great weakness – he could create but not administer,' said Sloan), Durant was later toppled by a complex stock market scandal involving GM shares. A three-man executive committee, under Pierre du Pont and including Sloan, replaced him. When du Pont retired in 1923, Sloan became GM president.

Assessing the state of the company and the contribution of its founder, Sloan later wrote: 'Thanks mainly to Mr Durant, General Motors had then the makings of a great enterprise. But it was in good part physically unintegrated and in management uncoordinated; the expenditures for new companies, plants and equipment, and inventories were terrific – some of them not to bring a return for a long time, if ever – and as they went up, the cash went down. General Motors was heading for the crisis, from which the modern General Motors Corporation would emerge.'

He also recalled: 'The problem for General Motors, as I saw it in 1922, was to get the advantages of volume by buying on general contracts such items as tyres, steel, stationery, rags, batteries, blocks, acetylene, abrasives, and the like, and at the same time to permit the divisions to have control over their own affairs.'

Central to Sloan's success was his 'Organization Study' which, according to one observer, appeared 'to have sprung entirely from his own head in 1919 and 1920'. The plan was initially put in front of Durant who, Sloan recalled, 'appeared to accept it favourably, though he did nothing about it'. Now the origins of Sloan's plan for GM's reorganisation are commonly attributed to similar ideas on decentralisation which came from du Pont at the same time. But as Sloan pointed out, the approaches were significantly different – du Pont was heavily centralised whereas GM was overly decentralised with little power emanating from its headquarters. The trick, Sloan realised, was to preserve the merits of decentralisation with a more co-ordinated approach.

That such a change was necessary was abundantly clear to Sloan, who labelled GM's previous methods as 'management by crony, with the divisions operating on a horse-trading basis'. The plan prepared by Sloan was labelled 'federal decentralisation'. It treated GM's collection of companies as 'operating divisions, responsible for all their commercial operations, but supervised by a central staff responsible for overall policy and finance'. Each division had its own engineering, production and sales departments. To simplify the process, Sloan explained it as 'co-ordinated in policy and decentralized in administration'.

Sloan based his philosophy on two basic principles which he described in *My Years with General Motors*:

1. The responsibility attached to the chief executive of each operation shall in no way be limited. Each such organization headed by its chief executive shall be complete in every necessary function and enabled to exercise its full initiative and logical development.
2. Certain central organization functions are absolutely essential to the logical development and proper control of the Corporation's activities.

In fact, his ideas made use of Fayol's functional approach. He believed jobs had to be impersonal and task focused. Assessing the impact of the organisation plan, Sloan wrote: 'It increases the morale of the organization by placing each operation on its own foundation, making it feel that it is a part of the Corporation, assuming its own responsibility and contributing its share to the final result.'

In the financial area Sloan explained the benefits as: 'It develops statistics correctly reflecting the relation between the net return and the invested capital of each operating division – the true measure of efficiency – irrespective of the number of other divisions contributing thereto and the capital employed within such divisions.'

And in terms of strategic investment Sloan wrote: 'It enables the Corporation to direct the placing of additional capital where it will result in the greatest benefit to the Corporation as a whole.'

Sloan gave the appearance of omnipresence. He personally selected every GM executive from manufacturing managers and controllers to master mechanics. He created, in his own words, 'a group management comprised of very competent individuals'. Sloan also developed a 'product policy' so that, by 1925, GM was changing its models annually and was able to overtake Ford and its ageing Model T.

The role of the individual executive was played down. 'I feel that we are all apt to exaggerate what a Director can contribute to any Corporation,' he wrote in a letter to Pierre du Pont. His belief in organisation rather than personnel management continues to provide annoyance to management theorists.

James O'Toole, a professor of management and editor of *New Management* magazine, offered a personal view of Sloan's book in *Inc.* (February 1988):

> Of all the biographies I've read in my life, none has affected me so profoundly as Sloan's autobiography. I've read it three or four times. What I find fascinating about the book is that it is internally so consistent, so well argued, so convincing that it became the model for how managers should think – indeed, the model for much management education. And the intriguing thing is that it's all wrong. For example: for the first 300 pages or so, Sloan seems oblivious to the fact that there are any employees in the company. At the back of the book, when he finally discusses 'labor', he focuses on the adversarial relationship between the company and the union. Even then he never mentions Walter Reuther, the great United Auto Workers leader, by name.
>
> That, in a nutshell, helps me understand what's wrong with the management of large companies in America. It helps me in dealing with my students, most of whom want to become entrepreneurs and run small companies. By reading this book they learn which management practices to avoid.

Yet, much emulated, Sloan's restructuring of GM put into practice what were basic concepts, principles and perspectives. The emphasis on Sloan's organisational thinking can detract from his solid and pragmatic business acumen. 'The task of management is not to apply a formula but to decide issues on a case-by-case basis. No fixed, inflexible rule can ever be substituted for the exercise of sound business judgement in the decision-making process,' he wrote.

Rather modestly, Sloan explained his leadership style: 'I simply exercised . . . power with discretion; I got better results by selling my ideas than by telling people what to do. Yet the power to act must be located in the chief executive officer.' At one meeting of a top GM committee, Sloan is reported to have said: 'Gentlemen, I take it we are all in complete agreement on the decision here.' Everyone around the table nodded assent. 'Then,' continued Sloan, 'I propose we postpone further discussion of this matter until our next meeting, to give ourselves time to develop disagreement and perhaps gain some understanding of what the decision is all about.'

For Sloan, organisation provided the framework; people made decisions. 'From decentralization we get initiative, responsibility, development of personnel, decisions close to the facts, flexibility – in short, all the qualities necessary for an organization to adapt to new conditions. From co-ordination we get efficiencies and economies.' This proved the case for GM. Shrewd marketing meant it was able to fulfil its motto of 'A car for every purse and purpose', while Ford persisted with a car for one purse.

Sloan's achievement is clear: the multi-division company is firmly established as the basic structure for modern large businesses.

Peter Drucker

Born Vienna, Austria, 1909
Writer

Peter Ferdinand Drucker, journalist, art scholar and Jane Austen enthusiast, is seen by many as the man who invented management. Indeed, a book about him takes this as its title. Since the publication of his first book *The End of Economic Man* in 1939, his impact on management thinking and practice has been considerable.

Appreciation of Drucker's brilliant and wide-ranging mind is easily canvassed. *Business Week* recently labelled him 'the most read, most listened to, most regarded guru in management'.

Tom Peters has said: 'Knowledge is cumulative. Our debt to Peter Drucker knows no limit.' James O'Toole, professor of management at the University of Southern California, is also full of praise. In a *New Management* magazine celebration of Drucker's work, he said: 'Much as Keynes recast the framework in which all economics would thenceforth be analyzed, Peter F. Drucker has broken the mold of the old management and forged the new. The major organizational ideas of today's leading managers, business scholars, consultants, and journalists were almost all originally created in the crucible of Peter Drucker's productive mind.'

O'Toole assesses some of Drucker's achievements:

- He was the first to define the role of top managers as the keepers of corporate culture, the first to say that success depends on the vision articulated by the CEO.
- He was the first to show that structure follows strategy.
- He was the first to argue that success comes from sticking with the basics, the first to say that it all boils down to consumer sensitivity and the marketing of innovative products.
- He was the first to suggest that quality is a measure of productivity.
- He was the first to foresee the coming of post-industrialism (that is, the imminence of knowledge workers and computers) and the first to suggest that both the new workers and the new machines would necessitate revised managerial practices.
- He was the first to advocate mentoring, career planning and executive development as top management tasks.

The son of a leading Austrian government official (remembered by Drucker for his attempts to control inflation in the country and his involvement in the founding of the Salzburg Festival), Drucker gained a law degree and worked as a journalist. He then spent three years as an investment banker in London between 1933 and 1936. 'I was supposed to be the economist. This meant I did everything, I cleaned up after them.' He later commented: 'If I had wanted to be a rich man I would have stayed there, but it bored me to tears.'

Instead, Drucker struck out to follow his increasingly wide

range of interests. In 1937 he emigrated to the United States. C. Northcote Parkinson has described the genesis of Drucker's management thinking: 'Finding that Americans are chiefly interested in business, he began to study it with German seriousness, seeking to find there a philosophy of management. Finding none, he had to invent it.' Drucker remembers it differently. 'There wasn't a philosophy,' he says. 'But I wasn't a bit interested in management on my arrival in the United States.'

Of management thinking in the late 1930s, Drucker says: 'Nothing had come together. It was like a jigsaw puzzle. I asked what was missing: why the hell do we do all these things; what's the purpose?' Few people had even contemplated his basic questions. 'The concern was with the factory floor. Nobody had asked the question – what is management? I invented the term top management and am not proud of it. It's a poor one but there was no term. It was taken for granted,' he recalls and then quotes a German proverb – 'Whom God gives office, he gives the knowledge to go with it'. He believes it is not quite true.

Initially Drucker's challenging questions had a larger response in Japan. 'One of the greatest differences between the Japanese and Europeans and Americans is that they don't take their mission for granted. They start off with, what are we trying to do? Not "How do we do it?" '

He points out that management is as old as man. 'There is a book about me titled *Drucker: The Man Who Invented Management*. This idea is nonsense. The CEO of Pyramids, Inc. who built the Cheops pyramid 6,000 years ago surely knew more about management than any CEO of today. And so did whoever conceived, planned, and managed the cave of Ajanta in India (which carried out a master plan for 600 years without making a single mistake) or, even much earlier, whoever designed and managed the prehistoric cave paintings in Spain and in the Dordogne Valley of France. It is perhaps a little closer to the truth to call me the "man who discovered management" – though I am at best a co-discoverer and the most junior one.'

Others are not so sure. Tom Peters claims: 'A true "discipline of management" really didn't exist before Drucker. There is no doubt that Drucker changed the face of industrial America. He brought us decentralization, management by objectives, and the idea of customer-first business strategies. All are sound, garden variety practices in 1984 (even if not always used effectively). But all three were truly novel when Drucker began writing about them. GM and Du Pont were models of decentralization, starting in the 1920s, but Drucker was the first to label the phenomenon, and he deserves a huge share of the credit for moving some 75 or 80 per cent of the Fortune 500 to radical decentralization.'

The End of Economic Man marked the beginning of Drucker's lengthy and prolific career. 'I knew in 1933 how Hitler would end, and I then began my first book, *The End of Economic Man*, which could not be published until 1939, because no publisher was willing to accept such horrible insights. It was very clear to me that Hitler would end up killing the Jews. And it was also very clear that he would end up with a treaty with Stalin,' he wrote later.

The End of Economic Man was followed by *The Future of Industrial Man* in 1942 which Drucker still considers 'a very radical book'. It was regarded, at the time, as combining too broad a range of subjects, including, as it did, political science and economics. Drucker was warned, 'You have a very promising academic career – this book will destroy it.' Over forty years later he recalls these early experiences with glee. 'My publisher only published my second book because he felt he owed it to an author. He was sure there wasn't any possible interest in a book on management.'

Drucker then decided to examine a single company more closely. It was not initially successful, he explains: 'I happened to be friendly with the chairman of a big company whose office was above mine in the building. He was very nice to me but when I came to him and said could I study his company he threw me out and gave strict orders to the doorman not to let me in again – I was obviously a Bolshevik.' But a change of fortune was imminent. 'I'd given up on it so took a flat in New York for the winter and decided to write and make one last try. Then one day there was a telephone call from the vice-president of General Motors.' It was Drucker's first consultancy job. In 1942, General Motors was the biggest company in the world. At the time Drucker was totally inexperienced in business and the organisational problems it posed. 'The nearest I'd come to business was to be a junior partner in a very small merchant bank in London, which can hardly be considered a model of organisation.' His work with GM resulted in the 1946 book *The Concept of the Corporation*. It aimed to show what constitutes the modern organisation and what the managers running it should do. Again, reviewers struggled to come to terms with Drucker. One commented: 'It is to be hoped that this promising young scholar will soon devote himself again to serious matters.' GM was also far from impressed. 'Nobody ever admitted to having been the one who invited me,' says Drucker. 'If a GM manager was found with it his career was over!'

Drucker's methods remain direct and, for some executives, disturbing. When he became a consultant another consultant advised him to ask people the question: 'What do you do that explains you being on the payroll?' It is a question Drucker still asks; good answers remain rare. In a typical aphorism he has assessed his style: 'Most corporations consider me harshly critical. My clients don't consider me a management consultant but a management insultant.'

His growing consultancy work and the success of *The Practice of Management* provided the launch pad for the 'Management by Objectives' (MBO) movement of the late 1950s and early 1960s, in which Drucker was the leading figure.

The Practice of Management was published in 1954, but its message holds true over thirty years later. In it, Drucker identified the seven tasks of the manager of tomorrow. He or she:

1. Must manage by objectives.
2. Must take more risks and for a longer period ahead. And risk-taking decisions will have to be made at lower levels in the organization.
3. Must be able to make strategic decisions.
4. Must be able to build an integrated team, each member of which is capable of managing and of measuring his or her own performance and results in relation to the common objectives.
5. Will have to be able to communicate information fast and clearly. He or she will have to be able to motivate people. He or she must be able to obtain the responsible participation of other managers, of the professional specialists, and of all other workers.

6. Must be able to see the business as a whole and to integrate his or her function with it.
7. Will have to be able to relate the product and industry to the total environment, to find what is significant in it and what to take into account in his or her decisions and actions. And increasingly the field of vision of tomorrow's manager will have to take in developments outside his or her own market and country. Increasingly he or she will have to learn to see economic, political and social developments on a worldwide scale and to integrate worldwide trends into his or her own decisions.

George Odiorne, the author of *Management by Objectives* (1965), found Drucker to be an inspiration. He told International Management in June 1983: 'The first time I heard the MBO concept explained was when I was studying for my MBA under Drucker at New York University. He has been a voice of sanity in graduate schools. Faculty members are still busy running mathematical models and measuring the distance between managers' eyeballs but Drucker has always focused on what managers actually do, the practice of management.'

Drucker takes a fairly pragmatic view of the entire thing. 'MBO is just another tool. It is not the great cure for management inefficiency,' he has said. 'Management by Objectives works if you know the objectives. Ninety percent of the time you don't. The only things that evolve by themselves in an organization are disorder, friction and malperformance.' Typically, Drucker points to government programmes over the last fifty years and argues that all, except warfare, have achieved the exact opposite of their intention.

The MBO trend ignited by Drucker can detract from the basic tenets of his work. He argues, and has done so for the greater part of this century, that management is all-pervasive and all-important. 'We are beginning to realize that management itself is the central institution of our present society, and that there are very few, and mostly minor, differences between managing a business, managing a diocese, managing a hospital, managing a university, managing a research lab, managing a labor union, or managing a government agency. All along, this has been the main thrust of my work, and the one that distinguishes it from practically all my contemporaries working in the field.' In recent years Drucker has spent more time working for organisations such as hospitals and churches than with companies.

To Drucker, management is a universal force. Rosabeth Moss Kanter has described his faith in its power (in *New Management*, Winter 1985):

> Good management, as Drucker sees it, is responsible management. Good managers are clear that their central purpose is to serve the customer, and that they can do this best through treating workers as resources capable of sustained and valued contribution. In Drucker's view, customer service rather than profit should dominate management. Indeed, profit is not an end but a means. Profit is only what permits innovation, or the development of ever-improved goods and services, because continued investment is dependent on profits. And investment in the new enhances the quality of life.

> Good management is also our best hope for world peace. In the Drucker perspective, imperatives for growth push organizations beyond national borders in the search for new markets. The world becomes interconnected by a series of crosscutting trade relationships in which the interests of managers in the survival of their multinational enterprises outweigh the interests of politicians.

> Quality of life, technological progress, and world peace, then, are all the products of good management. No wonder Drucker feels that 'management' plays such a central role in our lives. At root, Drucker is a management utopian, descended as much from Robert Owen as Max Weber.

Drucker frankly admits: 'I'm more interested in people than ideas, but I'm better with ideas.' Human relations may not interest him, but humans within organisations do. 'I have come to the conclusion that the decisive change which underlies the rise of organizations is the shift from viewing the worker as a cost center to viewing him as a "resource",' he recently said.

Management, to Drucker, belongs with the humanities. It is not a narrow discipline with enshrined specialisms, but a broad base for human existence: 'A knowledge of Dante or of the history of technology is just as important as a knowledge of regression analysis.' Developing this, Drucker argues: 'My main point, I would say, is that the organization is a human, a social, indeed a moral phenomenon. To me it was fairly obvious that the new phenomenon, the new organization – namely, the large corporation – had to be seen and studied as a social and political phenomenon rather than as an "economic" one alone. And, contrary to the approach to the study of political and social organization that has prevailed in the West since Machiavelli, I stressed all along that organization does not deal with power but with responsibility. This is the one keynote of my work that has remained constant over more than 40 years.'

Management, Drucker would argue, requires simplification, not prolix books written by unworldly (and tenured) university staff. Part of Drucker's success in communicating this profound and discomfiting message lies in the clarity of his thought and language. His books, of which over twenty have been published and millions sold, are individualistic, some would say idiosyncratic. Drucker is at home talking on Trollope or Jane Austen ('a refresher course in writing') as management. 'I don't read management books. I look at them,' he admits.

His style remains firmly rooted in his journalistic background. His motto, he says, is 'I perceive, therefore I am.' Like his friend Warren Bennis, Drucker claims to remain a journalist at heart: 'I have a retentive memory for trivia, like flypaper, plus the journalist's feel for what makes sense and what doesn't.' Tom Peters describes his writing as 'not scholarly in the traditional sense. It is impressionistic, anecdotal, and borders on the dogmatic.'

Drucker has remained steadfastly detached from academia. 'I love to teach and write. But I am not a scholar and I have always had a very large part of my life outside the university. One Ivy League university wanted me, but not without restrictions. They wanted me to make sure that my writing was of scholarly quality and to make sure that I didn't consult more than one day a week. I said, "Consulting is my laboratory." This didn't make any sense to them and they said, "Perhaps you don't belong at a university . . . certainly not in business school." '

In the 1940s, Harvard wanted him to join its faculty, but to teach human relations not management. Drucker turned the offer down because: 'Harvard, to me, combines the worst of German academic arrogance with bad American theological seminary habits.' The great British universities are seen in a similar light by Drucker. 'I've never been terribly fond of Oxbridge,' he says. 'If you fit the model you're encouraged. If not, you're not allowed to be who you are.' Economists, he says, have never had to worry about where the next meal would come from and university faculties are filled with people 'who have never found out about the brilliant marketing strategy that doesn't work because the consumer does not behave the way you think he ought to.'

Of business schools, Drucker recommends that nobody should attend them until over thirty. 'Business schools are suffering from premature success. Now, they are improving yesterday a little bit. The worst thing is to improve what shouldn't be done at all,' he says, before going on to predict their decline.

Drucker is clearly and deliberately separated from the mainstream of management thinkers. He does not write commissioned books and has refused to become a celebrity. Instead, he works alone free from teams of enthusiastic young researchers hanging on to his words of wisdom. As he says: 'In this country if you tell people you're writing a book you can do anything.' He has also remained studiously distant from the actual practice of management. In one interview he admitted: 'I have always been a loner. I work best outside. That's where I'm most effective. I would be a very poor manager. Hopeless. And a company job would bore me to death. I enjoy being an outsider.' Indeed, his autobiographical work is entitled *Adventures of a Bystander*. It remains the favourite of his many books.

Drucker's influence may not be fully appreciated – he is not, after all, a globe-trotting preacher in the Tom Peters mould. Popular management books often expand on ideas Drucker talked of decades previously. John Naisbitt's *Megatrends* (1983) can be compared to Drucker's *The Age of Discontinuity* (1969); William Ouchi's *Theory Z* (1981) goes over some of the ground of *Men, Ideas and Politics* (1971), and the best-selling *In Search of Excellence* (1982) repackages some of the critical ideas in Drucker's 1954 book *The Practice of Management*.

Rosabeth Moss Kanter has argued that his idealism is a flaw: 'There is no evil in the world Drucker shows us, just ignorance. There is no power, no politics, no greed. There is also no human frailty that interferes with the implementation of ideal practice. There are no organizational complexities or flaws in the concept of the corporation that defeat those managers eager to implement Drucker's teachings.' Drucker realises management Utopia is unachievable. 'I don't think there is any such thing as a well-managed company because there are no universal geniuses. The only one was Leonardo da Vinci – and there is no record of Leonardo ever having played the flute!' But without an ideal to aim for, change might not come at all. Over his career, Drucker has observed and precipitated change. 'We are at the point where new concepts are emerging. There has been a tremendous realisation that all of society is made up organisations.'

His current work is as much concerned with the future as ever. Recent articles have focused on the likely changes in management, in the same way that Drucker's books were predicting drastic changes thirty years previously. In the *Harvard Business Review* (January–February 1988) Drucker wrote:

> The typical large business twenty years hence will have fewer than half the levels of management of its counterpart today, and no more than a third the managers. In its structure, and in its management problems and concerns, it will bear little resemblance to the typical manufacturing company, circa 1950, which our textbooks still consider the norm. Instead, it is far more likely to resemble organizations that neither the practicing manager nor the management scholar pays much attention to today: the hospital, the university, the symphony orchestra. For, like them, the typical business will be knowledge-based, an organization composed largely of specialists who direct and discipline their own performance through feedback from colleagues, customers, and headquarters. For this reason, it will be what I call an information-based organization.

Drucker laments, 'We are very slow learners.' His ideas have consistently marched far ahead of conventional wisdom. When conglomerates were fashionable, he warned of the problems of reckless mergers and acquisitions. At the height of its popularity he questioned General Motors' 'federal decentralization'. It was, he said, insensitive to external change. Later he was to argue against large executive staffs, to encourage tolerance of dissent in organisations and to call for a greater sense of responsibility, when managers seemed too selfish and greedy. 'I have never offered managers the easy panacea. I have always demanded of them that they think and decide and take responsibility. Let me say very bluntly – and with considerable conceit – that this explains why I am still around after more than forty years. The single-shot artists get immediate results; but, come Monday morning, all their revivalist converts are already backsliding and taking their first drink.'

Assessing his contribution to management thinking and practice, Drucker is typically forthright: 'I was the first one to see that the purpose of a business lies outside of itself – that is, in creating and satisfying a customer. I was the first to see the decision process as central, the first to see that structure has to follow strategy, and the first one to see, or at least the first to say, that management has to be management by objectives and self-control.'

A critic provided another viewpoint on Drucker's contribution: 'He has done for several generations of managers what Dr Benjamin Spock did for young mothers – guided and reassured them. He taught the care and feeding of the enterprise. And, most important, managers listened and learned.'

Thomas Watson Senior (1874–1956) and Thomas Watson Junior (born 1914)

Businessmen

In *The Frontiers of Management* (1986) Peter Drucker turns the conventional wisdom of the history of IBM on its head: 'Everybody knows that Thomas Watson Senior built IBM into a big computer company and was a business leader. But "everybody" is wrong. Thomas Watson Senior did not build the IBM we now know; his son, Tom Watson Junior, did this after he moved into the company's top management in 1946, at only thirty-two years old.' He goes on to point out that under Watson Senior IBM was a medium-sized company; his son transformed it into an industrial giant. What makes Watson Junior's story interesting and relevant for this book is that many of the principles of management he laid down have emerged as fundamentals of 'modern' management theory in the past decade.

The cold statistics of Watson Junior's success are staggering. When he joined IBM in 1946, its revenue was $119 million. When he retired, IBM's gross income was over $7 billion and the company was among the largest not only in the United States but the world. In fact, the modern IBM is the size of a moderately large country. In 1987, its turnover totalled $54 billion; the gross national product of Greece only reached $40 billion.

From restricted beginnings, Watson Senior was also a hugely successful businessman. National Cash Register, the company for which he worked as a young man, was run by John Patterson who voiced the opinion, 'The best way to kill a dog is to cut off its head.' This, he said, explained the way he treated competitors. NCR's success owed a good deal to forceful selling and its aggressive marketing tactics resulted in it becoming the first victim of American anti-trust laws in 1912. Narrowly avoiding a year's prison sentence, Watson became general manager of the Computer Tabulating Recorder Company based in New York. It was 1914, the year of Watson Junior's birth, and at the age of forty Watson Senior was set on building a company which would become larger and more successful than NCR.

His aim to outstrip NCR was achieved. Computer Tabulator Recorder's revenues doubled from $4.2 million in 1914 to $8.3 million in 1917. In 1924, the company changed its name – rather ambitiously it seemed – to International Business Machines. 'You cannot be a success in any business without believing that it is the greatest business in the world,' said Watson Senior. The name neatly disguised the fact that its products included butcher's scales, meat slicers, coffee grinders, time clocks and punched card tabulating machines. By the 1930s, as the rest of American industry struggled, IBM had 90 per cent of the tabulating machines market and was highly prosperous. In 1934 Watson was thought to be the highest paid executive in the US with a salary of $364,432. By 1946 the company had grown thirty-eight-fold and it was actually able to take on staff during the depression.

Watson Senior's success was built around many of the lessons he had learned at NCR. He leased rather than sold machines and insisted customers used only his company's punched cards. But selling was deemed all-important and Watson went to great lengths to elevate the status of his sales team. 'I want my IBM salesmen to be people to whom their wives and their children can look up. I don't want their mothers to feel that they have to apologize for them or have to dissimulate when they are being asked what their son is doing,' he said.

IBM was further differentiated from other companies by its corporate philosophy. There was even a company song to encourage morale: 'With Mr Watson leading, to greater heights we'll rise and keep our IBM respected in all eyes.' Watson Senior summed up his outlook when he said: 'It is better to aim at perfection and miss than it is to aim at imperfection and hit.' IBM employees were well paid and offered far more job security than elsewhere. Mistakes were not punished by immediate dismissal. Watson's much repeated advice to salesmen was simple: 'Do right.'

For Thomas Watson Junior, IBM was a force in his life from early childhood. 'In a sense I grew up in the company,' he said later. He made his first speech at an IBM sales meeting when he was twelve and, when a graduate in geology from Brown University, he became an IBM salesman in downtown Manhattan. After piloting B-24s during the war Watson rejoined IBM and finally emerged from his father's formidable shadow in 1956 when he became IBM president. Later he was to become chief executive, chairman and, in 1989, emeritus chairman. His career with IBM has only been broken by a spell as US ambassador to the Soviet Union at the time of the invasion of Afghanistan.

When Watson Junior joined IBM immediately after the war, it had 22,492 employees. In 1952 it unveiled its first computer, the model 701 for scientists. In 1956, when he became chief executive, it employed 72,504. The following year IBM became a billion-dollar corporation. In 1961 Watson Junior became chairman; ten years later, when he became chairman of the executive committee, IBM employed 265,493. On Watson Junior's retirement in 1984 there were 490,000 IBM employees.

Watson Junior developed and continued much of what his father put into practice. The IBM philosophy towards employees and customers has become internationally recognised. In his book *A Business and Its Beliefs* Watson Junior wrote:

> I firmly believe that any organization, in order to survive and achieve success, must have a sound set of beliefs on which it premises all its policies and actions.
>
> Next, I believe that the most important single factor in corporate success is faithful adherence to those beliefs.
>
> And finally, I believe that if an organization is to meet the challenges of a changing world, it must be prepared to change everything about itself except those beliefs as it moves through corporate life.
>
> In other words, the basic philosophy, spirit, and drive of an organization have far more to do with its relative achievements than do technological or economic resources, organizational structure, innovation, and timing.

The cornerstones of the IBM philosophy developed by the Watsons are:

- The individual must be respected
- The customer must be given the best possible service
- Excellence and superior performance must be pursued.

IBM also has five business goals:

- To enhance customer partnerships
- To be the leader in products and services, excelling in quality and innovation
- To grow with the industry
- To be the most efficient in everything we do
- To sustain our profitability which funds our growth.

When Peters and Waterman were searching out 'excellent' companies for their book *In Search of Excellence*, IBM was probably the least surprising name on the list. Its commitment to excellence is frequently voiced and borne out by results over the greater part of the century. Watson Junior says in his book: 'We believe that an organization should pursue all tasks with the idea that they can be accomplished in a superior fashion. IBM expects and demands superior performance from its people in whatever they do.'

Putting this into practice took on a variety of forms during

Watson Junior's tenure at the company. In 1958, for example, IBM became the first major corporation to place hourly paid workers on weekly salaries and was among the first to pay employees for holidays. Its commitment to never making its employees redundant remains intact. 'We've spent more time worrying about human resources and human kinds of procedures than we have on electronics or sales procedures over the past two decades,' Watson Junior later observed.

In fact, IBM's explosive success owed much to Watson Junior's ability to select the right people. 'Tom was never a technical man,' said a colleague on his retirement, 'but he had the imagination and the vision to see what needed to be done, and to find people who could do it.' Watson Junior explains: 'I think that a continual willingness to restructure, change and promote was probably my greatest contribution.' And he goes on to say: 'We have found that an ingrained understanding of the beliefs of IBM, far more than technical skill, has made it possible for our people to make the company successful.'

Of course, IBM has been fighting from an exceptionally strong base for decades. Its risks were, to some extent, offset by its size. Indeed, the company has regularly been accused of pursuing monopolistic practices (the recent book *Big Blue* chronicles this side of IBM's history). 'Because we've been operating in a fortunate position all through our technological history compared with our competition, we have generally been able to take safe conservative steps, and our percentage of wins has been exceedingly high,' Watson says. Even so, he did take large risks while in charge of IBM. The company's present strength, for example, owes much to the System/360 family of computers launched in the 1960s. 'We bet the company on it,' says Watson. System/360 cost a mammoth $5 billion to develop – more than the atomic bomb.

The reorganisation of the company in the late 1950s also showed Watson Junior as capable of taking risks. Recollecting it, he wrote: 'In late 1956, after several months of planning, we called the top 100 or so people in the business to a three-day meeting at Williamsburg, Virginia. We went into that meeting a top-heavy, monolithic company and came out of it decentralised.'

Tom Horton of the American Management Association, and

a former IBM employee, provides an insight into Watson Junior's management style.

> I asked a lot of CEOs what were the unique things that can be furnished by a CEO and no one else. I sent him a five-page summary of the results; he added in the margin: 'I contributed fear.'
>
> He would reward and encourage as well. I was once in his office with a scientist who argued with him on a technical point. I intervened on the scientist's side and won the point. He called me into a side room and said: 'A great company is like a symphony orchestra.' Then he compared all the other executives to instruments. 'What instrument do you think you are? I think you are a violin. Do you know how to tune a violin? If you overtune it, one twist will break its neck. Would you like me to tune you?' Of course, I said yes. Thereafter he'd call me and say: 'I just saw a message you sent. I'd have phrased it this way . . .' At a certain point he decided I was in tune. He called me in and said: 'What do we pay you?' I told him. 'No we don't,' he said. 'It's XYZ.' That was a $10,000 raise.'

This individualistic management style was backed by a forceful commitment to marketing. IBM's marketing reputation was set early in its history and its marketing expertise was used by Japanese multinationals as a model after the war. (IBM Japan is the country's largest and oldest foreign investment, having been first established before the Second World War.) Buck Rodgers, former vice-president for marketing at IBM, has chronicled the company's marketing strengths in his best-selling book *The IBM Way*. 'At IBM everybody sells! Every employee has been trained to think that the customer comes first – everybody from the CEO, to the people in finance, to the receptionists, to those who work in manufacturing. Marketing and sales are so tightly woven into IBM's past, present, and future successes that they are inseparable.'

Customer care was regarded as a top priority by Watson Junior. 'We want to give the best customer service of any company in the world,' he wrote and believed the advertisement 'IBM Means Service' was the company's best. 'In its commitment to customer service, IBM learned that the best way to serve a prospect was to provide equipment adapted to his requirements, rather than ask him to alter his business to fit our machines.' Peter Drucker makes the point in his book *Management* that IBM's customer orientation spreads throughout the organisation:

> One of the reasons that IBM has been so successful in the computer business is that it realized early that many different people in a company have to buy a computer if there is to be a sale. The people who use the computer (which largely means accounting and financial people) have to buy it. But top management also has to buy. And so do the people who are to use the computer as their information tool, that is, operating managers. From the beginning IBM has sold to all these groups and has thought through what each looks for, needs to know and considers of value; and how each can be reached.

The strength of Watson Junior's achievement may be seen in the continuation of many of his and his father's ideas in the IBM of today. In the 1980s IBM experienced the worst slump in its history, but remained loyal to the principle of no lay-offs. Its marketing orientation remains strong. Current Chairman John Akers rose up through the marketing ranks and has said: 'The fundamentals that Tom Watson Senior built the business on: pursuit of excellence, superior service, respect for people . . . they are as alive and well today as ever.' And today, in every market economy except Japan, IBM is the dominant supplier of mainstream computer systems.

Charles Handy

Born Dublin, 1932
Educator

Charles Handy began life in Ireland, the son of a vicar. Educated at an English public school, to which he won a scholarship, Handy went to Oxford University. On his first day at Oriel College, he and his compatriots were advised by the provost: 'You can do everything in life twice except die and take an Oxford degree.' His experiences at Oxford have profoundly influenced Handy's thinking and approach towards organisations. 'I spent four years there,' he says. 'I'm not sure that I've ever recovered.' Handy received a first in 'Greats', an intellectual pot-pourri of classics, history and philosophy. 'It wasn't a conscious choice to study Greats. At the time I regretted it, but it gave me an ability to think, which I am now thankful for.'

Laden with concepts and apparently destined for an academic career, surprisingly Handy joined Shell International. 'They told me I had a well-trained but empty mind,' he recalls. He was sent to Malaysia and found himself, at the age of twenty-two, in charge of five airfield refuelling systems in Sarawak. The time-scale, he remembers, was short. 'Elated with the honour, scared stiff by the responsibility, I took myself first to the aviation manager, who congratulated and promised me a full-scale training course in airfield refuelling systems. "How long have you got?" he asked. "Twenty-four hours," I replied. "In that case," he said very quietly, "we had best both go down to the cathedral and pray." ' It was, Handy says, 'education by small catastrophe'.

Later Handy found himself as Shell's economist for South-East Asia despite his absence of expertise in the field. He bought *Teach Yourself Economics* and steered clear of further catastrophes.

Returning to Britain, Handy found life with Shell humdrum: 'In Malaysia I had my own fiefdom. In London I couldn't cope with the bureaucracy.' He was transferred to the staff training college where 'I discovered I adored teaching'. After two years he was asked to go to Liberia but, like Peter Drucker, Handy had discovered that he didn't feel comfortable working for a large organisation.

He was then approached by one of the people organising the establishment of the London Business School which, with Manchester, was opened in 1965. The school was laying plans to run a Sloan Management Programme similar to that at Massachusetts Institute of Technology, a sabbatical year for people in their thirties. Handy was recruited to direct the programme if it got off the ground. It was, he admits, 'a bit vague'. Filling in time, he worked briefly in the City, as an economist for the Anglo-American Corporation, before joining MIT's Sloan School of Management. 'At that time I was an oil executive who'd become interested in training managers,' says Handy. 'I thought mathematics and computers were the answers to management. I thought that they were going to be the secret of the future.' But after three days at MIT, Handy attended a meeting at which he was introduced to Warren Bennis, Chris Argyris, Ed Schein and Mason Haire. 'They said they taught organisational behaviour. I asked what was that?' recalls Handy. 'I sat at their feet and forgot about maths and computers. It transformed my life.' Schein became his supervisor; Handy's fascination with organisations has dominated his subsequent work.

In his first book Handy wrote:

> I came to the study of people in organizations expecting certainty and absolute knowledge in the behavioural sciences. I anticipated that I would find laws governing the behaviour of people and of organizations as sure and as immutable as the laws of the physical sciences. I was disappointed. I found concepts and ideas abounding. I found, too often, ponderous confirmation of the obvious and weighty investigation of trivia. But the underlying unalterable laws were not there, organizations remained only patchily efficient, and the most exciting of the ideas did not always work.

On graduating from MIT in 1967 Handy did indeed join the London Business School to launch and direct its Sloan Programme, which continues to run. Later he became professor of management development at the school.

Despite the attractions of academic life, Handy was keen to convert his knowledge and enthusiasm for organisations into a book. He packed his car boot full of books and went to France where he wrote his first book *Understanding Organizations* (1976). It broke new ground in bringing a variety of theories together for the first time. Says Handy: 'I wrote it as an exercise for myself. I was making sure I understood it all.'

Understanding Organizations carried the advice, 'I would encourage anyone else to burn this book after reading it and start to write their own – it's the only way to really own the concepts.' Handy does not argue that each individual organisation exists in a theory-free vacuum. 'There has to be some sort of framework to learn about management. You have to put your experience into the theories,' says Handy. He explains his work as 'a few concepts. Some may help you understand your own world. It's a question of interpreting experience.'

Handy emphasises that *Understanding Organizations* is a textbook for students (and it continues to be bought by them in large numbers). 'Policemen and teachers have read it. It's not a book about business; it's about organisations. I wouldn't dream of giving it to ordinary business people.'

Handy's next book *The Gods of Management* (1979) provided a more idiosyncratic insight into organisational behaviour. In *The Gods of Management* he develops an elaborate analogy between four Greek gods and certain characteristics of organisations. The gods Zeus, Apollo, Athena and Dionysus are used to illustrate the intangibility of organisations and management. Handy's point is that adopting ancient symbols is as pertinent as providing any other framework for organisations.

Explaining *The Gods of Management*, Handy says: 'It doesn't tell people what to do. It is for explaining and interpreting experience. Management is a soft theory area. It is not precise. I have a great dislike for people who are looking for a hard law for management.' Instead, Handy sees himself in the Peter Drucker mould as an intuitive interpreter of what goes on inside organisations. In *The Gods of Management* he wrote: 'Management is more fun, more creative, more personal, more political and more intuitive than any textbook. Nevertheless, whilst every organization is different, there are patterns which can be discerned, models to be imitated and some guidelines which can be followed.' He is arguing for a completely new approach to thinking and dealing with organisations.

Like Drucker, Handy does not limit his interest in organisations to business. He is, for example, interested in the organisation of schools and has written on the subject in *Understanding Schools as Organizations* (1986). Similarly, his interest in voluntary organisations resulted in *Understanding Voluntary Organizations* (1988). 'Today people want more out of life and more out of organizations,' Handy argues.

His personal fascinations have gradually come to the fore in his published work. In *Understanding Organizations* he recounted the thoughts of others. In *The Gods of Management* he wryly developed his thoughts on organisations around a thought-provoking pattern. In *The Future of Work* (1984), he wrote about his view of the future and it is a far more personal book than its predecessors. It argues that in the world of the future we must 'look beyond employment and beyond the status quo' and is a passionate call for wider awareness of how the world of work has, and is, changing. In 1988, Handy carried this theme forward in his highly influential *The Making of Managers* which investigated the international state of management education. The report compared American, Japanese, German, French and British approaches to management education, imploring Britain to overturn the sad fact that 'little is known in Britain of the facts of management development'.

The future, Handy predicts, will be one of 'discontinuous change'. The path through time, with society slowly, naturally and rationally improving on a steady course, is a thing of the past. The blinkers have to be removed. Handy tells the story of the Peruvian Indians who saw invading ships on the horizon. Having no knowledge of such things, they discounted them as a freak of the weather. They settled for their sense of continuity.

In order to adapt to such a society, the way people think will have to change fundamentally. 'We are all prisoners of our past. It is hard to think of things except in the way we have always thought of them. But that solves no problems and seldom changes anything.' He points out that people who have thought unconventionally, 'unreasonably', have had the most profound impact on twentieth-century living. Freud, Marx and Einstein succeeded through 'discontinuous' (or what Handy labels 'upside-down') thinking.

In practice, Handy believes that certain forms of organisation will become dominant. They are the type of organisation most readily associated today with service industries. First, what he calls the 'shamrock organisation' – 'a form of organisation based around a core of essential executives and workers supported by outside contractors and part-time help'. The consequence of such an organisational form is that organisations in the future are likely to resemble the way consultancy firms, advertising agencies and professional partnerships are organised now.

The second emergent structure identified by Handy is the federal one. It is not, he quickly points out, another word for decentralisation. He provides a new blueprint for federal organisations. The central function co-ordinates, influences, advises and suggests. It does not dictate terms or short-term decisions. The centre is, however, concerned with long-term strategy; it is 'at the middle of things and is not a polite word for the top, or even for head office'. Handy points to Hanson Trust as an example of a company with a small strategic centre supported by a plethora of front-line outfits.

The third type of organisation Handy anticipates is what he calls 'the Triple I'. The three 'Is' are information, intelligence and ideas. In such organisations the demands on personnel management are large. Explains Handy: 'The wise organisation also knows that their smart people are not to be easily defined as workers or as managers but as individuals, as specialists, as professionals or executives, or as leaders (the older terms of manager and worker are dropping out of use), and that they and it need also to be obsessed with the pursuit of learning if they are going to keep up with the pace of change.'

Handy believes that *The Age of Unreason* (1989) is the most personal of all his books to date. 'People are not human resources. They are living individuals with the right to be different. Organisations which are set up to exploit people are wrong. This moral tone seems to be creeping into my work.'

Handy is gradually attracting a wider audience. He has, among his varied activities, also done a brief radio slot called 'Thought for the Day'. 'I'm probably better known for doing that than for any of the books. I have to believe there is a meaning in life and I have to believe in a meaning for organisations. I want to be more than an interpreter of theories,' he says.

His motivation is apparently simple: 'I write books because I can't help it. It's the process of clarifying my ideas.' It is also, he says, inspired by his interest in getting people to think. He has been involved, for example, in St George's House in Windsor Castle, a centre concerned with the issues of ethics and values in society as a whole, and is currently chairman of the Royal Society of Arts.

Henry Mintzberg

Born Montreal, 1939
Professor at McGill University, Montreal, Canada

Henry Mintzberg's latest book includes a dedication 'to those of us who spend our public lives dealing with organizations and our private lives escaping from them'. Mintzberg stands resolutely apart from the mainstream of conventional wisdom. He has been labelled 'the scourge of strategic orthodoxy' and has resigned from teaching MBA students because he believes that they are thrust into the real world of business with little real industrial experience. 'I'm not a parer of toenails. I go for the jugular vein of international issues,' he has claimed. His work has challenged much conventional management thinking, from the nature and structure of organisations to strategy development. To Mintzberg, many accepted management practices are a hindrance to change and innovation.

International Management observed: 'Henry Mintzberg is something of an *enfant terrible* in the world of management thinking. He has made a name and a career from going against accepted management theories, championing the individual manager against the system, and exploring what he would call the obvious areas overlooked by more esoteric colleagues.'

Now Bronfman Professor of Management at McGill University in Canada, Mintzberg graduated in mechanical engineering from McGill in 1961. Even at that stage he had decided that there was more to the practical subjects than the theoretical. 'I was more interested in industrial engineering, but there wasn't a programme in that,' he explains. His working career began in operations research with Canadian Railways where he was hired by 'a biologist with a Castro beard'. This unconventional character in a conventional company was able to demonstrate to Mintzberg that bureaucracies functioned, when they functioned at all, because people subverted the rules, not because they behaved in a logical, prescribed manner – and he had a significant influence on Mintzberg's thinking: 'At Canadian Railways I learned about bureaucracy and politicking in large organisations. I'm a corporate voyeur. Being in a staff position, I was able to step back and look at the organisation almost as an outsider.'

Mintzberg says he was surprised to get into MIT: 'As an undergraduate at McGill I was more interested in extracurricular activities. I was sports editor of the daily newspaper. I helped to run the winter carnival. My grades at MIT (at Sloan School) were not bad, but not exceptional. I stayed on for my Ph.D. proposing to do it in the field of policy (or strategy as we now call it). But there was no professor teaching that subject, so I was basically doing my doctoral research on my own, working with professors, but not with anyone trained in that area. At the time, Harvard *was* a big centre for policy/strategy. But I didn't agree with its approach. I felt strategy needed a theoretical base. There was a lot of literature available, but no one had pulled it all together.'

Effectively given his head, Mintzberg took advantage of the opportunity to break the mould. But first, like all academics looking for tenure, he began work on a book. 'In my first year of teaching, I set out to write *The Theory of Management Policy*. As I prepared each lecture, that became the next chapter.'

What started as a textbook has over the years become a series of books, each based on a single chapter. Mintzberg says: 'That initial study set the whole pattern for how I chopped up the world.' *The Nature of Managerial Work*, his first published book, turned out to be 300 pages long. *The Structuring of Organizations* was 500 pages long. The next was 700 pages. It didn't take a genius to work out that the next would be 900 pages long and in two volumes.

The pattern of Mintzberg's thinking breaks into three periods, divided as he describes it 'by two gestalt shifts. The first was the concept of configuration, introduced to me by a colleague from Carnegie-Mellon, Pradip Cundwallah. Basically this says that organizations get things together in ways that fit their particular circumstances. They do not plan so much as have a coherent system for organizing the attributes of their organization. I wanted to write a book on structure. I found it all very confusing until I realised they were built around configuration. As a result, I was able to open up new categories of organization, to which I gave names such as adhocracy. Before I had just cut vertically through organizations. Configuration allowed me to cut horizontally.

'The second gestalt shift came from a student in 1980, who asked if I was playing jigsaw or Lego in my previous books. It made me ask: are all of these elements put together in a predetermined way, or can you build new structures with them?'

Out of this questioning emerged his latest book, *Mintzberg on Management*, in which he argues that 'society has become unmanageable as a result of management'. Management disciplines, he argues, have driven out intuition, which is a vital element in setting organisation direction and making effective decisions. He recounts the story of the Inuit hunters, who in times gone by 'could find their way across dozens of miles of flat white tundra to visit the camp of a friend, guided only by their intuition. A few years ago, the snowmobile of three young Inuit broke down only a few miles from their home and they froze to death because they could not make their way back.' Our organisations, both public and private sector, have become so large and bureaucratic that they, too, have lost the instinct for survival, he argues.

Looking at Mintzberg's major contributions to management thinking, his first impact arose out of his studies into the work of managers who run organisations. He 'found that there were tremendous pressures on them to be superficial and concluded that managers had to learn to be effective in their superficiality'. In *The Nature of Managerial Work* he points to the roots of his interest – his puzzlement as a child over what on earth his father, the president of a small Canadian engineering company, did all day.

Mintzberg's approach to this issue was straightforward. He simply observed a number of senior managers in different companies for a week each, as they dealt with the mail, held meetings and negotiations, discussed problems and agreed on actions to be taken. The dominant view of the executive's job at the time was summarised most eloquently by Peter Drucker, who described the organisation as an orchestra and the chief executive as the conductor. Mintzberg dismisses Drucker's analogy – not least because the orchestral performance an audience sees is the result of days or weeks of practice, during which co-ordination within the orchestra is far from polished.

Instead, he maintains: 'The manager works immersed in an unrelenting stream of callers and telephone calls. Jumping from topic to topic, he thrives on interruptions and, more often than not, disposes of items in ten minutes or less. Though he may have fifty projects going, all are delegated. He juggles them, checking each one periodically before sending it back into orbit.

'The manager spends as much time dealing with outsiders – his peers, customers, business contacts and government people – as with subordinates (or superiors). He is constantly alert for snatches of "soft" information – gossip, hearsay, speculation – that may keep him a step ahead – passing along such titbits to the right subordinate is an important part of his job.

'The manager shuns written reports, skims periodicals and merely processes his mail. He has a pronounced bias toward doing business face to face or by telephone – a mode enabling him to gauge emotions and move fast. But it also saddles him with the time-consuming chore of giving lengthy instructions whenever he delegates things.'

All of this is a long way from previous theories. Mintzberg divides these into eight basic concepts, starting with Henri Fayol's PODSCORB (effective managers plan, organise, direct, staff, co-ordinate, report and budget), which he names the classical school. The other schools are:

- the great man school, based on descriptions of their behaviour by very successful managers
  (interestingly, Mintzberg is now examining this approach as a means of understanding other issues of management)
- the entrepreneurial school, which sees the manager as a rational innovator
- the decision theory school, which focuses on how managers make decisions and sees this as the manager's primary role
- the leader effectiveness school, which concentrates on the manager's role as a leader
- the leader power school, which looks at how managers gain and use power
- the leader behaviour school, which looks at how managers behave in various situations
- the work activity school, which looks at the tasks managers do, from a work analysis point of view.

All of these theories, says Mintzberg, tackle only part of the problem. In his own analysis, which is closest to the last two categories, he looked not only at the activities, but at the reasons for them. That involved a systematic approach to examining:

- job content
- job characteristics
- job variations
- job programming.

From this came a definition of the ten key roles of a manager. These form three basic clusters:

- interpersonal roles – figurehead (representing the unit or the organisation, for example, for formal presentations); leader (providing direction and purpose); liaison (similar to Likert's 'linking pin' role)
- informational roles – monitor (making sure everything proceeds as planned); dissemination (giving other people the information they need to make decisions); spokesperson (to the outside world)
- decision-making roles – entrepreneur (seizing new opportunities); resource allocator (deciding which projects or activities to support); disturbance handler (correcting deviations from plan); and negotiator.

He argues that managers may adopt any or all of these roles within a short period, usually without thinking which particular role they are in at the moment.

Although initially attacked by some behavioural theorists as superficial, *The Nature of Managerial Work* gradually established Mintzberg's reputation. To many practising managers the results appealed because it made them feel less guilty about how they spent their time. When he summarised his findings in an article in *Harvard Business Review*, the text rapidly broke records for reprint sales. Articles in the *New York Times* and the *Wall Street Journal* also helped to spread his reputation.

Next came 'research on the processes by which organisations make their strategies – in other words how they establish basic directions for themselves. In my work and that of others, this turned out to be far more complicated than had been generally thought. In fact, the long favoured approach, called "strategic planning", proved to be a myth: there turned out to be no systematic way to create strategy. And so I came to describe two less systematic approaches, a centralised one based on entrepreneurial vision and a decentralised one based on "grass-roots" initiatives.'

The Structure of Organizations came about because Mintzberg wanted to understand how organisations formed their strategies. In order to do so, however, he reasoned that it was necessary first to understand how they were structured. The book contains two main themes: the importance of flows (of information, decision-making and so on); and how and why organisations configure themselves in particular ways. Mintzberg observed that traditional ways of analysing the variables that affected organisation structure were limited because they involved looking at issues two at a time, when, in reality, the mixture of influences was far more complex. By developing 'clusters' of influences, Mintzberg was able to identify five types of 'ideal' organisation structure:

- The simple structure: typically a small, entrepreneurial business still run by the owner or his family. Operating and management systems tend to be very basic; control is exercised as much by the manager going round talking to people as by formal reporting. The nature of the product or service tends to be craft and small batch rather than a mass production and assembly line. These firms are characterised by rapid response to external change and by cohesive teams on the shopfloor.

- The machine bureaucracy is a large, mass production operation that breaks jobs down into simple, repetitive tasks. It often has many hierarchical layers, a great many rules and procedures and numerous specialists. It has much less team cohesion and is much slower to react to change.

- The professional bureaucracy – for example, a hospital or an accountancy practice – places most of the power in the hands of key professionals whose allegiance is as much (or more) to their profession as to the organisation. These professionals have a great deal of freedom to decide how things should be done. The support staff, however, have very little freedom of action, so there is frequently conflict between the two groups.

- The divisionalised form describes the typical large company that has broken its activities into recognisable divisions, each – in theory – allowed a high degree of freedom to make its own decisions. The central headquarters exerts control primarily through financial targets, but it may also choose many other areas of control. The greater the central control, the more the divisions behave like machine bureaucracies.

- The adhocracy is an organisation designed to meet a continuous flow of new problems, rather than to produce standard goods or services. It is characterised by numerous project teams, that come together, change in membership as the project progresses and disband when the project is completed. (The development team for a new computer might be a good example.)

Within each of these organisations are five basic components. Each has:

- an operating core (the people who make the product or provide the service)
- support staff (people who provide the internal services needed to keep the operating core going – for example, personnel or canteen staff)
- a technostructure (people who design the systems and procedures to control what people in the operating core do)
- the middle line (the line managers responsible for operating core departments)
- and the strategic apex (the senior executives who define where the company is going, set strategy and oversee the activities of the line managers).

From structure, Mintzberg moved on to examine power in organisations, again as a step towards understanding the nature of strategy. Instead of focusing on individual power, as most previous theorists had done, Mintzberg looks at the power structure – how the roles people play in organisations give them power. He describes the main categories of power configurations as follows: 'I find it convenient to distinguish an external coalition (of outsiders) from an internal one (of essentially full-time employees). The former can be described as dominated, divided, or passive, and the latter as autocratic, bureaucratic, ideologic, meritocratic, or politicised. Putting together combinations of these two leads to six power configurations: the Continuous Chain (dominated, bureaucratic), the Closed System (passive, bureaucratic), the Commander (passive, autocratic), the Missionary (passive, ideologic), the Professional (divided, meritocratic), and the Conflictive (divided, politicised).'

Mintzberg's approach to strategy mirrors his approach to managerial behaviour. Having established the context in which managers develop strategy (the organisation structure and the power structure) he was able to track strategy-making as what he describes as 'a pattern in a stream of decisions'. Later, he amended that description to replace 'decisions' with 'actions'. Over thirteen years, he and his research students tracked the strategies of eleven organisations, looking for patterns in the most important decisions (such actions as store openings and closings for a retailer, new flight destinations for an airline, or new product introductions for a manufacturer).

The traditional view of strategy-making is, once again, a rational view. Managers analyse the problems and opportunities, decide upon a strategy and then seek the resources to implement it. The evidence for such an approach comes, he suggested, because researchers, having defined strategy in planning terms, went out and interviewed people who had plans. But, he says, that does not represent the reality of many organisations' approach to strategy. He explains: 'Our research suggests that no strategy is 100 per cent deliberate, that is, realised exactly as intended. Perhaps 95 per cent, but never 100 per cent. Every strategy seems to be at least partly emergent: that is, elements of it evolve over time.' He continues to say that in practical terms, formal methods of strategic planning in large organisations are so cumbersome that it is a wonder they ever work.

In his landmark *Harvard Business Review* article, 'Crafting Strategy', Mintzberg suggests an alternative description of the process, which he describes as strategy formation (as opposed to formulation, which implies deliberation).

Craft evokes traditional skill, dedication, perfection through the mastery of detail. What springs to mind is not so much thinking and reason as involvement, a feeling of intimacy and harmony with the materials at hand, developed through long experience and commitment. Formulation and implementation merge into a fluid process of learning through which creative strategies evolve.

He also draws the analogy of weeds growing in a garden. Eventually some turn out to be valuable plants.

Mintzberg says that in actually *forming* strategy, managers do the following:

- They manage stability, that is, they make sure that the strategies they have are pursued vigorously and that the implications are formally worked out. If they try to reassess strategy continuously they end up unable to implement anything.

- They detect discontinuity, that is, they look for changes that might make a serious difference to their business. Once again, intuition comes to the fore. 'The real challenge in crafting strategy lies in detecting the subtle discontinuities that may undermine a business in the future. And for that, there is no technique, no program, just a sharp mind in touch with the situation. Such discontinuities are unexpected and irregular, essentially unprecedented. They can be dealt with only by minds that are attuned to existing patterns yet able to perceive important breaks in them. Unfortunately, this form of strategic thinking tends to atrophy during the long periods of stability that most organizations experience (just as it did at Volkswagenwerk during the 1950s and 1960s). So the trick is to manage within a given strategic orientation most of the time yet be able to pick out the occasional discontinuity that really matters.'

- They know the business, not in an intellectual way, but by personal feel for what makes it tick.

- They manage patterns. When they detect beneficial patterns emerging, they intervene to help them take shape. This implies letting a large number of strategies germinate, then weeding periodically to allow the most promising room to grow.

- They reconcile change and continuity. They decide when

to hold back a strategy whose time has not yet come, and when to let rip with new strategies.

Much of Mintzberg's reputation as an iconoclast comes from the pungency with which he makes his statements about management. For example, his enthusiasm for getting into the heart of complex issues, by experiencing them: 'Engineers think analogically. They are not afraid of getting their hands dirty. . . . I can't say that for economists and other advocates of the rational model.' Or his opinions of MBA courses: 'We should not be in the business of training 22-year-olds to be MBAs. We should be making them into managers. You give people a case study on General Motors and tell them to read it overnight and come up next morning with what GM should do. The approach assumes that managers are decisive, but there's no basis for assuming that. Anyone who asks for more information is put down. Then you wonder why there is so much superficiality in the executive suites.'

In recent years, he says he has become more aware of the dangers of being too polemic. 'Some people will seize on anything you say.' None the less, he claims: 'The most outrageous things I've said are the truest.'

Mintzberg is also a confirmed collector of other people's aphorisms. Above his desk is a quote from Einstein. 'The confusion of ends and means characterizes our age.' Over the door is another sign. 'The higher the monkey climbs, the more you see its arse.' Elsewhere is a motto. 'God made Americans to test theories.' ('I'd much rather speculate about ideas than prove speculations,' he comments.)

Perversely, he rejects modern technology for writing purposes (although he does enjoy playing with a good data base). 'I write by hand. I don't use a word processor for writing anything serious – it discourages dramatic changes like throwing it all in the bin and starting over. Each word of my 700-page book on power was written five times over. I need something in front of me – some other literature or an empirical base. I can't write from my head.'

The originality that characterises all of Mintzberg's work (one critic has said: 'He sees meanings where rationalists would see only typos') is to a certain extent – perhaps entirely – a reflection of his individuality. 'I think of myself as the little Danish boy who pointed out that the Emperor had no clothes. If I've had any success it's more a matter of the blinkers on other people than any special insights of mine,' he says. 'I'm fascinated by organisations and I want to study them, but I choose never to do things in organisations if I can help it.'

Certainly, he *looks* like an eccentric. And while he is a keen sportsman, he is a constant loner. 'I won't go hiking in organised groups,' he says. In his sporting activities he is constantly searching for new challenges he can tackle with one or at most two companions. In recent years he has taken his bicycle with him to Spain, Holland, France and Japan. In Spain, he cycled from Barcelona to Granada, Gibraltar, and on to Casablanca. 'In the winter I do a lot of off-piste skiing with a compass. In summer I canoe. I like to hike in the mountains and I'm a bad mountain climber. I managed Mont Blanc on the fourth try. We climbed it from the lower refuge – 5400 feet in a day.'

Mintzberg's current work is focusing upon how leaders change organisations – hence his interest in business biographies. Part of the problem for organisations is that visionary managers tend to grow less visionary. He is also examining the problems of organisational size and social purpose. 'How can we create organisations that serve us and not vice versa?' he asks.

To identify his single most important contribution to management thinking is difficult. He himself says: 'My main impact has been to demonstrate that intuition is the soft underbelly of management.' And then, as befits a true iconoclast: 'It always amuses me when lay people say: "This is all obvious. What's the big deal?" I agree with them.'

CHAPTER 3

The Behavioural Scientists

The trouble with rational models of how organisations should work was that, in practice, they didn't. Clearly, the problem lay less in the systems than in the fact that people perverted them. The need gradually emerged to understand how people in organisations behaved and why. If managers could gain this understanding, they should be able to forestall and divert dysfunctional behaviours and strengthen behaviours in tune with the organisation's objectives. The obvious people to become involved in this effort were the behavioural psychologists.

Psychologists had had a brief period of glory during the First World War when the US Army adopted the principle of intelligence testing to identify potential officer material. Although there was relatively low correlation between IQ and leadership qualities, the tests did seem to provide a rough and ready measure of management potential. But it was not until after the Second World War that psychologists came into their own, as they searched for explanations as to why people in work groups behave as they do.

Some of the giants in this era are discussed in greater detail in the biographical sections that follow. Argyris, Maslow, McGregor, Herzberg and others have all earned longer mention from the sheer impact and visibility of their ideas, though not all would fit the definition of a guru as someone who continues to innovate in management thinking. We will concentrate here on some of the main themes of behavioural science and the people who shaped them.

Team-Building and Personality

In Britain controversy surrounds the place of Cyril Burt (1883–1971) in the canon of management thinking. In 1907, having recently graduated from Oxford, Burt became involved in a survey sponsored by the British Association for the Advancement of Science. The aim was to examine the existence and nature of intelligence. This subject was to become Burt's lifelong obsession and work.

Initially Burt carried out his work at Oxford and then at the University of Wurzburg. His first permanent post was at the University of Liverpool where he was appointed as a lecturer in psychology in 1908. On leaving Liverpool Burt became the psychologist to the London County Council – the first such position in Britain. While working with the council, which he did until 1932, Burt also spent time in the Ministry of Munitions, the National Institute of Industrial Psychology and the London Day Training College.

Burt's work concentrated on the distribution of intelligence throughout the population and to what extent it was determined by hereditary influences. His work, particularly at the Institute of Industrial Psychology, marked the birth of industrial psychology (and ran at the same time as Mayo and his associates in the United States were developing human relations elements in industry).

Peter Drucker has argued that Burt was of critical importance in the development of management theory. In *Management* he wrote: 'Cyril Burt, an Englishman, might be called the father of industrial psychology. During World War I he studied aptitudes, that is, the relationship between the demands of specific manual work and the physical skill, motor co-ordination and reactions of individual workers.'

From 1932 until his retirement in 1950, Burt held the post of professor of psychology at University College, London. There his attention switched to statistical methods. He developed the process of factor analysis to extract a small number of basic dimensions from a large number of variable figures. Since his death, this work has become highly controversial. Allegations that Burt fabricated statistics were found to be true. His biographer L. S. Hearnshaw has written: 'There was . . . a certain deviousness in his make-up, an inability to accept opposition or rebuffs, and an almost pathological intellectual ambition. In the last resort he chose to cheat rather than to see his opponents triumph. His downfall in later life was a tragedy, but it should not be allowed to eclipse his genuine contributions to the early development of applied psychology.'

Once psychologists became really interested in management, it was only a matter of time before they started to think in terms of remedial tactics for ineffective teams.

A particularly controversial concept in team-building was T-group training, developed by the National Training Laboratories at Bethel, Maine, immediately after the Second World War. The idea was that to change behaviours, people need to be 'unfrozen' from existing learned behaviours by becoming dissatisfied with them. Then they need to experiment with different patterns of behaviour until they find one that works better than the old; finally, they need to practise the new behaviours until they, in turn, 'freeze' and become the person's normal behaviour.

T-group training involves a great deal of personal soul searching as, usually for the first time, people spell out to others their fears and resentments and the effect other people's behaviour has upon them. This information is used to stimulate discussion about how the team could function more smoothly if people changed behaviours. In practice, however, many managers reported that the intense stress and embarrassment of such soul-baring could make the functioning of the team worse.

The T-group approach was pioneered by the highly influential but often underrated Kurt Lewin (1890–1947). Lewin, a German-born psychologist, was the founder of the Center for Group Dynamics in the United States and a force behind Britain's Tavistock Institute. 'He had more influence on the Tavistock than almost anyone else,' says the institute's Harold Bridger.

Lewin died before the Maine experiments took place, but he had structured and organised them as a result of ten years' previous work at the Harwood Manufacturing Company. One experiment in particular looked at overcoming resistance to change. It found that employees were more highly motivated and productive when they had participated in working out how the change should take place – a revolutionary idea to many managers at the time.

A similar, but less traumatic, theoretical approach lies behind Transactional Analysis, developed by Eric Berne (1910–70), a Canadian psychiatrist who settled in California. Berne held that people behave towards each other according to which of three 'ego states' they are in. These ego states – called child, parent and adult – could almost be described as three different personalities and they represent the way we have grown up to expect children, parents and adults to behave. In the child state, we are often rebellious, prone to tantrums, easily frustrated and yet able to switch mood to playfulness. In the parent state, we treat other people like children. We make decisions for them, administer punishments to correct their behaviour and spend time trying to nurture them. We don't expect them to challenge or answer back and we take offence if they do. The adult state is rational, open to discussion and re-evaluation as new information presents itself. When it operates efficiently, it allows us to keep our 'child' and 'parent' states under control, so that if we do adopt one, we do so for appropriate reasons.

Berne said that problems within a team frequently occur because people use the wrong state to deal with situations. For example, they may respond to a colleague's straightforward inquiry by snapping back that it is time they learned to sort that kind of problem out on their own. In Berne's terms that is treating the other person like a child. His or her reaction may well be to adopt the child role. Both parties now assume the other is being unreasonable. Berne's solution is to educate people to understand these 'transactions' and to make use of their knowledge to ensure that they are always 'complementary' (appropriate) rather than 'crossed' (inappropriate). The adult state is not appropriate at all times. On occasion, we may wish to use one of the other states to obtain particular reactions from other people. For example, banging the table at a meeting is ostensibly a childish action, but it may well be the only way to make other people recognise the importance of the point you want to make.

Ralph Coverdale (1918–75) drew his ideas about effective training from what he observed to be the shortcomings of sensitivity training and T-groups. Both techniques were weak, said Coverdale, because:

- they concentrated entirely on analysing the past, when a manager's job was to look forward
- they concentrated entirely on feelings, when a manager has to focus on rational thinking rather than emotion

- they put a great deal of emotional pressure on participants and could, in some cases, cause more harm than good.

Coverdale (a descendant of Miles Coverdale, one of the earliest Protestant translators of the Bible into English) had spent four years as a Jesuit novitiate, before joining the Army in 1942. He then studied psychology at Oxford, choosing thought as the subject of his advanced degree. He was told by a tutor that the best he might accomplish would be to become a social worker, but after several jobs he joined the Steel Company of Wales to work on management development and recruitment.

It was at the steel company that his ideas began to gel. One of the problems with managers was that they were so busy dealing with today's problems, they had not time to plan properly to avoid tomorrow's. It was a very similar problem he diagnosed to that experienced by some wartime pilots, who were so intent on aiming for the runway that they forgot to lower the under-carriage. They had, in technical jargon, 'task mesmerisation'. In spite of their education and excellent technical training, many of the managers (and particularly young recruits) also lacked the people-handling skills to get tasks done.

Coverdale and his colleagues looked for better solutions and turned to his Oxford psychology tutor, Bernard Babington Smith, who was unhappy at first with the idea of becoming involved with business. However, with volunteer teams of managers, they tested a variety of ways of helping people learn basic management principles for themselves. They discovered that working through case studies was neither motivating nor particularly effective. Far more effective was to focus on achiev-ing a clearly defined task, such as building towers of Lego bricks, which all the trainees could participate in and from which they could extract lessons about their own and other people's behaviour. Gradually, the method developed until people on the courses created and managed their own teams. This basic approach is now standard practice in many companies.

Coverdale's main contribution was to demonstrate that team-work and co-operation in management groups were achievable without trauma. As a man full of nervous energy, he suffered from his own task mesmerisation. A long-standing colleague, Tony Birbeck, recalls that on one thirty-mile drive, he drove through every red traffic-light without stopping, being so wrapped up in his thoughts. His two key mottoes were: 'men can learn from experience, but they rarely do' and 'give people the power to learn from what they do, to build up plans.' What drove him, says Birbeck, was 'the belief that he could bring about a situation where people would start listening to each other and co-operating with each other'.

Coverdale made the most direct impact in Britain, across the English-speaking Commonwealth and (via the World Bank and the International Monetary Fund) many developing countries. In the United States, the concepts seeped in through a variety of routes and his name is scarcely known.

Coverdale's work on learning was paralleled by that of Reg Revans (see page 123), although Revans went much further. He suggested that the games played in the artificial environment of a training course could never really substitute for involvement in real, important decisions. Revans advocated what he called Action Learning, where training courses gave managers enough theory to understand key processes and left the rest of the learning experience to the practical know-how that came from following a genuine project from concept to implementation.

One of the most useful tools for team-building and analysing why individuals behaved in the way they did was the Myers-Briggs questionnaire, developed by an American, Isabel Briggs-Myers. She based her observations of human behaviour on the four temperaments of Hippocrates – the sanguine, the choleric, the phlegmatic and the melancholic – and, with her mother (neither woman having had any formal training in psychology), developed the Myers-Briggs Type Indicator (MBTI). The MBTI aims to establish individual differences in basic functions and attitudes so 'types' can be encouraged to work better together and make the best use of their perceived strengths and weaknesses.

Berne, Coverdale and Briggs-Myers were important in the development of management thinking, not so much in the direct impact they had on the way people manage but because they set a pattern of transferring psychological therapy to business situations. More recent ideas and techniques following the same path are body language, the absurdly named neuro-linguistic programming (another method of identifying and learning to control communications styles) and the work on establishing positive self-image by Lou Theiss, an American. Currently, and particularly in Britain, a great deal of research is being conducted into the psychology of learning and of managers' motivation to develop themselves through self-study.

One of the first attempts to define the appropriate behaviours for a manager to extract the best from his subordinates was Blake and Mouton's managerial grid. Robert Blake (born 1918) was professor of psychology at the University of Texas. Together with Dr Jane Mouton (1930–87), his social scientist research colleague, he tried to measure management styles on two dimensions – concern for production and concern for people. These two dimensions are basically the same as those that underpin the theories of situational leadership. Concern for production refers to how much effort the manager puts into raising output and efficiency; concern for people refers to how far he is concerned with his subordinates' well-being, with achieving a pleasant working atmosphere. Blake and Mouton scaled each dimension from 1 to 9 and, in general, found that where individual managers appear on each of these dimensions depends upon the basic beliefs they have about people and production methods.

Blake and Mouton's grid allows for four extremes of management style. Someone who is low in concern for both production and people (a 1,1) has effectively abdicated his management role and is prepared to exert only the minimum effort to hold the job down. Someone with a high people score and low production score (a 1,9) is paternalistic and likely to compromise on any production issue that might stimulate conflict or upset the cosy atmosphere of the working group. At the opposite extreme, a person who cares only about production (a 9,1) is typically a slave-driver, who will probably not achieve any better results than the paternalist because he earns no respect from his subordinates. The ideal manager, say Blake and Mouton (by now rather inevitably), is the person who has an equally high concern for both production and people issues (a 9,9).

Both Blake and Mouton wrote a remarkable number of books – collectively over thirty, including a number of variations on the original grid idea which was applied to situations including managing stress, real estate sales, social work and marriage.

'We've studied ten or eleven different relationships,' explained Blake. 'In each one, we see the grid in different ways, but the structure remains the same.'

Another particular interest of Blake and Mouton's was an approach to learning they dubbed 'synergogy' – the methodology they used in their own seminars to teach grid teams. Its premise is that a trainer or facilitator can block learning so, to prevent this, learners follow steps designed into the training materials that enable them to help one another and critique their progress as they go. Scientific Methods, the company founded by Blake and Mouton, continues to propagate their theories from its offices in thirty-five countries around the world.

The Satirists

Some of the most illuminating insights into the behaviour of people in organisations came from non-psychologists, writing with a degree of satire. The three most influential writings have been *Up the Organization* (see page 209), *Parkinson's Law* and *Management and Machiavelli*.

When the book *Parkinson's Law* appeared, readers were wont to wonder if the author was the creation of an overly imaginative editor. In fact, the author was a British historian of academic, if not popular, repute. 'Rumours of my non-existence . . . proved to be unfounded or at least grossly exaggerated,' Parkinson said at the time.

C. Northcote Parkinson (born 1909) studied history at Emmanuel College, Cambridge, where he graduated in 1932. He studied for a Ph.D. at King's College, London, and then held a series of academic posts at Cambridge, Tiverton and the Royal Naval College at Dartmouth before the war. During five years of army service Parkinson began to formulate his administrative laws but he pursued his academic career at Liverpool University and the University of Malaya and had become Raffles Professor of History in Malaya by the time the success of *Parkinson's Law* began to make waves in 1958.

Parkinson exposes the ridiculousness of much bureaucratic behaviour. His targets include the committee which 'flourishes and blossoms, sunlit on top and shady beneath until it dies, scattering the seed from which other committees will spring'; the executive meeting (the less important the subject; the more animated the discussion); and offices (the more opulent; the less successful the company).

Parkinson's Law sold 100,000 copies in the United States and was translated into numerous languages from Italian to Icelandic. Parkinson has ascribed its appeal to the fact that 'it has double impact. It is read initially as a joke . . . but the sequel to laughter is the shock of realisation that the absurdity is based on fact, that the statistics are accurate, that the wildest statement is literally true.'

The book allowed Parkinson to pursue his career in the United States at Harvard, University of Illinois and Berkeley. *The Law and the Profits* (1960), the sequel to *Parkinson's Law*, discusses Parkinson's second law: expenditure rises to meet income. The *New York Times* labelled it 'twice as long and half as funny' as his previous work. In it Parkinson warns: 'the multiplication of public administrators is unchecked by any thought of total expenditure. . . . Politicians and economists see no reason at all to call a halt in the raising of taxes.'

Anthony Jay's *Management and Machiavelli* (1970) used the Italian prince's approach to make comparisons between the great empires of history and the modern corporation. Like Parkinson, Jay has interesting and amusing light to shed upon the nature and function of bureaucracy – in particular how the existence of clearly defined hierarchies ensures that the higher people go, the greater the likelihood of their seeking to do the minimum job possible because the odds against further progression increase exponentially. As an antidote to academic casuistry and intellectual pomposity, there is much to be said for the wisdom of the following: 'It is too late to change the word now, but "manager" is an insulting and belittling word. It carries a sense of someone put in by the owner to keep the thing going while he is not there. "Director" has a ring of opulence, even worker has an unpretentious dignity, but "manager" sounds dangerously like a euphemism for dogsbody.'

Motivation Studies

Inevitably, the roles of the manager and the managed were scrutinised again as a search began for new ways to define the relationship and for ways to understand what motivated people to work well or badly. One major outcome of this analysis was the concept of employee democracy and semi-autonomous work groups.

While Chris Argyris (born 1923), Frederick Herzberg (born 1923), Abraham Maslow (1908–70) and Douglas McGregor (1906–64) have gained widespread recognition, there was a host of less well-known names who made major contributions to new theories of management.

Russ Ackoff (born 1919) runs the Institute of Interactive Management in Philadelphia. He challenges the manifestations of Taylorism in management which have individual management skills being broken down into their component parts rather than regarding management as a single entity. The belief still holds that if individual units of management function well, the whole management apparatus will be similarly successful. Instead of separating out specialisms for ease of study, and later for ease of management, Ackoff argues for interaction.

'The performance of the system is never the sum of the performance of its parts taken separately. Performance is the product of their interactions,' says Ackoff. While no manager can fully understand the implications of every action and decision in a company, Ackoff believes there is a need to have general awareness of what is going on: 'This is what makes it necessary to have collective management in every sense.'

In Ackoff's view a balance has to be struck between individual autonomy of managers and managerial units and interaction between the different elements: 'Effective managers do not manage the actions of the units and individuals reporting to them: they manage their interactions and allow individuals and units to manage their own actions. Employees at any level who cannot do their jobs without supervision are unfit for their jobs.'

In the book explaining this approach, *Management in Small Doses*, Ackoff recommends forming committees and boards to bring about this sort of interaction.

Each manager creates a board and on that board minimally is himself, his immediate superior and each of the people who report directly to him. That board operates as a planning and policy-making group. It doesn't manage: it's not a managing committee. It operates like the board of a corporation does but it does this with a lower-level manager.

The board addresses issues of interactions and any issue of policy. For example, if the corporation wants to bring out a new product, which affects everybody, the question is 'What kind of interaction should be planned between R & D, production, marketing, finance, and so on to get the best final result from the whole?'

This board is supported by similar ones down the management scale so interaction is continually encouraged and focused by their activities. In fact the boards should be able to carry out the central core of managerial activity. Ackoff then argues that more management time should be taken up by what are commonly regarded as self-indulgent fringe activities. They should, for example, read books to keep up with contemporary ideas and not be afraid to talk about the ideas at work.

A remarkable amount of valuable work on motivation came in one way or another from the Tavistock Institute in London. Eric Trist, one of the Tavistock's founders, explained the Institute's inception in a speech to the US Academy of Management in August 1982: 'The Tavistock Institute was founded as the result of a linkage between psychoanalytically oriented psychiatry and the broader social sciences, which was effected during the Second World War. It grew out of the Tavistock Clinic, an out-patient facility founded as a result of a link between psychiatry and dynamic psychology effected in the First World War. The staff became sociologically as well as psychologically minded as a result of the Depression, and they were ready therefore to take the initiative when a crisis occurred in management and utilization of human resources in the Army after Dunkirk.' The Institute, Trist explains 'brought together an interdisciplinary group – psychiatrists, psychologists, sociologists, anthropologists – which wanted to pursue the problems of organisational and societal change as well as personal change'.

The Tavistock's debt to the work of Lewin is acknowledged as substantial by Trist: 'Our approach was closely akin to action-research as conceived by Kurt Lewin, except that it had a socio-clinical basis. It depended on a collaborative relation being established between ourselves and the organisation with which we worked on problems of change needed and, when understood, desired by them.' The emphasis was on managers being able to learn and develop themselves. Unfortunately Lewin died shortly before the Tavistock began to operate in 1947.

Trist and his colleagues' work belongs at least in part to the previous chapter, because it starts with a systems approach. Their two main areas of research were focused on working groups and the organisation as a part of its environment. Taking the latter first, they define an enterprise as an 'open socio-technical system'. This jargon phrase means that organisations take in inputs (goods, materials, information and so on) from the external environment; do something with them; then output them back into the external environment. This interaction takes place across the whole surface of the organisation, wherever the internal world deals with the external (for example, answering telephone calls, making sales calls, paying bills). They argue that, far from spending their time managing the internal conflicts, top management should focus on managing the interfaces with the outside world, changing the organisation's shape according to external stimuli. This has a good deal in common with Stafford Beer and directly contradicts traditional wisdom about top management's role.

The idea of the work group as a social system goes beyond the relatively simple team-building approaches of Blake and Mouton and their contemporaries. Trist developed his theories by observing what happened in the Durham coal mines, with the aid of a colleague, Kenneth Bamford, himself a former miner. This was one of the most powerful studies of how the nature of work and supervision could affect both motivation and productivity. The miners had traditionally worked in small groups, selecting their own members and dealing with discipline problems within the group. They set their own work targets and, though the working conditions were unpleasant, the members of each team worked well with each other. Then they were faced with mechanised production in the form of longwall mining. The teams were broken up and each person did his own task as the machine moved along the coal-face. Under the new system, there was little opportunity to talk to other team members, even though each relied on the others to do their part of the job before he could do his. When the promised productivity improvements did not materialise, the managers' immediate assumption was that the equipment was at fault. What they failed to realise was that it was the *human* systems that had broken down. The social integration between the workers had vanished and along with it most of their motivation to perform well.

Trist and his colleagues gradually defined what was happening in terms of how organisations respond to change in their environments. Basically, there are two options: to make tasks so simple that it is relatively easy to slot a new person into a job, where he or she can rapidly perform; or to provide employees with a wider range of skills, so that change is accommodated by the increased flexibility of the people available. The former, which they call *redundancy of parts*, stems from Taylor and from Weber's bureaucracy. Its disadvantage is that the drive towards simplicity is frequently out of tune with an environment that is growing more complex. In the end the system must break down. The latter, which they call *redundancy of function*, forms the starting point for much of the theories of job enrichment, quality of working life and industrial democracy. It involves creating jobs of greater variety and skill, where, they argue, people are much more able to motivate themselves to high performance.

Working closely with Trist was Fred Emery, now based at the University of Canberra. Emery joined with Norwegian Einar Thorsrud to take the Tavistock's ideas further. The Tavistock's basic approach to job enrichment (the socio-technical approach, as Herzberg has called it) was to help the worker gain a sense of personal worth from the accomplishments of the group and the social relationships within it. Emery and Thorsrud's approach, which has come to be called industrial democracy, was concerned more with taking decision-making down to a level where a large proportion of employees would be willing to participate. The theory was that, the further away from the action a decision was taken, the less likely it would be to take all the necessary factors into account and the longer it would take. If the people who did the work could be given sufficiently wide skills and a broad enough job, and could be persuaded to take greater responsibility, then the quality of decisions should improve.

Thorsrud is remembered as an exceptionally modest man who was reluctant to accept many of the accolades he was awarded. On his return to Norway in 1964, he set up the

Arbeidspsykologisk Institut in Oslo. The institute rapidly became the focal point for Scandinavian experiments in industrial democracy.

Scandinavia had had worker participation, in the sense of worker directors, for some time. But the system had had little impact on the shop floor. Thorsrud's own motivation was not to help companies improve productivity; he simply wanted to make people's working lives more fulfilling. He was adamant that, in some cases, job satisfaction must take precedence over purely economic considerations. Given that his objectives were at best tangential to those of the companies that endorsed his idea, he was clearly highly persuasive.

Emery, who collaborated with Thorsrud in the authorship of several books and papers, including *Form and Content in Industrial Democracy*, credits the Norwegian with 'the vision to see what was possible and the courage to take up the challenge'. 'What we counted on,' he adds, 'was the trust and respect that Einar inspired in people at all levels.'

The initial experiments in Norway were carried out with the help of the Tavistock in 1963. They identified six criteria that every job should have to maintain the employee's interest. It must:

- be reasonably demanding in terms other than sheer endurance, yet provide a certain amount of variety
- allow the worker to learn as he works
- give the worker an area of decision-making or responsibility which he can call his own
- increase the worker's respect for the task he is doing
- have a meaningful relationship with outside life
- hold out some sort of desirable future, and not just in terms of promotion, because not everyone can be promoted.

Thorsrud's thinking took shape in large part as a result of his experiences as a resistance fighter in the Second World War. Living and hiding in the mountains, he became part of what was, in effect, an autonomous work group. Responsibilities were only loosely defined and the group acted largely on its own initiative. Most of the help they received was from small farms where people had very little. 'Everywhere we went we found that ordinary people could be ingenious,' he recalls, 'and we found leadership in places you would least expect it. And these were not always the people who got the medals. This is the type of person companies should look for, people with a combination of leadership and modesty.' Another wartime example of people organising themselves occurred in the schools. 'A lot of teachers were arrested,' says Thorsrud, 'but school went on. The pupils themselves did much of the teaching. I learned that even in school there is more open space than you think.'

The problem, as Thorsrud saw it, 'was how to change the way work was organized so that you could both work effectively and at the same time have a good, rather than bad, effect on the people performing the tasks. People have tremendous resources of fun. Even factory work can be a source of pleasure, if the atmosphere is right. Sometimes we have marred some of our experiments by being too serious.'

In Thorsrud's world, managers and specialists such as engineers adapted their roles to become teachers as well. Instead of giving orders, they delegated as much decision-making as possible to the people actually doing the work and helped them develop the skills to make decisions. One result of this in the experimental companies was that several layers of management could disappear.

In one experiment, everyone in a ship's crew took on two jobs instead of one. Many of the rank barriers were discarded, opening up social interaction. People became less isolated in their spare time and maintenance was kept at a higher level than before and at a lower cost. A second stage redesigned the ship to fit this informal organisation.

Employee democracy as proposed by the Tavistock was largely ignored by British and American industry until the late 1970s. There were, however, a number of significant experiments which laid the groundwork for many of the current attempts to push responsibility and creativity down to the shop floor by major manufacturers such as General Motors.

Among the many books and texts published by the Tavistock during this period was a detailed study of a medium-sized British manufacturing company, Glacier Metals. The Glacier research team was led by the Tavistock's Elliott Jacques (born 1917) and gained support within the firm from Wilfred Brown, then chairman and managing director. The project lasted from 1948 until 1965 (though only the initial part was under the Tavistock's auspices) and examined a number of organisational and human relations issues. Assessing it Eric Trist said: 'The findings of this project, which were far-reaching, were presented in a book, *The Changing Culture of a Factory*, by Elliott Jacques and published in 1951. It became a classic. Yet the project itself produced none of the successors we had anticipated. It was a decade ahead of any form of organisational development.' Ahead of its time and unique in approach, the Glacier Project had few emulators.

Douglas McGregor

Born Detroit, 1906
Died 1964
Social psychologist

Douglas McGregor was an academic – the president of Antioch College and between 1954 and 1964 professor of management at the Massachusetts Institute of Technology. He is best known for his work *The Human Side of Enterprise* in which he created Theories X and Y, which have been much emulated in theory and practice.

Evaluating McGregor's work, former protégé Warren Bennis says: 'The McGregorian chant is still profoundly true. If you look at the work of Peters, Waterman and others, they all grow out of that initial McGregor theory.'

In *The Human Side of Enterprise*, McGregor's argument was forcefully compact: 'Every managerial decision has behavioral consequences. Successful management depends – not alone, but significantly – upon the ability to predict and control human behavior.' McGregor argued persuasively that managers' behaviour towards workers is strongly influenced by their assumptions. He separated the extremes of our views of human behaviour at work into Theory X and Theory Y. Theory X – what McGregor calls 'the traditional view of direction and control' – involves three basic assumptions:

1. The average human being has an inherent dislike of work and will avoid it if he can.
2. Because of this human characteristic, most people must be coerced, controlled, directed, threatened with punish-

ment to get them to put forth adequate effort toward the achievement of organizational objectives.

3. The average human being prefers to be directed, wishes to avoid responsibility, has relatively little ambition, wants security above all.

If a manager makes these assumptions about his staff (whether correctly or not) then he is likely to behave in an autocratic manner towards them, becoming obsessed with controlling uncooperative employees. He will supervise each worker closely, impose all kinds of controls on him and generally display a lack of trust in him. In all probability the workers will resent this approach, resist the pressure and do as little work as they can get away with. The manager will then feel that his original opinion about them has been confirmed and, in all probability, he will impose even greater constraints.

At the other extreme, McGregor set Theory Y, which argued:

1. The expenditure of physical and mental effort in work is as natural as play and rest.
2. External control and the threat of punishment are not the only means for bringing about effort toward organizational objectives. Man will exercise self-direction and self-control in the service of objectives to which he is committed.
3. Commitment to objectives is a function of the rewards associated with their achievement.
4. The average human being learns, under proper conditions, not only to accept but to seek responsibility.
5. The capacity to exercise a relatively high degree of imagination, ingenuity and creativity in the solution of organizational problems is widely, not narrowly, distributed in the population.
6. Under the conditions of modern industrial life, the intellectual potentialities of the average human being are only partially utilized.

If managers adopt these assumptions, then their behaviour towards employees is likely to be different, and so will the reciprocal reaction of the employees. Theory Y assumptions and subsequent behaviour may well lead to a much more co-operative relationship between managers and workers.

Assessing the two theories, Peter Drucker wrote: 'Theory X assumes immaturity. Theory Y assumes that people want to be adults.'

Psychologist Abraham Maslow was an ardent supporter of Theory Y. His work with a small Californian company attempted to put it into practice and was reported in his book *Eupsychian Management* (1965). Maslow, however, criticised Theory Y for making inhuman demands on the weak members of the organisation.

In *Management* Drucker also provides a critique of McGregor's ideas: 'Things are far less simple than McGregor's followers would have us believe. In the first place, we have learned that Theory Y is not by itself adequate. Management by Theory Y is not "permissive". On the contrary, managing worker and working by putting responsibility on the worker and by aiming at achievement makes exceedingly high demands on both worker and manager, a fact that McGregor noted only somewhat later.'

Harold Geneen comments in his book *Managing*: 'The beauty of Theory X and Theory Y was that they so neatly encompassed all of business management.' But he adds: 'The trouble with these neat theories, however, is that no company that I know of is run in strict accordance with either Theory Y or Theory X. Not even the Army.'

McGregor was arguing that the basic beliefs of managers actually dictated the way an organisation was run. 'All managerial decisions and actions rest on assumptions about behavior,' he wrote. The challenge was to unite theories of management with effective practice. 'Science is concerned with the advancement of knowledge; management, like any other profession, is concerned with the achievement of practical objectives. The issue is whether management can utilize scientific knowledge in the achievement of those objectives.'

Although Theories X and Y have been repeatedly interpreted as dogma, McGregor regarded them as opposite poles. Like Charles Handy today, he saw organisations as hugely complex but ultimately pragmatic and versatile, and he eschewed rigid approaches, arguing for an ethical framework within which management could successfully operate. He maintained:

Management's freedom to manage has been progressively curtailed in our society during the past century. Legislation with respect to child labor, the employment of women, workmen's compensation, collective bargaining and many other matters reflects society's concern with the ethics of management. One approach to these problems is to see all restrictions on management as unreasonable and to fight blindly against them. This was fairly typical of industrial management a generation or two ago. The other approach is to become more sensitive to human values and to exert self-control through a positive, conscious, ethical code. It is this latter approach which characterizes the concept of the 'social responsibility' of management about which we hear so much today.

McGregor contributed to the idea of a hierarchy of needs. 'Man is a wanting animal – as soon as one of his needs is satisfied, another appears in its place. This process is unending. It continues from birth to death. Man continuously puts forth effort – works, if you please – to satisfy his needs' he wrote. 'A satisfied need is not a motivator of behaviour!'

Management knows today of the existence of these needs, but it is often assumed quite wrongly that they represent a threat to the organization. Acceptance of Theory Y does not imply abdication, or 'soft' management, or 'permissiveness' . . . such notions stem from the acceptance of authority as the single means of managerial control, and from attempts to minimize its negative consequences. Theory Y assumes that people will exercise self-direction and self-control in the achievement of organizational objectives to the degree that they are committed to those objectives.

As president of Antioch College, McGregor found translating his theories into practical and effective leadership an immense challenge. (It is interesting to note that his pupil Warren Bennis went through a similar process as president of the University of Cincinnati.) On his departure from the college, McGregor wrote: 'I thought I could avoid being a boss. . . . I thought that maybe I could operate so that everyone would like me – that "good human relations" would eliminate all discord and disagreement. I couldn't have been more wrong. It took a couple of years, but I finally began to realize that a leader cannot avoid the exercise of authority any more than he can avoid the responsibility for what happens to his organization.' Even so, McGregor continued to champion the human element of management. He affirmed: 'Fads will come and go. The fundamental fact of man's capacity to collaborate with his fellows in the face-to-face group will survive the fads and one day be recognized. Then, and only then, will management discover how seriously it has underestimated the true potential of its human resources.'

Abraham Maslow

Born Brooklyn, New York, 1908
Died 1970
Psychologist

Maslow's 'hierarchy of needs' provided the starting block for the behavioural science boom which followed. Maslow argued that man's expectations begin with the basic needs of food, warmth, sleep and sexual fulfilment. These must be satisfied before other needs become pressing. The other needs identified by Maslow were safety, a sense of belonging and love, esteem and the realisation of personal potential. He argued that the human acts as an integrated whole – motivation has to appeal to the whole and is, as a result, complex, continuous and fluctuating.

Maslow was trained as a psychologist at the University of Wisconsin, becoming Carnegie Fellow of the College Teachers College in 1935 and then associate professor of psychology at Brooklyn College. From 1947 until 1949 he gained first-hand business experience as plant manager of the Maslow Cooperage Corporation but he returned to academia becoming an associate and then full professor at Brandeis University in Massachusetts. Eventually he became head of department and then tried his hand in business again with a Southern Californian electronics company. There, as he studied motivation and self-fulfilment, his Utopian ideas became coloured by reality. In describing his experiences, Maslow created the word 'Eupsychian', which he defined as 'the culture that would be generated by 1,000 self-actualising people on some sheltered island where they would not be interfered with'.

The electronics company was, in effect, trying to convert Douglas McGregor's Theory Y into practical reality. This theory, which Maslow enthusiastically backed, argued that people had a deep-rooted need to work. Such idealism, Maslow soon realised, did not accord with what he saw in practice. From a year's work with the company he wrote *Eupsychian Management*, criticising Theory Y for its 'inhumanity' and concluding that even the strong in society require the security of order and direction, while the weak require protection from the burden of responsibility. He did not, however, dismiss Theory Y completely. Instead, he argued that the security and reassurance offered by Theory X had to be created by alternative means. Theory Y alone could not offer a suitable structure but could not coexist with Theory X.

Maslow's idealistic strain has been criticised. Of the hierarchy of needs, one psychologist commented: 'They are simple categories and have a certain universality. But they are gross, non-definitive and no research has derived from them.'

In his book *Management* Peter Drucker wrote:

What Maslow didn't realize is that a want changes in the act of being satisfied. As the economic want is satisfied, that is, as people no longer have to subordinate every other human need and human value to getting the next meal, it becomes less and less satisfying to obtain more economic rewards. But economic rewards do not become any less important. On the contrary, while the impact of an economic reward as a positive incentive decreases, its capacity to create dissatisfaction, if disappointed, rapidly increases. Economic rewards cease to be 'incentives' and become 'entitlements'. If not properly taken care of – that is, if there is dissatisfaction with the economic rewards – they become deterrents.

Reg Revans

Born Portsmouth, 1907
Educator

Revans is a prophet long unrecognised in his own country and now perhaps the bitterest of gurus. He says: 'No British management consultant, professor of business, polytechnic reader in administrative science, proactive facilitation module counsellor, nor their manifold colleagues will touch anything that has my name on it.' The *bête noire* of the traditional business school case study approach to management education, he had to take his ideas to Belgium to see them put into practice. The generation of rising middle managers who experienced 'action learning' at his hands has been widely credited as the driving force behind Belgium's dramatic expansion in the 1960s.

Revans's development of the concept of 'action learning' has its roots early in his lengthy career. In 1938, he was the education officer responsible to the Essex County Council for all technical colleges and major professional training wanted throughout the authority. It was from there that he wrote his first paper on the training of student nurses. Since then six hundred more papers have appeared by him.

From the start, Revans challenged the status quo. In a 1949 symposium, 'Education in a Changing World', he wrote:

> Although industry and trade are both more widely recognising that the efficiency of production is still in the end merely the efficiency of the producers, there still lurks a fear that the processes of education may bring fortl. ...me undesirable by-products. We must all remember that, in addition to ordered thinking having its dangers, education has a strong literary tradition; it has been designed more in the interests of those who write letters about things than of those who do them; it has not infrequently tended to train for responsible administrative positions men who have either positively despised the skill of the engineer, or deliberately kept themselves in genteel ignorance of the risks of the market and the exchange.

It was when Revans became responsible for recruiting and training colliery managers that he first started to examine how managers learn. His proposals were radical. Instead of bringing them together to be taught, classroom style, by a management or behavioural expert who would have less knowledge of their jobs than they did, why not let them teach each other? Over a number of years this led Revans to the conclusion that: 'Members of small working teams can learn quickly from each other and they support each other in getting out the work.' Revans projected this idea in 1957, arguing the case for small working groups on the factory floor. He was ridiculed in the West, but the Japanese incorporated his ideas into their developing quality circle techniques. His ideas were then picked up by the British National Health Service. Medical, nursing and administrative teams met together to learn from each other and, over a period of five years, impressive results began to emerge from ten London hospitals. Again, Revans insisted that only the hospital staff knew their own problems and could solve them.

The concept of 'Action Learning' developed by Revans forms the cornerstone of his work. Action Learning primarily focuses on the acquisition of a 'questioning insight', which can only be achieved if people become used to asking 'useful and discriminating questions in conditions of ignorance, risk and confusion'. Learning this may require a 'combiner', a supervisor (not a facilitator) who has a direct involvement in the outcome and who makes clear from the start that he or she needs to learn as much about his or her own supposed abilities as all others in the group. 'Since experts cannot grasp the meaning of such truth they respect all genuine action learning,' says Revans. Action Learning has three major objectives:

- To give attention only to real problems with elements of risk, confusion and opportunity.
- To give members scope to learn for themselves, in the company of colleagues doing the same thing, how best to approach ill-structured challenges to which nobody can, at the outset, suggest a satisfactory response.
- To encourage 'management developers' to perceive their missions afresh as having to contrive with senior managements the conditions in which all managers and all management developers, including those from the top, learn with and from each other in the pursuit of their common and everyday duties.

Revans acknowledges that this is nothing new: 'The idea must be, in fact, of great antiquity: that nobody learns merely by talk or discussion – and, for my argument, talk includes case studies, management games, discussion groups, seminars, role playings and all other forms of social interaction that fall short of taking operational responsibility for one's real decisions in a real world.' In fact, it is so ancient that Revans cites Buddha as 'an early believer in action learning, teaching others that it is from their own real experiences that the most fundamental truths are most likely to be learned'.

Revans cites two of the achievements of action learning as saving the palm-nut oil mills in the jungles of Nigeria, and keeping Belgium as first of all OECD countries in building manufacturing productivity and exports. However, his ideas provoked general derision. 'The book *Action Learning* did not sell. I bought most as scrap,' admits Revans. 'It made the "experts" quake with merriment.' In response, Revans left for Europe, becoming president of the European Association of Management Training Centres. A later EEC Report *Management Education in the European Community* in 1978 provided sober testimony to Revans's contribution.

It was at the Fondation Industrie-Université in Belgium that Revans's theories were most notably put into practice. He recalls: 'The feeble and ill-informed concepts that I had struggled to distil from what went on in the mines and hospitals were replaced by the clear and decisive enunciation of Belgian scientists, engineers and bankers.' His achievements in Belgium have been described enthusiastically. Dr Jonathan Rosenhead, 1987 president of the Operational Research Society said of the Revans-inspired programme: 'This programme has been credited (and not only by Reg Revans himself) with some of the responsibility for Belgium's exceptional growth in industrial productivity during the 1970s – up 102 per cent in the decade to 1981. Compare Japan at 85 per cent and Britain at 28 per cent.' Belgium was the only manufacturing nation to increase significantly its rate of growth in the 1970s, despite the fact that for twenty-five years it had the lowest ratio in Europe of capital investment to gross domestic product; the smallest reserve of labour in Europe; and was devoid of natural resources.

In 1973 Revans's concepts were picked up by Sir Arnold Weinstock at GEC and, before long, companies all over Britain were experimenting with the Revans approach. Projects sprang up in Egypt, India and Africa. Action learning became integrated into the management training of many institutions and a few, notably the International Management Centre from Buckingham, have made it the core of their activities.

To some extent, Revans now feels his approach has been vindicated. He expresses 'total indifference to the opinions of our economic and related experts, above all, those into management consulting or business school education. The facts now are that all I have been on about these fifty years is slowly being seen to have been right.' He believes support for his ideas is growing. For example, in February 1988 Sir Douglas Hague wrote: 'We are in a new industrial revolution which requires management trainers to develop "action learning" from real experience within business and industry, rather than getting tied up with theory and academia.' Revans himself continues to travel the world giving lectures and spreading the action learning gospel. He is, says Igor Ansoff, 'an amazing and underestimated man'.

Frederick Herzberg

Born Lynn, Massachusetts, 1923
Professor of Management, University of Utah

Now in his sixties, Frederick Herzberg is Distinguished Professor of Management at the University of Utah. Assessing the inspiration for his work, Herzberg explains: 'The central core of my work stems from Second World War experiences in Dachau Concentration Camp, where I realised that a society goes insane when the sane are driven insane. As a psychologist, I believe that sanity requires as much professional attention to nourishing the humanistic content of character and ethics as to showing compassion for differences in personality. The insane also require care and compassion but their insane actions should never be reinforced by ethically neutral strategies. My theories have tended to emphasise strategies for keeping the sane sane.'

Herzberg joined the Army in his senior year at the City College of New York. He had left home when the rest of his family moved to the south and paid his own way through school. When his money ran out, he enlisted. At the college he began by studying history, a subject he still regards as his first love, but found the teaching impersonal. 'It was a sequence of events, depersonalised. But history is made by people. I went to the psychology department to understand people so I could understand history.' Wartime provided Herzberg with a harsh education in people. He was posted to Dachau when it was liberated: 'What I saw at Dachau made me more adamant about studying history and psychology. I was looking for answers about the obscenities in human society,' he has said. After the war he completed his studies in New York, before obtaining Master's and Ph.D. degrees at the University of Pittsburgh. In the mid 1950s, he began working for the US Public Health Service in various research projects.

Herzberg worked in clinical psychology, becoming research director of a non-profit-making psychological consulting company. To assess current thinking on mental illness, Herzberg and his colleagues created a bibliography of works on industrial psychology. What Herzberg discovered was disappointing – 'a paucity of conceptual thinking'. It is this gulf that he has attempted to fill. 'I decided I needed to look at the mentally healthy, who at least were functioning,' he says. 'My goal was not so much to relieve the pain of industry as to keep people healthy there. How do we keep the healthy from going sick? It was a positive approach.' His scope is wide. He calls for a 'higher level of understanding' and suggests, 'We need Renaissance men as managers – broadly educated men who can see the interrelationships of sociology, psychology, technical aspects.' He surrounds himself with post-doctoral assistants from a variety of disciplines.

Herzberg's human behaviour theories are, he believes, as relevant to the humanities as management science. In taking an overall view, Herzberg argues: 'Individual needs and expectations of satisfaction are shaped by the religious/philosophical system in which one lives' (*Industry Week*, 12 November 1984).

Consultant Roy Walters has worked with Herzberg over many years. It was Walters who brought Herzberg into AT&T to test his theories in an industrial situation. 'Fred Herzberg is driven by a desire to assist organisations in improving the utilisation of their human talents. His commitment to this objective is intense,' says Walters. 'Why else would a person physically punish himself by acquiring such a heavy load of speeches, consultation assignments and numerous public appearances? When working with Fred at AT&T and later in my own consulting firm, I saw him take late night flights across the country in order to make early morning appearances, or staying up most of the night discussing work philosophies, issues and problems.'

George Tsatsos of Investment Finance provides this assessment of Herzberg: 'The main characteristic of Herzberg I would say is the very youthful and irreverent approach he has to the world. He sees the world with great humanity but in the same way as a child or a very young person would and he questions established theories which he does not take at face value. By seeing things from a funny angle – and he is one of the funniest people I have met – he brings out major characteristics in the same way as a caricaturist exaggerates certain traits of his subject. This, in management and human relations, which have generally been handled with great sobriety and with moralistic attitudes, is in itself a very novel way of seeing things. Of course novelty, a fresh approach and humour are not enough and Herzberg has also made a synthesis of his observations and has formulated his original theories.'

Herzberg's fame was achieved in the late 1950s when he separated the elements of work into two sets: those that serve people's animal needs (hygiene factors) and those that meet their unique human needs (motivation factors). He explains: 'I did a lot of interviews trying to establish what made ordinary sane people sick. I found that it was what they were doing. That led to more studies, which led to motivation theory.'

The book *Motivation to Work* expressed the basic hygiene-motivation theory. It was translated throughout the world and brought Herzberg consultancy work with large companies and private organisations. Its theories provided two challenges for managers:

- To look after employees by serving their animal needs
- To make the most of them by appealing to their inner motivation for self-development.

Herzberg and his associates' research found that workers derived satisfaction from what Herzberg termed 'satisfiers' or 'motivation factors'. These were achievement, recognition, the work itself, responsibility, advancement and growth. Dissatisfaction, however, was usually related to environmental factors, which were labelled 'dissatisfiers' or 'hygiene factors'. These were company policy and administration, supervision, working conditions, relations with superiors, subordinates and peers, salary, status, job security and personal life.

Information was drawn from interviews with two hundred Pittsburgh engineers and accountants. They were asked to recall times when they felt exceptionally good about their jobs. The interviewers then investigated why they felt that way. The workers were also asked if the feelings of satisfaction had affected their performance, their personal relationships and their well-being. The process was repeated to also discover negative feelings about work. The results were then classified by topic to find what type of events led to job satisfaction and dissatisfaction. The major finding of the study was that the events that led to satisfaction were of quite a different kind from those that led to dissatisfaction. Satisfaction and dissatisfaction were *not* opposites.

In *Motivation to Work* Herzberg and his co-authors Mausner and Snyderman wrote:

> Hygiene operates to remove health hazards from the environment of man. It is not a curative; it is, rather, a preventative. . . . Similarly, when there are deleterious factors in the context of the job, they serve to bring about poor job attitudes. Improvements in these factors of hygiene will serve to remove the impediments to positive job attitudes. Among the factors of hygiene we have included supervision, interpersonal relations, physical working conditions, salary, company policies and administrative practices, benefits, and job security. When these factors deteriorate to a level below that which the employee considers acceptable, then job dissatisfaction ensues.

Merely looking after hygiene factors, the book argues, is not enough. 'All we can expect from satisfying the needs for hygiene is the prevention of dissatisfaction and poor job performance.'

Herzberg believes his theories have had positive impacts on business and are now standard in many companies – so much so that the theoretical source has been forgotten. 'Flexitime, annual wages, cafeteria, compensation are all derivatives of motivation theory (the hygiene part). So are job enrichment, job design and flatter organisations, to give people more opportunities to express themselves,' he says.

The impact of Herzberg's work on hygiene and motivation factors is assessed by George Tsatsos: 'At the time his theory was revolutionary and represented an example of lateral thinking. He suggested that instead of trying to motivate people through rewards or pressure, companies should motivate them by improving the content of the job itself. This theory was of course no panacea. In itself, it does not solve all management problems, nor does it work in every case. In the years that followed, many of Herzberg's disciples pretended, however, that this was the case. The over-application and the pretence that this is a unique solution to problems of management risked turning job enrichment theory into a passing fad. But this is not so. In countless ways today the aspects of job enrichment are an integral part of our current management practice and enter into any equation regarding the application of successful management.'

Herzberg coined the term 'job enrichment' which called for responsibility to be distributed down the line – an idea which is still much discussed. For Herzberg, job enrichment requires people to have a 'client relationship' with employers, managers and colleagues and to be engaged in a constant learning process. Both ideas have resurfaced strongly in different forms in the 1980s.

As part of his interest in motivation, Herzberg was a precursor of much of what is today covered with the umbrella term 'participation'. However, Herzberg stands apart from the way participation works at present. To him it is dehumanising, because it extols the virtues of group over individual action. 'What we have today is participation by lobbyists. Everybody wants to participate to get what he wants,' he wrote in *Industry Week* (15 September 1980). Training is ignored for the temporary satisfaction of working as part of a group, and at best the group will prove mediocre.

'I believe in one man, one vote in terms of civil rights; I don't believe that some oligarchy should tell me that I'm unequal. But I do not translate that into participative management in terms of people having equal knowledge,' says Herzberg. 'I believe that people should participate on the basis of know-how. I don't believe the stewardess should have a vote equal to that of the captain of the plane as to whether or not they should land in a storm. I do believe, however, that her expertise in terms of the passengers' condition should be communicated to the captain,' he said in the same article.

The final piece Herzberg wrote about his early theories was an article for the *Harvard Business Review* in 1968 entitled 'One More Time: How Do You Motivate Employees?' It has sold 1.2 million copies and is the *Review*'s biggest-selling article. In it, Herzberg introduces the acronym KITA (kick in the ass) and argues, 'If you have someone on a job, use him. If you can't use him on the job, get rid of him, either via automation or by selecting someone with lesser ability. If you can't use him and you can't get rid of him, you will have a motivation problem.'

The article examines motivation:

> What is the simplest, surest, and most direct way of getting someone to do something? Ask? But if the person responds that he or she does not want to do it, then that calls for psychological consultation to determine the reason for such obstinacy. Tell the person? The response shows that he or she does not understand you, and now an expert in communication methods has to be brought in to show you how to get through. Give the person a monetary incentive? I do not need to remind the reader of the complexity and difficulty involved in setting up and administering an incentive system. Show the person? This means a costly training programme. We need a simple way.

The article re-examined Herzberg's hygiene and motivation factors. He identified them in this way: 'The growth or motivator factors that are intrinsic to the job are: achievement, recognition for achievement, the work itself, responsibility, and growth or advancement. The dissatisfaction-avoidance or hygiene (KITA) factors that are extrinsic to the job include: company policy and administration, supervision, interpersonal relation-ships, working conditions, salary, status, and security.'

In the October 1987 edition of the *Review*, the article was reprinted with Herzberg's thoughts on how his theories stood up nearly a decade later. Explaining the impact of the article Herzberg wrote: 'For this article, I invented the acronym KITA (kick in the ass) to describe the movement technique. The inelegance of the term offended those who consider good treat-ment a motivating strategy, regardless of the nature of the work itself. In this plain language I tried to spotlight the animal approach to dealing with human beings that characterizes so much of our behavioural science intervention.'

Now Herzberg observes: 'There are very few people out there trying to make the living experience an enjoyable experience. People who enjoy their work do better work. KITA is always short term.'

Herzberg has become increasingly angry at the failure of organisations fully to satisfy humanity, man's creativity and passion. He is strongly opposed to Taylor's scientific view of man. 'Science can only help us invent more glasses to see the boundaries of the physical system better. We develop bigger and bigger encyclopedias, but they are still bounded by hard covers,' he said in a recent interview. He gives scientific and systemised methods short shrift. 'To get reliable, empirical knowledge, mankind has developed scientific methods for determining which knowledge is reliable and which is not. The first, and still the most pervasive, method of gathering reliable knowledge is experience: *observation*,' he argues. In his eyes you cannot manage people scientifically, no matter how hard you try. 'We will have to have broader training, more cross-training and earlier training for people. We must extend psychological life for people and that can only come from what they are doing. With an ageing population, what are we going to do with these people? Since industry is the dominant institution in the world we have to look to industry to provide the remedy.'

In 1976, Herzberg wrote *The Managerial Choice: To Be Efficient and To Be Human*, in which he tried to bridge the gap between human concerns and economic factors. The emphasis on profits and accounting procedures rather than people has become a preoccupation with Herzberg. 'Our love affair with numbers is the root cause of the passionlessness of the '80s,' he argues. 'We try to escape the nihilism of zero by putting our dreams and emotions into greater and greater numbers. How many pieces of information will fit on the computer chip? How many channels will play on our TV sets? How many billions can we add to or cut from the budget?

'Numbers numb our feelings for what is being counted and lead to adoration of the economies of scale. Passion is in feeling the quality of experience, not in trying to measure it.'

Passion is one of the essential facets of innovative people as identified by Herzberg. The full list is:

1. Intelligence quotient
2. Subject matter expertise
3. Unconventionality
4. Effectiveness in ambiguity
5. Feeling the self
6. Ability to separate motivator from hygiene values
7. Control of anxiety
8. Control of careerism
9. Intuition
10. Passion

Roy Walters assesses Herzberg's work: 'His main contribution to management theory has been to expose management to a new area, that is, that motivation comes from the "work itself". Often this was a painful process because it flies in direct opposition to the historical ways of managing, and is antithetical to the historical management belief systems. But his belief system and his tenacity have allowed him to prevail.'

David Whitsett, professor of psychology at the University of Northern Iowa, comments on Herzberg's world view: 'He was driven by a compassion for people's pain. He has probably seen himself that way all of his life and believes that personal pain is unsolvable, that is, inescapable. He believes that a focus on growth opportunities or learning and development opportunities is really the only thing worth living for and makes life worthwhile in spite of the fact that one has to endure a significant amount of discomfort or pain.'

Assessing his own achievements, Herzberg has identified

them thus: 'First, I've created more consulting firms and new activities for consulting firms. In creating job enrichment, I've given employment to a hell of a lot of consultants, by giving them new products to sell.

'I've rescued behavioural science from the morass of the human relations movement.

'Third, I've given a new public relations dimension for companies. They come out with enriched machines. You've seen those tremendous ads: "We have happy workers."

'My most instrumental feat was pointing to work itself as the focus of infection. More hygiene aspirin was not effective.

'As a corollary of this, I created a new vocabulary – KITA, motivation and so forth.

'Sixth – and seriously – I gave theoretical behavioural science justification to meet new social mores and values, as we change to a freer culture, emphasising the quality of life.

'In creating job enrichment, I resurrected social technical systems which had been dead for twenty-five years. My activity pointing to the nature of work revived the social technical work of groups such as Tavistock Institute in England. It led to re-evaluation of appraisal systems, and training being related to work motivation rather than being a Tayloristic concept of turning a person into a function.

'Eight, I differentiated between pathology and ideology. When lower-level workers didn't work, they'd say it's the nature of the person. They'd say the lower classes don't want to work, you can't motivate them. I showed they were not the great, dirty, unwashed. Behaviour is pathology, a sickness we created. What was called ideology was a self-confirming system.

'Ninth, I've put hygiene in its proper place in life. It was normal to say, "Give someone more money and they'll be happy". But I've shown that's incorrect.'

Chris Argyris

Born 1923
Professor of Education and Organizational Behaviour, Harvard Business School

Both as an academic and as a consultant, Harvard Business

School's Chris Argyris has devoted his career to attempting to marry the needs of the individual with those of the organisation.

His consulting work has taken him into a broad range of organisations. Among the large concerns that have retained him are International Business Machines, DuPont and Shell Oil. He has served as a special consultant to the US State Department and numerous other US government bodies. His advice on problems of executive development and productivity has been sought by the governments of the United States, France, Norway, Sweden, Germany, Italy, Greece and the Netherlands. His research findings have been the basis of twenty-four books and innumerable articles which have kept him at the forefront of the behavioural science movement.

Argyris currently lectures in education and organisational behaviour. His academic achievements demonstrate his versatility – a baccalaureate in psychology, a master's degree in economics and a doctorate in organisational behaviour. He taught at Yale in the 1950s and became a Professor of Industrial Administration there in 1961, before joining Harvard in 1968.

His early research focused on the unintended consequences for individuals of formal and organisational structures, executive leadership, and control and management-information systems – and on how individuals adapted to change those consequences. His book *Personality and Organization*, published in 1957 and regarded as a classic work of behavioural science, was followed by *Integrating the Individual and the Organization* (1964).

Argyris has pointed to the mismatch between individuals and organisations, and between the information managers need and receive. 'Developing skills for even simple activities such as riding a bicycle is an extremely complex process for the human mind. The human capacity for information processing is quite limited in comparison to the demands of the environment in which it is embedded,' he says.

Observing that 'Formal organisations, alas, are unintentionally designed to discourage the autonomous and involved workers', Argyris argues the case for a multi-dimensional view of people and organisation, and the relationship between them. He writes: 'Organisations depend on people. Thus, many organisational variables are designed around an explicit or implicit model of man. Taylor's molecularised jobs, for example, took a one-dimensional view of man and assumed that one could hire a hand; by contrast, the champions of vertical and horizontal job enrichment assume that one hires a whole human being.'

Argyris criticises formal systems which stem from the scientific management movement for neglecting both the social and egotistical needs of the individual. He believes every individual should achieve his or her potential. Each of us has 'psychological energy' which provides motivation. The problem of motivation, as Argyris sees it, is not how to create it but where to channel it.

In the 1960s, Argyris turned his attention to ways of changing organisations and wrote *Organization and Innovation* (1965). He moved on to focus on the role of the social scientist as researcher and interventionist in *Inner Contradictions of Rigorous Research* (1980). He has also developed, with Donald Schon, a theory of learning in which human reasoning, not just behaviour, becomes the basis for diagnosis and action. Their book, *Organizational Learning*, was published in 1978.

Schon gained fame, in Britain at least, through his 1970 Reith lectures. Then president of the Organization for Social and Technical Innovation at Massachusetts Institute of Technology, he argued there was a mismatch between the need for change and the yearning for stability in society. 'Belief in the stable state serves primarily to protect us from apprehension of the threats inherent in change. Belief in stability is a means of maintaining stability or, at any rate, the illusion of stability. I would propose Schon's Law: no idea in good currency is appropriate to the circumstances of its time. And since you can only get money on the basis of ideas in good currency, you can never get money to work on any problem that's real.'

The lectures were met with criticism from *The Times*, among others. It hammered Schon's 'close attention to the doings of computer programmers, hippies and medical sociologists' and labelled his thesis 'both unoriginal and profoundly unsatisfactory, because it provides no guide to the evaluation of the diversity of our feelings nor does it help us to distinguish those which should be used as a basis for public action from those which should not'. Despite such comments Schon and Argyris anticipated many of the preoccupations of management writers in the next twenty years – change, using technology to provide useful information and questioning the relentless search for expansion.

The concept of the learning organisation (also explored in Britain by Bob Garratt) in Argyris's and Schon's view starts from a definition of what an organisation is. What distinguishes an organisation from a mob, they say, is the way it devises procedures for making decisions in the name of the collectivity; delegating to individuals the authority to act for the collectivity; and setting boundaries between the collectivity and the rest of the world.

These procedures or rules may be written or unwritten. Either way, they form a basis for decision-making and action, a set of 'norms, strategies and assumptions' that are generally accepted as the right way of doing business. Every person in the organisation creates an image of himself or herself in line with his or her perception of those norms. Their perception is rarely complete; they are constantly testing it and reassessing it as they use it to describe their role and how they interact with other people. This learning by the people within the organisation is the basis of the organisation's learning, because the changes in people's perceptions are inevitably reflected in changes in the norms that govern the organisation's behaviour.

Argyris and Schon identify two types of learning in organisations which they call single-loop and double-loop learning. Single loop learning refers to situations where employees 'respond to changes in the internal and external environments of the organisation by detecting errors, which they then correct, so as to maintain the central features of the "theory-in-use" '. In practice, the organisation only learns when the employees themselves absorb lessons from this experience – when the new knowledge becomes sufficiently part of the norms, strategies and assumptions to remain even if the employee who initiated it should leave.

In one article Argyris provided this analogy: 'When a thermostat turns the heat on or off, it is acting in keeping with the program of orders given to it to keep the room temperature, let us say, at 68 degrees. This is single-loop learning, because the underlying program is not questioned. The overwhelming amount of learning done in an organization is single loop because it is designed to identify and correct errors so that the job gets done and the action remains within stated policy guidelines. The massive technology of management information systems, quality control systems, and audits of the quality control systems is designed for single loop learning.'

Whereas single-loop learning merely changes strategies and assumptions within a fairly constant set of norms, double-loop learning also questions the norms. It frequently involves conflict, either between established requirements or between individual managers and departments, and can result in significant changes of the image that people have of the business (and therefore of their roles in it). The process by which this change of image occurs begins with a recognition of the conflict of values, and continues with an inquiry phase, in which organisational norms become reconstructed, often along with related strategies and assumptions. Failure to learn occurs when this restructuring is blocked – for example, when people take entrenched positions that prolong conflict. On the other hand, each cycle where double-loop learning takes place helps create patterns for future learning.

Constantly looking for new ways of putting the point across, Argyris wrote in 1982:*

> Learning may be defined as occurring under two conditions. First, learning occurs when an organization achieves what it intended; that is, there is a *match* between its design for action and the actual outcome. Second, learning occurs when a *mismatch* between intention and outcome is identified and corrected; that is, a mismatch is turned into a match. . . .
>
> Single-loop learning occurs when matches are created, or when mismatches are corrected by changing actions. Double-loop learning occurs when mismatches are corrected by first examining and altering the governing variables and then the actions.

Much of Argyris's and Schon's subsequent work has focused on how to help managers make use of organisational learning. From observations of what managers actually do, they have found, for example, that:

* 'Problems in producing usable knowledge for implementing liberating alternatives', an address to the International Congress of Applied Psychology, July 1982.

The executive mind seems to work in bewildering ways. . . . First, the reasoning executives use to manage people and technical issues leads simultaneously to productive and to counterproductive consequences. Second, they are unaware of this feature because they are disconnected from their own reasoning processes while making tough decisions. Third, they are disconnected from their reasoning processes because of the skills they have mastered to solve tough problems. The skills that lead to success will also lead to failure. . . .

Surprisingly, executives (or anyone else, for that matter) are usually unaware of their reasoning processes. There are two reasons for this. First, they have great reasoning skill – the activity is second nature to them, and they are rarely aware of it while they are doing it. Indeed, as is true of most skilled behavior, they rarely focus on it unless they make an error. Second, when they do make errors, other people – especially subordinates – may feel it is safest to play down the error, or may ease in the correct information so subtly that the executive will probably not even realize that he did make an error. . . .

Our research indicates that when executives deal with difficult, threatening, underlying issues, they use reasoning processes that, at best, simultaneously lead to immediate success and long-range problems. Often the problems go unsolved, compounding the long-range difficulties. Much of this occurs without executives' realizing it.*

Argyris believes that recognising such problems is a good way towards resolving them. Developing interpersonal competence in organisations will help both the individuals and the organisation itself to learn; they will then become more mature in outlook and begin to use their full psychological energy for the organisation's goals.

* 'The Executive Mind and Double-loop Learning', *Organizational Dynamics*, Autumn 1982.

CHAPTER 4

The Strategists

The word strategy has been applied to the business world only in recent decades. Until the 1940s, strategy was seen as primarily a matter for the military. It is no coincidence, then, that the language of business strategy resounds with military terminology and analogies. In *Business Wargames*, Barrie James identifies many of these similarities and it is perhaps significant that the current most aggressive global strategists, the Japanese, make the most use of martial terms in their routine communications.

The concept of business strategy started out as 'business policy', a term still in widespread use at business schools today. The word policy implies a 'hands-off', administrative, even intellectual approach rather than the implementation-focused approach that characterises much of modern thinking on strategy. In *The Evolution of Management Thought* (1979), Daniel Wren traces the first coherent approach to business policy to Arch Shaw, a Chicago businessman and publisher who lectured at both Northwestern and Harvard Universities. Shaw persuaded senior executives of large companies to discuss with students the policy (or strategy) problems they were facing, and how they approached the process of planning solutions.

Various authors divide the progression of strategic thinking into three eras:

- long-range planning
- strategic planning
- strategic management.

As artificial as these divisions are, they provide a useful starting point for placing the evolution of strategic theorists into context. One of the most helpful definitions of the differences comes from Professor Bernard Taylor, editor of *Long Range Planning* magazine, who explains that:

- *Long-range planning* was simply an extension of one year financial planning into five-year budgets and detailed operating plans. It involved little or no consideration of social or political factors, assuming that markets would be relatively stable. Gradually, it developed to encompass issues of growth and diversification.
- *Strategic planning* aimed to ensure that managers engaged in debate about strategic options before the budget was drawn up. Here, the focus of strategy was in the business units rather than in the organisation centre.
- *Strategic management* aimed to give people at all levels the tools and support they needed to manage strategic change. Its focus was no longer primarily external, but equally internal – how can the organisation seize and maintain strategic advantage by using the combined efforts of the people that work in it?

This evolution began in the early 1960s, when a flurry of authoritative texts suddenly turned strategic planning from an issue of vague academic interest into an important concern for practising managers. Before this, discussion of strategy was extremely limited recalls David Hussey of management consultants Harbridge House, a close follower of the development of strategic thinking and one of the first non-American authors in this area. 'There were no books on the subject for managers to read. Drucker made some references, while Stanford Research Institute was publishing a lot of useful, basic materials', but strategy wasn't part of the normal executive vocabulary.

Two giants emerged in the 1960s. Business historian Alfred Chandler (born 1918) advised splitting the functions of strategic thinking and line management (see Chapter 2). His influential book *Strategy and Structure* was published in 1962, appealing to many large companies that were having difficulty in coping with their size. In recent years it has come under heavy attack from critics, who maintain that strategy must be a line responsibility, decided as close as possible to the action, with corporate planning staff operating as advisers and co-ordinators within a broad strategy set at the top.

Igor Ansoff, the second of these early strategy giants, is particularly scathing: 'It resulted in a lot of concern with boxes of the structure,' he declares, 'but generally ignored organisational capability.' Nonetheless, Chandler did help to focus managers' attention on the necessity to create a coherent strategic plan before drawing up an organisation chart. As he put it succinctly, 'structure follows strategy'.

Ansoff has his own section (see pages 151–8). His influence stems from his erudite *Corporate Strategy*, published in 1965. One observer remarks wryly: 'Igor created a kind of one-upmanship: those who claimed they could understand his book and those who admitted they didn't.' It was Ansoff who introduced the term strategic management into the business vocabulary.

Before and between Chandler and Ansoff were a number of lesser-known writers who opened up the idea of planning and strategy to wider discussion. At Harvard a research team had been producing a steady flow of articles for *Harvard Business Review* and these were eventually published as a collection in 1963. Bernard Taylor says the credit for developing strategy as a serious subject at Harvard goes to Ken Adams, whose case work after the Second World War has also provided the core of business policy courses at many other US business schools. However, the earliest real impact on managers was made by John Gardner's *Self-Renewal*, published in 1964, which pointed out that organisations constantly need to reassess themselves. Like people, they need to keep renewing their skills and abilities – something they can only do effectively through careful planning. Also in the early 1960s an Australian, Bruce Scott (son of Sir Walter Scott, founder of Australia's largest management consultancy), published his observations of how a number of companies carried out their long-range planning. Shortly afterwards, Kirby Warren at Harvard took a different tack. Instead of gathering the consensus of wisdom on how to plan, as Scott had done, he looked in depth at what happened in a small number of companies to see what worked well and what didn't. He identified a number of common errors that had been hidden by vagueness in the executive suites as to what strategy was. In several companies, for example, he found that the managers confused the strategic plan with its components – in particular, the marketing plan was often assumed to be the same thing as the overall corporate plan.

This specific theme was developed in much greater depth by

Wickham Skinner (born 1924), who pointed out that an excessive focus on marketing planning frequently led companies to forget about manufacturing needs until late in the day, when there was little room for manoeuvre. Skinner argued for a clear manufacturing strategy to proceed in parallel with the marketing strategy. In many ways he was ahead of his time, for the concept of technology strategy or manufacturing strategy has only really begun to take root in the 1980s and many manufacturing companies still have no one in charge of this aspect of their business.

One particularly influential idea from Skinner was the 'focused factory'. He demonstrated that it was not normally possible for a production unit to focus on more than one style of manufacturing. Even if the same machines were used to produce basically similar products, if those products had very different customer demands that required a different manner of working, the factory would not be successful. For example, trying to produce equipment for the consumer market, where a certain error rate in production was compensated for by higher volume sales at a lower price, was incompatible with producing 100 per cent perfect product for the military. The most likely outcome was a compromise that satisfied no one.

Skinner has been based at Harvard since 1960. Also at Harvard were Paul Lawrence and Jay Lorsch, whose contingency theory of organisations is discussed in Chapter 2. Their work forced many managers to understand that organisations were not fixed; that strategy and planning had to be adapted to each segment of the environment with which they dealt.

While the theorists were arguing, one large US company was quietly innovating. General Electric Co. had begun to develop the concept of strategy business units (SBUs) in the 1950s. The basic idea – now largely accepted as the normal and obvious way of going about things – was that strategy should be set within the context of individual businesses which had clearly defined products and markets. Each of these businesses would be responsible for its own profits and development, under general guidance from headquarters.

Stung by its failure to compete effectively with the rapidly growing IBM in the computer market, GE recognised that its planning processes were inadequate, because they relied largely on financial data. A new chief executive, Fred Borth, took the courageous step of inviting 'soft' scientists, such as economists and sociologists, to help compile a data base that would allow it to identify which strategies worked in various situations. The source of the data was the hundreds of SBUs in the group. Among the researchers was Sid Schoeffler, economics professor at the University of Massachusetts, who had written a seminal book, *The Failure of Modern Economics*, shortly before. Schoeffler's theme was that economic theories failed to explain how markets worked because they focused on the industry sector of the company, when all the real decisions were taken at the business unit level.

Like most other industrial economists of the time, Schoeffler was heavily influenced by operational research. He believed that if only you had a broad enough data base, you could model the behaviour of markets sufficiently well to pull the right levels and be reasonably sure of the profits that would result. In practice, it has become clear that the number of factors that influence what happens in markets is too huge and the market forces are too dynamic to make such accurate predictions. Nevertheless, Schoeffler persuaded a number of companies that the data base should be expanded to include thousands of business units and he set up what is now the Profit Impact of Market Strategy (PIMS) data base at Harvard. PIMS – which did produce a good many observations on what strategies resulted in best perform-ance *in general* – moved out of Harvard in 1975.

GE's data base was instrumental in developing a variety of benchmarks and portfolio planning approaches. For example, the largest, most established management consultancy McKin-sey worked with GE to develop a matrix based on industry attractiveness and competitive strength. This was widely seen as McKinsey's answer to Boston Consulting Group's Boston Box.

The Boston Box is a device to help companies balance the amount of resources invested and the types of product they have in various types of business according to their market share and the predicted rate of growth of their markets. In theory, they should be able to use cash-generating businesses (cows) to finance businesses with high growth potential, while disposing of those in mature markets where they have low market share.

The origins of the box go back to the concept of the experience curve, which was the real innovation of BCG's founder, Bruce Henderson (born 1915). Henderson is a Harvard Business School graduate who went to work for Westinghouse Electric Co, where he eventually became general manager of the air-conditioning division in the mid 1950s, before joining A. D. Little in 1959. One of the companies he was working with had a technical breakthrough. It would have been expensive to develop it to the stage where it could be marketed, but no one was able to predict what the pay-offs for various levels of investment would be, in terms of market share and profitability. While looking for a way of providing answers, he came across the US defence industry, which had found that the more aeroplanes it made, the less time each unit took, and therefore the cheaper it became to produce.

Henderson took this concept and applied it to electronics. Much the same cost curve emerged. He wrote his ideas up in a small booklet in 1967. 'Perspectives On Experience' has never been formally published or advertised, but it rapidly sold 25,000 copies. The experience curve, he explains, is a means of measuring probable competitive cost differentials. It assumes that a difference in market share of two to one compared to the nearest competitor is worth 20 per cent or more in terms of pretax costs on value-added, or at least 5 per cent more on after tax profits. This led to the next question, he says: 'If we double output, that means investing twice as much money into capacity – where's the money going to come from?' The answer was that companies had to invest cash from mature profitable businesses with large market share (which should be producing more profits than they need to maintain market position and continue to develop the product) into younger businesses where market share can still be bought relatively cheaply. Henderson founded BCG in 1963 to develop these ideas and put them into practice.

BCG describes its portfolio management terms as follows:

The growth share matrix is a diagram of the normal relationship of cash use and cash generation.

Stars are in the upper left quadrant. They grow rapidly and therefore they use large amounts of cash. However, since they are leaders, they also generate large amounts of cash.

Normally, such products are about in balance in net cash flow. Over time all growth slows. Therefore, *stars* eventually become *cash cows* if they hold their market share. If they fail to hold market share, they become *dogs*.

Cash cows are in the lower left quadrant. Growth is slow and therefore cash use is low. However, market share is high and therefore comparative cash generation is also high. *Cash cows* pay the dividends, pay the interest on debt and cover the corporate overhead.

Dogs are in the lower right quadrant. Both growth and share are low. *Dogs* often report a profit even though they are net cash users. They are essentially worthless. They are cash traps.

Question marks are the real cash traps and the real gambles. They are in the upper right quadrant. Their cash needs are great because of their growth. Yet, their cash generation is very low because their market share is low.

Left alone, *question marks* are sure losers. They can require years of heavy cash investment. Yet, if they do not develop a leading market position before the growth slows, they become just big *dogs*.

Question marks are very difficult to convert into *stars*. Increase in market share compounds cash needs. The cost of acquiring market share doubly compounds the cash needs. *Question marks* are sometimes big winners if backed to the limit. But most *question marks* are big losers.

The Boston Box has been criticised in recent years as being far too simplistic. Henderson, however, points out that it was never meant to be prescriptive. The intention of portfolio management was, he says, 'to give people a way to talk about their businesses that they hadn't had before. It helped them think about their businesses in new ways; of exploring what would happen, if we did this or that. A business is a dynamic system with a great many interactions between its parts.'

Henderson, still active in his seventies, now teaches in Nashville. A large part of his lectures is devoted to examining organisations as dynamic systems.

BCG's concepts were marketed in a very subdued manner through small pamphlets with thought-provoking articles on aspects of strategy and through private conferences on similar themes. As a result, even though it grew at 40 per cent a year, it was not noticed – or, at least, was not taken seriously – by McKinsey, until the early 1970s.

Although today there are hundreds of strategy consultants, with a wide variety of specialisations, and every major consultancy has a strategy arm, in the 1950s there were very few. James McKinsey (1889–1937), founder of the global management consultancy that bears his name, was a professor of cost accounting at the school of business at the University of Chicago. His most important publication, *Budgetary Control* (1922), is quoted as the start of the era of modern budgetary accounting. He was only with the consultancy he founded in the mid 1920s for a few years (when he was offered and accepted the job of managing director of Montgomery Ward, he felt the two activities were not compatible), but in the time he was there he wrote what he called his General Survey – a thirty-page check-list for effective management consultancy that all new recruits to McKinsey are still told to memorise.

McKinsey's successor, Marvin Bower (born 1903), had only been with the company for three years when he took over. Bower is not a management guru yet he belongs in this book because he created a climate from which so many genuinely innovative management thinkers emerged. A lawyer by background, his stamp is on everything McKinsey does, down to the layout of letters and reports, which has been unchanged for more than forty years. Still active in the business, although officially long retired, he is known for his uncompromising standards ('He once shouted at me for trying to sign a contract with a ballpoint pen,' recalls one senior executive) and for his habit of responding to short memos with lengthy, considered replies. 'Whenever he came across an example of good or bad practice, he wrote a memo to everybody,' recalls Henry Strage of McKinsey's London office.

One of Bower's characteristic decisions was to give away his majority shareholding to his colleagues around the world. Recognising that many professional firms falter because the founder loses his vision or fails to provide for a visionary successor, when he reached the formal retirement age of sixty he appointed a three-man executive to run the company while he contemplated the best way to ensure its survival. Ironically, Bower's successor, Archie Macdonald, was recommended to McKinsey by none other than Bruce Henderson, then still at Westinghouse.

Next to Harvard Business School, McKinsey has probably generated more original thinkers in management than any other institution. Among them are Arch Patton, originator of much now common practice in executive compensation, Peters and Waterman, and Kenichi Ohmae.

McKinsey's portfolio planning developments at General Electric were paralleled in Britain and Holland by international oil giant Shell. Shell also pioneered another new concept – scenario planning. Creating one single strategic plan to be followed with military precision simply didn't work in practice. As circumstances changed, the strategic plan also needed changing and executives were either constantly going back to the drawing board or trying to push through a plan that was no longer appropriate. The longer the planning horizon, the worse the problem became. Shell's answer was to make not one but a number of sets of assumptions about the future environment. At its simplest, these would be optimistic, pessimistic and straightline. Any one of these scenarios *could* happen, but managers now drew up plans that followed the most likely series of events, while building in frequent evaluation points where one of the alternative scenarios could take over. In effect, what they were doing was thinking through the implications of necessary deviations from a plan sufficiently far ahead to be able to implement them at minimum cost and effort.

In the early 1970s, a further batch of writers, such as George Steiner of the University of California at Los Angeles and John Argenti in Britain, tried to pull together the strings of research into strategy that were going on around the world and particularly in the United States. Although Wickham Skinner had done most of his research in the 1960s, he only published seriously at this later stage with *Manufacturing in Corporate Strategy* (1977), followed by *Manufacturing: The Formidable Competitive Weapon* (1985). One of the most influential pieces of research in the 1970s (though still far less influential than it should have been) was by John Kitching, an Englishman with a strong interest in the process of acquisitions. Kitching analysed what happened in US acquisitions in the late 1960s and in European acquisitions in the early 1970s. The results were very similar: the betting odds for success were 50 per cent or less.

In the past decade, the number of powerful and influential thinkers in the strategy field has increased dramatically. Among those whose influence has been particularly felt are Michael Porter (see pages 167–72) and, in the marketing field, Theodore Levitt (see pages 158–63), both of Harvard. Within South-east Asia, the most prominent strategist is McKinsey's Kenichi Ohmae. The study of strategy has become a truly international phenomenon. The North American and British academics still predominate, but there are now centres of excellence in strategic studies in France (at INSEAD), Spain, Sweden and Switzerland.

The sheer diversity of research into business strategy during the 1980s makes it an invidious task to select a handful of key players. It is perhaps more helpful to isolate the most significant themes of the decade:

- *globalisation* (how companies can react to global threats and opportunities) – Porter and Ohmae's contributions are buoyed up by other missionaries such as Gary Hamel at the London Business School.
- *strategic alliances* and *joint venture strategy* (how to obtain resources through partnerships) – promoted strongly by Kathryn Rudie Harrigan of Columbia.
- *the role of headquarters* – Michael Goold and Andrew Campbell, founding directors and fellows of the Ashridge Strategic Management Centre, a research body established late in 1987 have recently identified three fundamentally different management styles (strategic planning, strategic control and financial control), each of which can be a viable approach for a parent company.
- *new product development strategy* – Richard Foster of McKinsey and Ian Macmillan of the Wharton School have achieved recognition in this area. (Macmillan, however, sees his main contributions as being in political strategy, competitive dynamics and entrepreneurship.)
- *manufacturing strategy* – where concentration has

increasingly focused on concepts such as computer-integrated manufacturing, production cycle time reduction and quality.

The trend in strategy research is clearly for increasing specialisation as every functional area of business, from human resources (that is, people management) to factory location, becomes drawn into the strategic planning net. We are therefore less likely to see gurus of general strategy in future – at least until the mass of theory and data is sufficient for another Mintzberg-like iconoclast to pull it all together and tell everyone that they have got it all wrong.

Igor Ansoff

Born Vladivostok, Russia, 1918
Academic and consultant

One reviewer of Igor Ansoff's books has commented: 'Ansoff's work is at the apogee of hard management theory. He is rationalist to a fault, insisting that everything quantifiable should be quantified.'

Ansoff takes partial exception to the reviewer's comment. He says: 'Indeed I am a rationalist, but I do not insist and do not seek to quantify everything. I prefer a comment contributed by Henry Mintzberg to the cover of my last book, in which he said "Ansoff is the father of strategic management. His book *Corporate Strategy* remains the most elaborate model of strategic planning in the literature." Rather than quantify, I seek patterns in complexity which can help managers to do their work in the overwhelmingly complex and turbulent world of today and tomorrow. During the past twenty-five years, since my first book *Corporate Strategy* was published, I have progressed to a broader perspective which embraces economic, psychological, sociological and political rationalities. These are all necessary to an understanding of today's world of organizations and their behaviour.'

In his search for a broader perspective, it was Ansoff who was the first to recognise the need for strategic management. Starting with *Corporate Strategy* (1965), his books *Acquisition Behavior in the US Manufacturing Industry, 1948–1965* (1971), *From Strategic Planning to Strategic Management* (1974), *Strategic Management* (1979), *Implanting Strategic Management* (1984) and *The New Corporate Strategy* (1988) trace this progress from economic rationalist to multi-disciplinarian.

Ansoff's books *Business Strategy* (1969), *Strategic Management* (1979) and *Implanting Strategic Management* (1984) have led the way in the field. Bernard Taylor of Henley Management College has said: 'Ansoff is among the few pioneers who have developed and tested new concepts and techniques which have advanced the art of corporate planning.' Gay Haskins of *The Economist* is a friend of Ansoff's and reflects, 'He is the father of corporate strategy and business policy. He really isn't given enough credit.'

In bringing strategic management to a wider audience, Ansoff has forged a truly international career. Conceived in Japan, born in Vladivostok, Ansoff started life on the move. His mother was '400 per cent Russian', his father an American diplomat. Initially marooned in Vladivostok when the Russian Revolution took place, Ansoff spent his youth in Moscow. When he was sixteen, the family left for the United States. 'We came to the United States alone,' Ansoff recalls. 'My father had great difficulty finding employment, so I had to scratch for every bit of education. This produced an enormous drive to succeed.'

Ansoff had been taught English by an Englishman in Moscow and, for the first two months at New York's Stuyvesant High School, he could hardly understand a word. Two years later he passed with the highest honours in his class because, he says, 'I worked my ass off.'

Next, he studied mechanical engineering and physics at Stevens Institute of Technology before becoming a teacher at the college. He went to war for two years (as a deep-sea diver amongst other things) before returning and taking advantage of a generous government sponsorship of education for ex-servicemen. This time he studied applied mathematics.

Upon graduation in 1948, he joined the Rand Foundation, a brain trust which had been created by the Air Force. Surrounded by some of America's finest brains, Ansoff had second thoughts about his chosen subject. 'I came to the conclusion I would not make a great mathematician.' At Rand Ansoff took part in 'sophisticated operational research' including studying the vulnerability of NATO air forces to enemy attack. 'One of the first lessons I learned was that it's not all about technology, it's about organizations and people,' he says. This particular study triggered off many of his later concerns. 'I began to learn that rational decision-making is the tip of a large pyramid which describes the processes by which organizations move and change.'

Rand provided the genesis of much of Ansoff's later thinking. He read management theorists Fayol and Barnard and was deeply influenced by Norbert Wiener's pioneering book on cybernetics. But such pursuits weren't enough. 'Somehow, despite the success of my work at Rand, I wasn't living in the real world. The recommendations to the Air Force, which we worked so hard to provide, were highly regarded but had no visible consequences.'

In search of reality, Ansoff joined Lockheed as a long-range planner and later became responsible for the diversification of the company. He divided his interests into three categories: learning how business works, perceiving the key variables and relationships in complex problems and learning to manage. 'I was fortunate that my first job at Lockheed gave me ample opportunity for the first two kinds of learning,' says Ansoff.

Opportunity to learn the realities of management occurred when part of one of the firm's diversification moves went wrong. Ansoff was sent to sort it out. 'It was a major and traumatic experience,' he recalls. 'For the first time in my life I found myself managing lives of people. The division in trouble was in seventeen different hi-tech businesses with a total of 150 engineers. It didn't take a genius to see what was wrong. It was relatively easy to reduce seventeen business areas to three, but confronting the soul-wrenching task of disrupting careers and personal lives of 100 engineers who had to be laid off was one of the most difficult experiences of my life.'

Losses were transformed into profits. 'Things began to hum and then one day I was shaving, looked at myself in the mirror and realised that, while I managed my division strategically,

I had no idea of what I wanted to do with the rest of my life.'

Ansoff took off with a case of whisky and grew a beard. Things fell into place. 'It was exhilarating but tough and it helped me extraordinarily.' The conclusion, the strategic plan, emerged. It was simple enough: 'I decided to become a college professor.'

Within six months of Ansoff's decision to change direction, the prestigious Graduate School of Industrial Administration at Carnegie-Mellon University invited him to join its faculty.

Ansoff recalls this event as his first proof of the value of having a clearly formulated strategy: 'If I hadn't made a decision to change careers, I would have turned down the offer. My division was profitable and there were many attractive opportunities to be pursued by remaining in business.'

Ansoff accepted the offer (and a 50 per cent loss of salary) in order to pursue his strategy.

Work on his first book was not an easy process, he admits: 'My secretary told me, "Ansoff, you're going to write your book." She virtually locked me in the office.' The result was *Corporate Strategy* (1965) which Ansoff remembers as 'a creative book – I was working it out bit by bit.'

Corporate Strategy contains detailed and systematic planning procedures, though Ansoff later commented, 'I was arrogant enough to believe that all a company had to do was to maximise its strengths and minimise its weaknesses. That of course made organisations not more flexible but more rigid. That is the last thing a company wants in these turbulent times.'

Corporate Strategy was finished during the first year at Carnegie-Mellon. It was well received and, within a few years, was translated into fourteen languages. But after six years of teaching, Ansoff became progressively concerned that Carnegie, along with all other business schools, was not responding to the growing need in industry for women and men who are creative change-makers and entrepreneurial risk-takers. 'They were graduating risk-controlling profit-seekers,' says Ansoff.

Again, opportunity knocked when Vanderbilt University invited Ansoff to become the founding dean of its Graduate School of Management. 'As a result of negotiations with the university I obtained a brief to build a school for change managers and change agents.' Ansoff went about the task with gusto. 'By this time I was convinced that such schools must be thoroughly multidisciplinary. But I also learned that, to make interdisciplinary interaction work, for every "quantitative" faculty member I had to recruit two "behavioural" types.'

Ansoff and his faculty spent four months designing the school's curriculum. The word 'teaching' was replaced with 'learning', a new concept of different length courses was introduced, new subjects were introduced, and traditional subjects were assigned time in relation to their importance in the repertoire of a successful change manager.

Within a year the school admitted its first class of students. Ansoff is particularly proud that the class was multinational, with 37 per cent of its students from outside the United States.

While building and managing the school, Ansoff continued his research on the problems of strategy. But he increasingly found himself out of step with the academic research which blossomed in the 1960s. Instead, he focused on elaborating and expanding the concept of strategy.

'My interest has always been in the application of research to practice. I observed that, as firms became increasingly skilful strategy formulators, the translation of strategy into results in the market-place lagged behind. This created "paralysis by analysis" in strategic planning and suppression of strategic planning in many firms.'

Claims were increasingly made by practitioners and some academics that strategy planning did not contribute to the profitability of firms. In the face of these claims, Ansoff and several of his colleagues at Vanderbilt undertook a four-year research study to determine whether, when paralysis by analysis is overcome, strategic planning increased profitability of firms.

The result of the research was Ansoff's second book, forbiddingly titled *Acquisition Behavior of US Manufacturing Firms, 1945–1963*.

The research proved that planned acquisitions produced significantly better financial performance than opportunistic, unplanned ones. Ansoff observes: 'This result presented me with a question which guided my thinking, writing, and research during the following fifteen years – "What are the reasons for the paralysis by analysis and what can be done to eliminate them?" '

An early and fundamental answer perceived by Ansoff was that strategic planning is an incomplete instrument for managing change, not unlike an automobile with an engine but no steering wheel to convert the engine's energy into movement.

In 1972 Ansoff published a pioneering paper titled *The Concept of Strategic Management*, which was ultimately to earn him the title of the father of strategic management. The paper asserted the importance of strategic planning as a major pillar of strategic management but added a second pillar – the capability of a firm to convert written plans into market reality. (The third pillar – the skill in managing resistance to change – was to be added in the 1980s.)

Ansoff obtained sponsorship from IBM and General Electric for the first International Conference on Strategic Management, which was held at Vanderbilt in 1973 and resulted in his third book, *From Strategic Planning to Strategic Management*.

As the school for change managers attracted a growing number of students and began to receive increasing recognition among its business clients, Ansoff encountered resistance and opposition from other schools of the university, which claimed that his school was breaking academic norms. Resistance also came from Nashville's business community.

'It got to a point where I was spending most of my time on fending off criticisms and opposition and a minor portion of time on what I was supposed to do: manage my school, help my students learn, and contribute to knowledge about management,' says Ansoff. He resigned from the deanship six years after its founding and took himself and his family to the European Institute for Advanced Studies in Management in Brussels, where he was responsible for developing a European community of teachers and scholars in strategic management. His research proceeded in two parallel streams. 'Enough knowledge had accumulated by the 1970s to make an effort to develop a comprehensive theory of strategic behaviour which would explain what kinds of behaviour lead to success, and why so much behaviour is unsuccessful.' Between 1974 and 1979 Ansoff developed a theory which embraces not only business firms but other environment-serving organisations. The resulting book, titled *Strategic Management*, was published in 1979.

'Building this theory was the most important phase of my

intellectual development. In search for a theory which would faithfully produce reality, I was forced to recognise that my initial training in rational business analysis was totally inadequate and that a multidisciplinary perspective was essential. I begged, borrowed and stole concepts and theoretical insights from psychology, sociology and political science. And I attempted to integrate them into a holistic explanation of strategic behaviour.'

The book received little attention at first. Ansoff's reasons are two. 'First, the title was a misnomer – the result of a protracted argument with the publisher. My preferred title was "Applied Managerial Theory of Strategic Behavior". Second, the book was before its time. Academia was still focused on strategy formulation and there was little interest in the holistic perspective I offered.' Ansoff feels that now, ten years later, the book is more likely to receive attention, and he is busy incorporating new theoretical developments in the expectation of publishing a revised version.

Ansoff's second focus, while in Europe, remained on the development of practical tools for managing adaptation of firms to turbulent environments. In 1980 he published a paper which represented another step in the development of practical strategic management. The paper, called *Strategic Issue Management*, presented a way of adapting a firm to the environment, when environmental change develops so fast that strategic planning becomes too slow to produce timely responses to surprising threats and opportunities.

Ansoff and his family returned to the United States in 1983, when he became Distinguished Professor of Strategic Management at the US International University (USIU).

In 1984 he published a comprehensive book on the state of the art of strategic management called *Implanting Strategic Management*. In 1988 an updated revision of his 1965 book appeared both in the United States and in Britain.

At USIU Ansoff focused his energies on working with doctoral students who began empirical research on hypotheses advanced in *Strategic Management*. The first concern was with proving the 'Strategic Success Hypothesis', which specifies the strategic behaviour, which optimises a firm's return on investment. The hypothesis asserts that there is no universal prescription for success; that success depends instead on the firm's ability to match its external strategic behaviour to the turbulence in its environment and to develop an internal capability which supports this strategy. Ansoff proudly points out: 'To date we have completed four theses, performed on different types of organisations and in different countries. All of them give very strong statistical support to the hypothesis.' Ansoff has translated the hypothesis into a practical diagnostic instrument which has been used by many managers to determine whether their present strategy and capability will be responsive to the turbulence of their future environment.

Having shown what kinds of strategies and capabilities lead to success, the next major subject on Ansoff's agenda is to extend knowledge to help firms behave successfully. Several doctoral theses are already under way.

When asked to summarise what he considers his major contribution to strategic management, Ansoff cites two contributions: 'First I would like to be known as one of the first to bring a multidisciplinary approach to both exploratory theory and practical tools for helping environment serving organisations to succeed in turbulent environments. Second, I would like to be recognised as one of the first to offer a scientific proof that the age of universal prescriptions (like "stick to your strategic knitting" or "return to basics") is over; that the solution depends on the characteristics of the organisation's environment; that each organisation needs to diagnose its future environment and then devise its own appropriate solutions; and that I contributed a practical tool for matching a firm to its environment.'

Theodore Levitt

Born Vollmerz, Germany, 1925
Editor of Harvard Business Review

Theodore Levitt arrived in the United States with his parents in 1935 at the age of ten. Today, he is probably the world's best-known marketing thinker (described by one manager as 'the Copernicus of American business'); he has been based at Harvard Business School for nearly thirty years.

Having studied economics, Levitt became a marketing expert by default. In the late 1950s, as a consultant in Chicago, he carried out a survey of the retail gasoline business. Approached by Harvard, his interests remained ill-defined. 'The work I had done meant marketing was where I was at the time, though I didn't realise this,' says Levitt. 'I had become interested in business practice but I hadn't really narrowed anything down.' In his first year at Harvard, Levitt was assigned to teach marketing, even though he had never read a book on the subject. He recalls with typical understatement, 'I didn't volunteer. Some people at Harvard thought marketing was a subject I might be able to handle.'

Levitt's reputation was soon established with the 1960 *Harvard Business Review* article 'Marketing Myopia', which has now sold more than 500,000 copies in reprints. He criticised short-sighted managers, who regarded marketing as 'a step-child', arguing that 'an industry is a customer-satisfying process, not a goods-producing process'. He traced the chronic problems of the railroads to top management's belief that it was in the railroad business, not transport; similarly managers in the film industry were carried away by the movies when they were in the entertainment business.

Nearly three decades on, Levitt believes things have changed – that marketing is no longer a stepchild. However, he says, 'What is fascinating is that even today in company after company people recently given high responsibility suddenly discover that something has to be done to improve marketing orientation. It keeps getting discovered again and again.'

In 'Marketing Myopia' Levitt also emphasised the difference between selling, which he regarded as 'tricks and techniques of getting people to exchange their cash for your product', and marketing, defined as 'a tightly integrated effort to discover, create, arouse and satisfy customer needs'. Levitt observed: 'The seller takes his cues from the buyer, in such a way that the product becomes a consequence of the marketing effort, not vice versa.'

The importance of customer orientation has remained a preoccupation of Levitt's work. As for 'Marketing Myopia' (still the piece he is best known for) Levitt calls it 'a lucky shot', before putting its success into perspective: 'I thought I said something important, said it pretty well and I think I carried it off. I wasn't particularly surprised, but I was also not particularly aware of how influential it had become.'

Levitt's marketing wisdom has since been distilled into five major books as well as a steady stream of articles (he has had more articles in the *Harvard Business Review* than anyone else). The 'Marketing Myopia' article was included in the 1962 book *Innovation in Marketing*. Levitt points to *The Marketing Mode* (1969) as his favourite, while not necessarily recommending it. 'I like it a lot because in it I indulged myself – I took a lot of curious detours.'

It is *The Marketing Imagination* (1983) that Levitt regards as his most important work. 'It has by far the most important and enduring subjects of all my books and they will last a long time because they deal with things that won't go away.' Competitive success, Levitt argued, demands realisation of five things:

1. The purpose of a business is to create and keep a customer.
2. To do that you have to produce and deliver goods and services that people want and value, at prices and under conditions that are reasonably attractive relative to those offered by others, to a proportion of customers large enough to make those prices and conditions possible.
3. To continue to do that, the enterprise must produce revenue in excess of costs in sufficient quantity and with sufficient regularity to attract and hold investors in the enterprise, and must keep at least abreast and sometimes ahead of competitive offerings.
4. No enterprise, no matter how small, can do any of this by mere instinct or accident. It has to clarify its purposes, strategies and plans, and the larger the enterprise the greater the necessity that these be clearly written down, clearly communicated, and frequently reviewed by the senior members of the enterprise.
5. In all cases there must be an appropriate system of rewards, audits, and controls to assure that what's intended gets properly done and, when not, that it gets quickly rectified.

Asked how to develop a marketing imagination, Levitt

provides a simple formula: 'Expose yourself to your environment and ask questions to develop your sensitivity and sensibility.' This, he believes, is the chief source of his ideas and success. 'I see things all the time. I go into factories, offices, stores and look out the window and just see things and ask why? Why are they doing that? Why is it this way and not that? You ask questions and pretty soon you come up with answers. When you begin to try to answer your own questions you become much more receptive to reading things which help you to answer questions.' Like Peter Drucker, Levitt makes an important distinction: 'Seeing is one thing but perceptiveness requires cognitive effort and personal involvement. You bring something to what you see.'

In recent years Levitt is probably best known for his work on the globalisation of markets, increasing standardisation of products and the role of 'global brands'. In a 1987 interview he said: 'Everybody around the world speaks a common language now of science and technology. I'm not just speaking about the semiconductor business. Steel-making today is high-tech – all over the world. So is paper making. The proletarianisation of communication, travel and transport is bringing the world much closer together.'

The concept of global brands, while rapidly endorsed by some of the largest advertising agencies, has come under fire from other academics. While there may be global markets where the same high-tech products can be sold in much the same manner to diverse customers, there are many consumer products, they argue, where local differences are everything. Writing in *Issues* magazine, Volney Stefflre, another US marketer, declares:

In my experience the same product in a different country is often very different in terms of its competitive advantage, so much so that it might as well be a different product. The competitive array is different, consumers may pay attention to and focus upon different product attributes with differing degrees of product knowledge and the consumers' expectations of how the product should be used or who should use it can be quite different from those in the originating country. Coca-Cola, though a global brand, has very different patterns of usage in different countries, in terms of usage occasions.

This whole area is now the subject of fierce debate. Theodore Levitt has recently argued in favor of global brand products with one positioning worldwide. In a recent discussion of Ovaltine, William Tragos argued that since Ovaltine is used to put the British to sleep, send the French kids off to school and in Nigeria makes people go off to bed and have good sex, regional positionings that highlighted local meanings might be appropriate. Professor Levitt's quoted rejoinder is that Ovaltine should be advertised as an aphrodisiac in Britain.

Levitt's comment is a typical illustration of his impassioned desire to stir discussion in a world where most managers spend most of their time avoiding asking themselves probing questions.

Levitt has always championed the simple approach. He has little time for academics who travel the world preaching their particular gospels. 'I've given all that up,' he says. 'I just don't think it's very much fun to listen to oneself talk a lot, and especially saying the same things over and over like a performer. It's just doing it for money. It's boring and unsatisfying. I prefer playing tennis or reading and writing what I've thought my way through.' He talks and writes sparingly. Ideas cannot simply be tossed away on to the lawns of Harvard; they have to work. 'There's a strong "back to basics" motion in management. People are enormously disenchanted with elaborate paradigms about how to manage a business – portfolio planning rules, hortatory check-lists, grids and charts. People are beginning to believe that what really counts is thinking – thinking with energy and courage. Courage is very important to get major things to happen,' he says.

Levitt's formidable intellect is put to the test as editor of the *Harvard Business Review*. True to form, he is taking a controversially forthright and populist approach. Inevitably, customers are at the forefront of his strategy. 'We've tried to clarify what we're trying to do; what business are we in; and for whom. Who are the customers? And tried to understand the customers and the competitive environment and the customer's own internal environment, their cognitive systems and what pressures they work under, what their lives are like and from that try to determine how we should function. We have a clear notion of what we're trying to do and what our unique positioning is and why it should be that way. This has been reflected in the kind of articles we run, the design and the editing of the magazine.' Unfortunately, being a full-time editor means Levitt no longer spends his time on research. He writes an editor's page only after being encouraged to do so by his magazine colleagues.

Levitt explains his way of working simply. 'I do what I do and things happen. What I've achieved, I think, is to make myself effective in some way, kept myself intellectually curious, alive and productive and made myself interesting to myself.'

It is, he makes clear, a continuing battle, 'a constant state of becoming better with problems that need to be solved and solutions that need to be corrected, because solutions bring their own problems.'

Kenichi Ohmae

Born Kyushu, Japan, 1943
Consultant

Kenichi Ohmae is one of the most prodigious modern writers on strategy (he has some thirty books to his name already). His messages are of interest to Western managers because they reflect how the Japanese plan and they provide insight into the strategies Japanese companies have adopted to make rapid inroads into world markets. He appears both chauvinistically Japanese and remarkably American. The *Financial Times* described him as 'a personality in a land where outspoken personalities are rare. And while most Japanese are anxious not to offend, Ohmae is blunt and often downright rude . . . he is Japan's only successful management guru.' Ohmae himself is reported as saying, 'I don't have the feeling that I am "a Japanese". I see myself as a global citizen. I like people from all around the world. I like the Japanese people but not those Japanese who stick only to traditional interests. I like Americans, too, but I reserve my right to disagree. You have to take me as I am.'

Ohmae trained as a nuclear physicist and as a concert flautist. Given the choice of which career to follow, he went to Massachusetts Institute of Technology on the grounds that there were more jobs for nuclear physicists than solo flautists. Recruited by management consultants McKinsey in 1972, he is now managing director of its Tokyo office and has carved out an extraordinary role for himself as both an adviser to Japanese ex-prime minister Nakasone and an outspoken champion of the new Japan in the Western world.

Ohmae's two most valuable books for the Western reader are *Triad Power* and *The Mind of the Strategist*. In *Triad Power* he argues a strong case for companies in international markets to establish a strong foothold in all three main economic zones: the United States, Japan and the Pacific, and Europe. The company that fails to do so becomes vulnerable because its global competitors can use their strengths in major markets where there is less competition to resource attacks in its home markets. The keys to success in these markets that contain together some 630 million consumers, are three Cs – commitment, creativity and competitiveness. The last two depend on several factors, among them the level and quantity of education and training and a willingness and capability to find good joint venture partners.

He claims that the new global enterprise has found that attractions of cheap labour in the newly industrialising countries (NICs) were at best ephemeral. As labour becomes a smaller and smaller proportion of overall production costs and as NIC wages rise, it pays to keep the jobs nearest the markets. In future, the global company should be more deeply and strategically involved in fewer countries, choosing a few and getting to know their institutions and leaders well. It will distinguish its global-scale operations in these locations from opportunistic, small-scale plants that companies used to build to enter restricted markets. It will be as prepared to contribute to the host nation's goals as to its own home country. Over time, it will build relationships with neighbouring countries for raw materials and supplies of low-cost components, as well as marketing and distribution.

The Mind of the Strategist: The Art of Japanese Business might better be called 'The Mind of the *Japanese* Strategist'. It explores the mixture of logic and intuition that drives strategic planning in many of Japan's most successful companies. He explains this in the following terms: 'In strategic thinking, one first seeks a clear understanding of the particular character of each element of a situation and then makes the fullest possible use of human brainpower to restructure the elements in the most advantageous way. Phenomena and events in the real world do not always fit a linear model. Hence the most reliable means of dissecting a situation into its constituent parts and reassembling them in the desired pattern is not a step-by-step methodology such as systems analysis. Rather, it is that ultimate nonlinear thinking tool, the human brain. True strategic thinking thus contrasts sharply with the conventional mechanical systems approach based on linear thinking. But it also contrasts with the approach that stakes everything on intuition, reaching conclusions without any real breakdown or analysis.'

The key to the analysis phase, he believes, is identifying the critical issues. It requires the use of issues diagrams that follow an issue through the algorithm of possible actions and their implications. A good business strategy, Ohmae says, 'is one, by which a company can gain significant ground on its competitors at an acceptable cost to itself'. There are four main ways of doing this:

- By focusing on the key factors for success (KFSs). Certain functional or operating areas within every business are more critical for success in that particular business environment than others. If you put especial effort into these areas and your competitors do not, this is a source of competitive advantage. The problem, of course, is identifying what these key factors for success are – which comes back to identifying the critical issues. 'The most effective shortcut to major success seems to be to jump quickly to the top of the rank by concentrating major resources early on a single strategically significant function. . . . All of today's industry leaders, without exception, began by bold deployment of strategies based on KFS.'
- By building on relative superiority. When all competitors are seeking to compete on the KFSs, a company can exploit any differences in competitive conditions. For example, it can make use of technology or sales networks not in direct competition with its rivals.
- By pursuing aggressive initiatives. Frequently, the only way to win against a much larger, entrenched competitor is to upset the competitive environment, by undermining the

value of its KFSs – changing the rules of the game by introducing new KFSs.

- By strategic degrees of freedom. By this, Ohmae means that the company can focus upon innovation in areas which are 'untouched by competitors'.

He explains: 'In each of these four methods, the principal concern is to avoid doing the same thing, on the same battle-ground, as the competition.'

Ohmae argues that an effective strategic plan takes account of three main players – the company, the customer and the competition – each exerting their own influence. The strategy that ignores competitive reaction is flawed; so is the strategy that does not take into account sufficiently how the customer will react; and so, of course, is the strategic plan that does not explore fully the organisation's capacity to implement it.

Henry Strage of McKinsey, London, describes Ohmae as 'the most extraordinary thinker we have. He has tremendous insight and creativity and sheer intellectual output. I've seen him writing away at meetings, but he's not taking notes: he's writing his next chapter. He questions everything. He's always asking why?'

Ohmae has also attracted a fair deal of controversy by saying what for many is unthinkable. Henry Strage continues: 'In recent years, he has become very political. It was his idea to move all the Japanese rice farmers to Alabama, where they could buy land cheaply, then sell the vacated land in Japan for building.' The heavy subsidies to Japanese farmers are holding back development and making the cost of rice artificially high. Ohmae's solution, he claimed, would cut the price by two-thirds and stimulate the economy at the same time. 'He has the knack for the dramatic. He gave a lecture in London and pulled out a handkerchief, saying, "We've just sold that much land in Tokyo for $1 million." '

Ohmae has a singular, and challenging, international perspective. 'It was a high risk to come to McKinsey and Co. in 1972, but I'm glad I did,' he has said. 'I'm now more interested in society, social systems and large corporate activities on a global basis. This is where I think I can do the most good.' His world view strips economics down to first principles: 'Interdependence is the key to making our world work. To protect its steel industry, Japan should invest in Australian iron ore and coal mines. We should stop subsidising our rice farmers and free them to go wherever they want.'

Among his most controversial claims is that there is no trade imbalance between the United States and Japan. As he told a group of executives in 1987, 'The sales of US companies in Japan plus imports from the United States equal the sales of Japanese companies in America plus exports to the United States. So what is the problem?' This is the theme of one of his most recent books, *Beyond National Borders*. He also argues for Japan, Europe and the United States to share global economic power and proposes 'a common community – cultural, monetary, a political system – a communal arrangement similar to the Treaty of Rome thirty years ago'. The book has been a run-away best seller in Japan, with more than 250,000 copies sold.

Other writings by Ohmae have attacked common perceptions of Japanese management by Westerners. For example: that Japanese companies make decisions from the bottom up; or that Japanese companies have a much longer-term planning horizon than their Western counterparts. Even so, Ohmae is truly international in outlook. 'We are experiencing the emergence of the global citizen,' he says. 'If anyone in the future ever looks back, I would like to be known as someone who worked for establishing a global village, regardless of racial prejudice or national bias.'

Michael Porter

Born Michigan, 1947
Professor at Harvard Business School

'My work has been aimed at improving the ability of firms and other organisations to compete, drawing on a rich understanding of the principles of competition. I have tried to bring a new level of sophistication to the understanding of competition by combining the tools of an economist with a strong awareness of and interest in the problems of the practising manager.'

One of the youngest full professors in the history of Harvard Business School, Porter is extraordinarily talented. He could have been a professional golfer and has an interest in what he calls 'the aesthetics and business of contemporary music and art'. He has sponsored rock bands, including one called Reckless, and has found time to play a leading role in a Presidential Commission on Industrial Competitiveness.

It was the business strategy lectures in the economics courses he took as an undergraduate that convinced Porter that here was a subject with great potential for original thinking. The lectures seemed from a different world. Ever since then, he says, 'I've been trying to bring the richness of companies' real experience to bear on the world of economics.' In doing so, he has created a following that is probably stronger among business practitioners than economists.

Encouraged by an inspirational teacher, Roland Christensen, Porter joined the Harvard faculty. 'My ideas on strategy were not initially accepted well by some of my colleagues,' he recalls. So he started an elective course, built around his emerging ideas. 'The course was so popular with the students that my colleagues began to understand there had to be something good here.'

Porter's first book for practising managers, *Competitive Strategy: Techniques for Analyzing Industries and Competitors*, was published in 1980. Drawing heavily on industrial economics (a field of study that tries to explain industrial performance through economics), he was trying 'to take these basic notions and create a much richer, more complex theory, much closer to the reality of competition'. The book defines five competitive forces that determine industry profitability – potential entrants, buyers (customers), suppliers, substitutes and competitors within the industry. Each of these can exert power to drive margins down. The attractiveness of an industry depends on how strong each of these influences is.

Competitive Strategy brought together in a rational and readily understandable manner both existing and new concepts to form a coherent framework for analysing the competitive environment. It sold more than 200,000 copies in English alone. A section that attracted a great deal of attention – about generic strategies – was virtually an afterthought. 'It occurred to me late in the process of writing the book that this was a missing piece; I hadn't been focusing on choice of competitive positioning.' This work led in turn to his interests in the concept of competitive advantage, the theme of his next major book, *Competitive Advantage: Creating and Sustaining Superior Performance*.

Porter says that *Competitive Advantage* starts with the question 'Given the industry a company is in, how can a company understand in a rigorous way how to gain competitive advantage?'

One of the most important concepts he explores is the value chain. He explains: 'A systematic way of examining all the activities a firm performs and how they interact is essential for analysing the sources of competitive advantage. . . . The value chain disaggregates a firm into its strategically relevant activities in order to understand the behaviour of costs and the existing and potential sources of differentiation. A firm gains competitive advantage by performing these strategically important activities more cheaply or better than its competitors.'

Each of these activities can be used to gain competitive advantage on its own or together with other strategically important activities. Here, the concept of linkages ('relationships between the way one value activity is performed and the cost or performance of another') becomes relevant. These linkages need not be internal – they can equally well be with suppliers and customers.

Porter describes the development of his thinking since then as 'a succession of asking and answering questions'. Each book is a direct outcome of issues raised in the previous book but too large to answer fully at that time. The process, as he describes it, is as follows: 'When I start work on one of these problems, I begin by trying to write down all I know, given all my research and consulting experience. I start writing very early. Then I try to build a theory and systematically expose myself to more and more data to test it. The 20 per cent of my time I spend consulting contributes to this. I sometimes write and rewrite many times. When I see that the process is confirming the theory rather than raising new questions, I stop. A book takes me three or four years.'

Since May 1986 his research has concerned the nature of competitive advantage between nations. He explains the ten-nation project in these terms: 'Most work on national competitiveness has taken a broad macroeconomic perspective and involved the study of one or two countries. I believe that a nation's competitive advantage can only be explained today by understanding the microeconomic perspective – why firms from the nation succeed internationally in particular industries. Broad macroeconomic factors such as exchange rates, interest rates and average unit labour costs are significant, but are rarely decisive in creating competitive advantage. I also believe that only by investigating a range of countries with different circumstances can one separate the fundamental principles of competitive advantage from the peculiarities of a particular nation.

'The starting point for my research is the view that the classical theory of comparative advantage, based on the factor endowment of countries, is less and less important in explaining competitive advantage, as economists have increasingly come to recognise. Technological change and the globalisation of competition have conspired to decouple factor advantages from firm success. Firms can either nullify the role of factors (for example, automate to eliminate labour, purchase low cost foreign inputs) or locate activities in countries with low factor costs. Today, competitive advantage is increasingly driven by innovation in the broad sense of the word. The firms who are the most dynamic in terms of product and process improvement are the ones who ultimately sustain international success, not those who rest on cheap labour or other factor cost advantages.'

He told the Conference Board in an interview that he had discovered: 'there are no competitive nations, only those that are competitive in some things and uncompetitive in others. The hope is that a nation can sustain competitive advantage in enough industries to employ its work force and support a rising standard of living.'

He found that for a wide variety of industries the international leaders tend to be concentrated in one or two countries. In addition, the successful industries in a nation are 'clustered', linked by supplier, buyer, and other relationships. Entire clusters are often geographically concentrated in regions or even cities, something Porter's theory tries to explain. Bigger economies, such as the United States or West Germany, have more clusters than smaller countries, such as Denmark, where most internationally competitive businesses tend to be associated with the food industry or, to a lesser extent, housing and household products. One lesson for governments is that they should direct their efforts to help these and similar industries to grow – that is, to build on existing competitive advantage. Another lesson is that the great spate of merger activity may do more harm than good. 'There's a view today that since competition is global, it doesn't matter if there are a lot of mergers in the home country. Yet in my study I found that the most competitive industries in a country were ones in which there were three or four (or more) domestic rivals fighting it out. This environment produced a hothouse for innovation, not to mention stimulating supplier industries, local universities and the like. The view that merging at home makes you more competitive abroad doesn't seem to hold.'

The fruits of Porter's labours will be published under the title *The Competitive Advantage of Nations*. The book challenges many of the ivory towers of international competitiveness. For example, Porter argues that competitive advantages can be extracted from what are usually perceived as disadvantages. Japan's lack of domestic raw materials, for example, stirred the country into greater innovatory activity in many sectors. Porter also argues that local competitiveness is far more important than was once thought. Parochialism is viewed by him as as potent a force in business as internationalism.

Once he has completed working in this area, which will also involve looking at less developed countries, Porter expects to move on to the diversified firm, asking the question: how do you develop overall corporate strategy for a multibusiness firm?

Why has he had such an impact? 'I was lucky. There aren't (or weren't) many people working on this subject. Also, I've been working on it in a period when the interest in competition has been very strong around the world. There was an appetite for anything useful in this area. My forerunners were mostly consultants, who proposed somewhat simplistic ideas designed for easy packaging with potential clients. By the early 1980s, the field had matured to the point where work like mine was acceptable to managers.

'In the 1970s, most companies' idea of strategic positioning was that you had to have the largest market share, to plot your business on the experience curve and do portfolio analysis. We've come a long way from there. There are few major companies today in the United States, Japan or Europe, who have not moved to the next generation of ideas in the way they think about strategy.

'I've tried to write complicated material in a way that is clear and has a minimum of complicated language. I've tried to write books that are somewhere in between a light business book and a theoretical academic work. I want to challenge the reader but be accessible and practical.'

One of his former pupils, Kathryn Rudie Harrigan – now an emerging guru in her own right – summarises his success in this way: 'Mike had a vision concerning a book he would be writing (*Competitive Strategy*) that sounded like exactly what was needed at that time – a rigorous examination of the forces that make some industries more amenable to strategic restructuring than others as well as a careful look at what firms could do to improve the profitability potential of the industries where they competed. The ideas in this book (as well as in the next blockbuster, *Competitive Advantage*) are required reading in every business school and most executive education programmes. The framework he popularised forms the cornerstone for the next decade of research concerning strategy formulation. More importantly, those ideas mobilised managers to *do something* about sick industry situations. The first chapter of the book he edited about global competition provides what has become the dominant framework for looking at issues in global strategy.'

Like Peter Drucker, Porter does not see his ideas as confined to business. 'I like to apply strategic concepts to unusual organisations, such as art museums,' he declares. He decided against becoming a golf pro 'because it was too boring'. Similarly, 'I was all set to get a doctorate in engineering, but I changed my mind. . . . I believe that whenever you are getting comfortable in what you are doing, you should find a way to make yourself uncomfortable, because that's the way innovation takes place.'

Kathryn Rudie Harrigan

Born Minnesota, 1951
Professor of Strategic Management, Columbia University,
New York

Columbia University's Kathryn Rudie Harrigan is a fast-emerging strategic management guru. Once labelled 'the very incarnation of the no-nonsense businesswoman', Harrigan specialises in industrial survival strategies, mergers and acquisitions and joint ventures. Her message is often harsh, challenging the preconceptions of managers. 'My material can be used by a thoughtful manager, but it's not the sort of thing you read on the train to work in the morning,' she says.

Harrigan has a theatrical background and this has undoubtedly helped in communicating her message. 'Harrigan is intensely dramatic. . . . As soon as she saw the camera, she became Sarah Bernhardt,' the *New York Post* has said of her. She has a simple explanation for forsaking the theatre for academia: 'The theatre doesn't pay all that well. It's an industry with easy entry barriers. There's always someone who is willing to buy their way in. I have something unique which works well in this market but may not work as well in another.'

She provides this assessment of her career: 'I am very much a self-made woman. I earned every one of my educational degrees without parental assistance – through scholarships, holding jobs while working, and by borrowing heavily. I hold a bachelor's degree in theatre arts and studied for a master of fine arts degree. My first venture was the creation of a theatre company: the North Suburban Young People's Theater. I have probably been an entrepreneur since birth. All of my life I've been able to wheel and deal and persuade people to see my point of view. All four of the ventures I started made money. I finally took an MBA to legitimise what I had been practising since 1966.'

After obtaining her MBA, Harrigan worked under Michael Porter at Harvard where she admits, 'I didn't fit into any of the pigeon-holes.' Her first book (*Strategies for Declining Businesses* (1980)) focused on a subject dear to her heart – declining businesses. Harrigan explains: 'Growing up in Minnesota and looking at the industries which made it great, I was always affected very much by the sight of depleted mines and all the people who had to relocate. If you're a miner there's not much you can do when the mines go.'

'I don't think that employees are disposable though a lot of companies act as if they are,' she says. 'I have a very strong sense of stewardship. Managers are entrusted with resources and they should make the best possible use of them.'

Harrigan believes there is a life-cycle for businesses and they need to revitalise themselves constantly to prevent decline. 'Everybody wants to talk about growth, but few people want to talk about declining businesses,' she admits. 'Too many managers refuse to face the ugly reality that they are in a dying business.'

From declining businesses, Harrigan moved on to the subject of vertical integration and the development of strategies to deal with it. 'My research explored how firms managed their needs for a stable supply of raw materials and stable access to ultimate consumers of their products. A central premise of the framework I developed and tested was that, as firms strived to increase their control over supply and distribution activities, they also increased their ultimate strategic inflexibility (by increasing their exit barriers).' It is this inflexibility which so enrages Harrigan. In search of more flexible approaches she carried out lengthy research into joint ventures. Despite their boom, Harrigan's research showed that between 1924 and 1985 the average success rate for joint ventures was only 46 per cent and the average life span a meagre three and a half years.

In her two books on joint ventures ('separate entities with two or more actively involved firms as sponsors'), Harrigan argues they will become a key element in competitive strategy. The reasons for this are: economic deregulation, technological change, increasing capital requirements in connection with development of new products, increasing globalisation of markets. 'A new language of cooperation, not warfare, is mandatory,' she wrote in *Strategies for Joint Ventures*.

She predicts:

1. One-on-one competition will be replaced by competition among constellations of firms that routinely venture together.
2. Teams of co-operating firms seeking each other out like

favourite dancing partners will soon replace many current industry structures where firms stand alone.
3. To cope with these changes, managers must learn how to co-operate, as well as compete, effectively.

This, to a large extent, runs contrary to current trends, which Harrigan disparagingly describes as 'When you are looking for a quick fix, what you do is buy something.'

More recently, Harrigan's work has focused on mature businesses. She has coined the phrase 'The last iceman always makes money', which she explains as 'The last surviving player makes money serving the last bit of demand, when the competitors drop away.' *Managing Maturing Businesses* (1988) examines 'the second half of a business's life' or, as it is more dramatically put, the endgame. The importance of her work in this area is given credence by the fact that over two-thirds of the industries within mature economies are experiencing slow growth, no growth or negative growth in demand for their products.

'For the typical American executive, maturity (alternatively described as slow growth or no growth) is synonymous with stagnation, which is equated to decline, and which in turn is a simple euphemism for death,' Boris Yavitz, former Columbia dean, points out in his introduction to this book. Harrigan's argument is that endgame can be highly profitable if companies adopt a coherent strategy sufficiently early.The strategic options are:

- divest now – the first company out usually gets the highest price; later leavers may not get anything
- last iceman – focusing on customer niches which will continue long-term and will be prepared to pay a premium
- selective shrinking – taking the profitable high ground and leaving the less profitable low ground to the competitors
- milking the business – the last option, but none the less a practical alternative in many situations.

Ameliorating the pain and avoiding premature death are the motivating factors of Harrigan's work. 'The real heroes of the 1980s are the managers who worked with competitors to strengthen their mature industries and retain their manufacturing skills by improving their firms' working practices,' she concludes.

CHAPTER 5

Leadership Under the Looking Glass

Writing in the *McKinsey Quarterly*, Louis Barnes and Mark Kriger cite one book that lists a mere 130 definitions of the term leadership and another book that 'notes over 5000 research studies and monographs on the subject'. One of the most influential writers on leadership, James McGregor Burns, describes it as 'one of the most observed and least understood phenomena on earth'.

Just about every major writer on management has felt that he had to devote at least some pages to expound his or her view of leadership – Argyris, Mintzberg and Drucker have all pronounced on the nature of effective leadership and how it links into the achievement of organisational objectives. But relatively few have focused on leadership as a prime element in their observation and theorising.

Among the most influential writers in this area are (in alphabetical order): John Adair, Warren Bennis, Blake and Mouton, James McGregor Burns, Fred Fiedler, Paul Hersey, John Kotter, Harold Leavitt, Kurt Lewin, Rensis Likert, Bill Reddin and Abraham Zaleznik.

This list is far from complete and certainly excludes some writers, who, though less well known, have significantly altered our understanding of what leadership is and how it functions. It also excludes revealing current studies by observers such as Andrew Kakabadse and John Nicols in Britain, neither of whose work has yet been very widely circulated. However, for our purposes we will confine ourselves to those in the list above, only one of whom has his own section in this book. Because it is so difficult in many cases to establish who influenced whom, we have kept to an alphabetical order.

John Adair made one of the first attempts to bring together multiple studies and theories of leadership. Adair is currently professor in leadership studies at the University of Surrey (the only such post in the United Kingdom). His colourful career includes spells in the army in a Bedouin regiment and as a lecturer at the Royal Military Academy, Sandhurst; working as a deckhand on an Arctic trawler and as an orderly in an operating theatre.

In an interview in *The Director* (November 1988), Adair explained: 'Leadership is about a sense of direction. The word "lead" comes from an Anglo-Saxon word, common to north European languages, which means a road, a way, the path of a ship at sea. It's knowing what the next step is.' He goes on to provide an important differentiation. 'Managing is a different image. It's from the Latin *manus*, a hand. It's handling a sword, a ship, a horse. It tends to be closely linked with the idea of machines. Managing had its origins in the nineteenth century with engineers and accountants coming in to run entrepreneurial outfits. They tended to think of them as systems.

'But there are valuable ingredients in the concept of management that are not present in leadership. Managing is very strong on the idea of controlling, particularly financial control, and administration. Leaders are not necessarily good at administration or managing resources.'

Adair's contribution to leadership studies is twofold. First, it is essentially *practical* (anyone who has led training expeditions of soldiers across the Jordanian desert by camel must have some practical knowledge of leadership). Second, he provides a neat analysis of other theories, which he categorises as the qualities – situational, and group or functional. The qualities approach assumes that leadership traits are built in at birth or during childhood – there are 'natural leaders'. By extension, this means that people who are not natural leaders will find it difficult to learn leadership qualities, most of which tend to be vague, such as courage or vision.

Situational approaches assume that different tasks or situations demand a different type of leader. Evidence for this can be seen in the difficulty many 'company doctors' experience in handling the subsequent consolidation and growth of the companies they save. A different style of leadership is needed. Adair points out that, taken to its extreme, this theory requires a constant change-over of leaders to fit changes in the situation.

While scathing about much of the literature covering laboratory observations of groups at work, Adair's own theory starts from the same basic question – what needs to happen for the group to fulfil its task? In analysing the functions every group has to carry out, he identifies three critical needs:

- Task needs – the overall objective and the actions and behaviours necessary to make it happen
- Team maintenance needs – things that help the group retain its cohesion, motivation and general willingness to work on the task
- Individual needs – things that help the individual feel part of the group and enable him or her to make the maximum contribution.

The leader's role, says Adair, is to look after all of these needs at the same time. Potential leaders can learn to do so by practice and by observing how other leaders behave.

James McGregor Burns is referred to by several of the major management gurus as the person who spelt out for them the difference between transactional and transformational leaders. Burns explains: 'The relations of most leaders and followers are transactional – leaders approach followers with an eye to exchanging one thing for another: jobs for votes, or subsidies for campaign contributions. Such transactions comprise the bulk of the relationships among leaders and followers, especially in groups, legislatures and parties.

'Transforming leadership, while more complex than transactional leadership, is more potent. The transforming leader recognises an existing need or demand of a potential follower. But, beyond that, the transforming leader looks for potential motives in followers, seeks to satisfy higher needs, and engages the full person of the follower. . . . Woodrow Wilson called for leaders who, by boldly interpreting the nation's conscience, could lift a people out of their everyday selves.'

A political scientist, Burns stood for Congress as a Democrat and wrote biographies of both Franklin D. Roosevelt and John F. Kennedy. He argued the American need for strong leadership and played an active role in Kennedy's presidential campaign.

Robert Blake and Jane Mouton's managerial grid (see pages 109–10), is widely regarded as one of the first systematic attempts to define situational leadership.

Fred Fiedler belongs firmly in the situational leadership camp, but, with his co-author Martin Chemers, he stressed the task side of the situational matrix. His 'least preferred co-worker' test aimed to identify whether leaders were more oriented towards the people side of management or the task side. Depending on their orientation they would be more or less suitable to provide the kind of leadership needed in various situations. Fiedler defined those situations in terms of three dimensions:

- how well the leader got on with the members in his team and how willingly they would do as he asked
- how closely or loosely defined the team's task was (the more closely defined, the more control he can exercise)
- how much authority the organisation delegates to him – his 'position power'.

In short, no matter what leadership style he adopts, the manager who is disliked by his subordinates cannot define the team's task precisely and doesn't have the authority to compel compliance is unlikely to be very effective.

Paul Hersey rose rapidly to fame as the result of a single book, published in 1984 – *The Situational Leader*. Hersey had learned a significant lesson from Robert Blanchard's *The One Minute Manager* – old ideas, packaged in a simple, lively manner as a short read, can appeal to an audience of managers who have neither the time nor the inclination to read more than they absolutely have to. It would be easy to dismiss *The Situational Leader* as too simplistic to be taken seriously. Its definition of leadership, for example ('any attempt to influence the behaviour of another individual or group'), could be taken as an apt description of the advertising industry but not of leader behaviour. However, like *The One Minute Manager*, Hersey's book had a single but significant advantage over more academically credible publications – large numbers of managers not only bought it but read it as well.

John Kotter, professor of organisational behaviour and human resource management at Harvard Business School, first achieved wide notice with a study of the activities of general managers, published as *The General Managers* (1982). He has also written on power and influence as aspects of leadership, arguing that 'many of the complex skills and personal assets that general managers possess are also needed by a growing number of middle-level managers and professionals, because their jobs are increasingly demanding the kind of leadership required in general management jobs'. In his latest writings, he focuses on how companies acquire strong or weak management and the implications in each case.

Kotter's theories have been succinctly summarised by Warren Bennis in a review in *Fortune* magazine: 'According to Kotter, not everyone has leadership potential. Leaders are born, and then made. As ever, that's easier said than done. Developing leaders is harder than developing managers, Kotter says, and developing managers who can lead is even harder.

'He believes that leadership potential is based on inborn traits, such as a high energy level, that are then built on in early childhood, in college, and through experiences on the job. A lot of people have the potential, but business's efforts to develop them have been mostly insufficient.' Kotter believes there is a critical shortage of leaders in US business today.

Harold Leavitt is Walter Kilpatrick Professor of Organizational Behavior at the Graduate School of Business at Stanford University. He divides managers into three types:

- implementers, who are concerned with action, tend to be highly social, fast talking and get their own way by persuasion, commanding and manipulation
- problem-solvers, who are happiest carrying out analysis, tend to be logical and rational, exerting the cautious influence of the intellectual; they spend much of their time in pursuit of 'right' answers to problems
- pathfinders, who are visionaries; often stubborn, impractical, impatient of rules (which they either ignore or go round when they get in the way) and impulsive, the pathfinder is predominantly concerned with asking the right questions.

Kurt Lewin was a European immigrant to the United States. Professor of philosophy and psychology at Berlin University until 1932, his studies in the United States initially concentrated on children. He was professor of child psychology at the Child Welfare Research Station, Iowa, until 1944 when he went to the Massachusetts Institute of Technology to found a research centre for group dynamics.

Lewin's experiments took place in boys' clubs, where he asked the adult leaders to adopt one of three different styles and to vary those styles as they moved from group to group. The three styles were essentially authoritarian (parcelling out information, not leaving the group members opportunity to think or decide for themselves); participative (where the leader discussed the task with them and was present to offer help and advice but didn't insist how they proceeded); and aloof (the leader explained the task, told them to come to him with any questions and left them to it). The studies showed that it was the style of leadership rather than the individual leader that conditioned behaviour in the groups, causing significant variations in the level of aggression and productivity. It is interesting that in Lewin's experiment the aloof leadership style was the least productive, but in a similar experiment thirty years later, using adults, the aloof style proved the most effective.

William (Bill) Reddin was really concerned with managerial effectiveness. But the aspect that intrigued him most was how managers persuaded other people to do things for them. To the two dimensions of situational leadership, he added a third – effectiveness – that allowed him to identify four basic styles of management. These were:

- related: where the manager is most strongly concerned about his relationships with other people and spends much of his time talking, counselling and listening
- separated: where the manager doesn't spend much time getting to know his co-workers but prefers to get things done through rules, procedures and memoranda
- dedicated: where the manager is concerned mostly about productivity; he tends to dominate his department, giving lots of orders and focuses very closely on the current task, often at the expense of issues with longer time horizons
- integrated: where the manager is equally concerned for people and for achieving the task.

All these styles can be appropriate in different situations. When they are appropriate, the manager is effective; when they are inappropriate, the manager is ineffective. In practice, of course, people tend to use a mixture of styles, but they also tend to have one dominant style. Reddin names the two extremes of effectiveness in each case as:

	Effective	*Ineffective*
Related	Developer	Missionary
Separated	Bureaucrat	Deserter
Dedicated	Benevolent autocrat	Autocrat
Integrated	Executive	Compromiser

Abraham Zaleznik made a stir with a controversial article in *Harvard Business Review* in 1977. In 'Managers and Leaders: Are They Different?' he had the temerity to suggest that there was a major difference between managerial and leader behaviour. At its most basic, the distinction between the two had much in common with that between transactional and transforming leaders.

Leaders:

- are active rather than reactive, shaping ideas rather than responding to them
- adopt a personal and active attitude towards goals
- develop fresh approaches to long-standing problems and open issues for new options
- are more interested in what events and decisions mean to people than their own role in getting things accomplished
- are often viewed with strong emotions by others
- tend to feel somewhat apart from their environment and other people.

Managers:

- focus on the decision-making process rather than ultimate events
- act to limit choices
- avoid solutions that might cause confrontation
- focus subordinates' attention on procedures rather than on the substance of decisions
- communicate in signals rather than clearly stated messages
- play for time to take the sting out of win–lose situations
- need to feel that they belong to a team, fulfilling a clear and useful role within the organisation.

The influential article (later extended into the book *The Managerial Mystique*) argued 'because leaders and managers are basically different, the conditions favourable to one may be inimical to the growth of another'. In the article Zaleznik observed: 'Managers tend to view work as an enabling process involving some combination of people and ideas interacting to establish strategies and make decisions. Managers help the process along by a range of skills, including calculating the interests in opposition, staging and timing the surfacing of controversial issues, and reducing tensions.' He continued: 'Where managers act to limit choices, leaders work in the opposite direction, to develop fresh approaches to long-standing problems and to open issues for new options.'

It would not be appropriate to leave a discussion on leadership without at least some mention of business leaders themselves. By and large, most businessmen have preferred to get on with the business of business and let others write the theory. In the past a few have felt sufficiently strongly about their particular style of management to want to spread it through books and articles – several of the early pioneers did so, among them Alfred P. Sloan in the United States and Wilfred Brown in Britain, who co-authored with Elliott Jacques a book about the experiments at his company, Glacier Metals. But in the 1980s there has been a flood of top executives explaining their particular management philosophy. They include Sir Michael Edwardes, who turned around ailing British Leyland by taking a firm stand against militancy both amongst unionised workers and amongst middle managers; Sir John Harvey-Jones, former chairman of ICI; Jan Carlzon of airline SAS; Lee Iacocca of Chrysler; Akio Morita, chairman of Sony; Sir Marcus Sieff of exemplary British retailers Marks and Spencer; and H. Ross Perot, the controversial former head of EDS. The latter did not write his own philosophy. Instead, he poured it out to Ken Follett. The result was *On Wings of Eagles*, a true-life adventure story of how Perot and his executives rescued their beleaguered staff in Iran. Perot's management style emerges as highly militaristic. From among these we have one, Harold S. Geneen, whose leadership style made him a unique manager.

One explanation for this phenomenon is that, given the opportunity to reassert their authority and influence in recession-born crisis, managers actually began to exercise leadership. This made them more interesting as people (or heroes, as Deal and Kennedy (see page 198) would say), both to other managers and to the general public. None of these authors (a high proportion were, of course, ghosted) has much to add in the way of theory, but they can provide inspiration in terms of practice.

In the next chapter, we examine how the excellence movement expanded from an interest in corporate culture to embrace quality, customer care, change management and *leadership*. The current preponderance of books and papers on the nature of leadership is no accident. It is based upon the realisation that controlled culture change can only happen through skilled leadership.

Harold S. Geneen

Born Bournemouth, England, 1910
Businessman

'Putting deals together beats spending every day playing golf,' Harold Geneen has said. Geneen's deal-making career was certainly one of the century's most dynamic. He has been labelled 'the corporate world's most famous workaholic' and his management record with International Telephone and Telegraph (ITT) is legendary. Harvard Professor Wickham Skinner has labelled him 'a model of scientific management'.

Geneen, the archetypal bullish American executive, was born in Britain to an opera-singing mother and an impresario father. Moving to the United States at an early age, his career was highly independent. He settled in New York, working as an errand boy, a page on the floor of the New York Stock Exchange, a door-to-door book salesman and a bookkeeper (Geneen later admitted he remained 'an old-fashioned bookkeeper at heart'). Studying at night, Geneen was able to qualify as an accountant. After progressing up the management scale by degrees, he was eventually put in charge of an engineering company, Raytheon. Earnings trebled in his four years there but his managerial triumphs were just beginning.

While Geneen was boosting the fortunes of Raytheon, a company twice its size was making slim profits and heading for stagnation. The company was ITT, founded by Colonel

Sosthenes Behn in 1920. Behn died in 1957 after the company – with most of its operations overseas – had fared badly during the war. His successor was General Edmund Leavey who had only two years to go to retirement. In his two years in charge he was briefed to designate a successor. He chose himself. The board was not convinced and Geneen was brought in.

Geneen became president and chief executive of ITT in 1959 and remained with the company until 1979, after which he continued as a consultant. He turned ITT into a multinational conglomerate. When he took over the company was dependent on overseas earnings and had poor profit margins. By the time he retired, Geneen had bought, merged or acquired 350 companies. ITT grew from a relatively unstable $760 million corporation into a $22 billion giant with 375,000 employees in eighty countries. In 1959 ITT's sales were $765.6 million and its profits $29 million. By the late 1960s ITT was the ninth largest industrial company in the United States and by 1977 sales were $16.7 billion and profits $562 million.

Geneen claims this corporate resurrection was achieved through a belief in practice rather than theory. He set an example of driving motivation and relentless hard work which few are capable of matching, and also the trend for hard-working executives to move dynamically across the globe work in hand. His management style is competitive and practical. 'Theories are like paper hoops,' he says, 'you cannot run a business, or anything else, on a theory.' He provides a three-sentence course on management: 'You read a book from the beginning to end. You run a business the opposite way. You start with the end, and then you do everything you must to reach it.'

To achieve his aim of 10 per cent profit growth every single year, Geneen instituted monthly management meetings at which the chief executives of all ITT operations from a particular continent were gathered. The meetings lasted all day and often late into the night. Despite this rigorous planning and discussion Geneen writes in his book *Managing*: 'My own style of leadership at ITT was not deliberately calculated to accomplish set goals. In fact, it was not calculated at all. It was much more instinctual.'

Geneen's instincts called for open communications; he intensely disliked petty bureaucracy. His own files were destroyed within ninety days. Under this regime, Geneen claimed to have converted ITT into 'an exciting place in which to work'. The central criticism made of his management style is of a soulless preoccupation with figures and results. Geneen argued, 'The drudgery of the numbers will make you free', and for ITT executives there were numbers in abundance.

Geneen encouraged a continuous flow of factual information and expected absolute commitment from senior managers. ITT's personnel department monitored performance and the psychological development of every aspiring manager. To stimulate growth, Geneen instituted salary incentives, open communications, close financial monitoring and regular monthly reports. ITT's 120-strong top management team became, in his words, 'a working think tank . . . a problem-solving mechanism in business management'.

Geneen plays down the scientific and analytical aspects of his management style. In *Managing* he says:

We had an enormous staff of experts to analyse the figures that poured into our headquarters. But we never fooled ourselves. We never believed that any or all of this made our management of ITT scientific. All the computers, reports, surveys, and staff analyses provided us with only one thing: information – factual information and, sometimes, misinformation. When it came time to make a decision, I would ask one, two, or several people, 'What do you think?' From the interchange of ideas, one sparking the other, based upon the facts at hand, we would reach a decision, for better or worse.

The short-term quest for improved quarterly results was unquestionably a dominant factor in Geneen's style. It worked. It was only in early 1974 that ITT's earnings declined after fifty-eight straight quarters of profit gains. 'There will be no more long-range planning,' read a famous Geneen memo. His year's activities were meticulously planned. 'We spent three weeks in February and March on our preliminary, rough business plans and budgets for the coming year, and then twelve weeks at the end of the year reviewing and agreeing on those plans. That's fifteen weeks. One general managers' meeting in Brussels and one in New York, a week each, ten months of the year, and you have another twenty weeks. That's thirty-five weeks of time. Add four weeks for vacation and holiday time, and you have thirty-nine weeks. That left a scant thirteen weeks of "other" time in which to run the company,' he wrote in *Managing*.

A significant proportion of Geneen's 'scant' management time was spent in acquiring other companies. Initially, under Geneen, ITT acquired companies such as Jennings Radio, National Transistor, General Controls, Cannon Electric and Gilfillan, all in similar businesses. Soon, however, ITT's interests went far beyond its traditional telephone and telegraph equipment. Its empire stretched to insurance, publishing, hotels, confectionery and beyond. The idea, according to Geneen, was to have unified management with multi-products.

Success was not, Geneen argues, achieved through acquisitions. They had to be managed, after all: 'People have said ITT grew because of our rapid acquisition programme. But we spent 90 per cent of our time managing the company, including the acquisitions, so that it would grow internally, which enabled us to trade our stock for the assets of other companies. We spent only about 10 per cent of our time in making acquisitions.'

Assessing Geneen's contribution is a demanding task. His unrelenting management style is not easily copied. Reviewing Geneen's book in *Management Today* (May 1985), Robert Heller wrote: 'Geneen had built a system, which could only be worked by one brilliant driven and driving man: Harold S. Geneen.' Most executives would need a month in a health farm after a few weeks' work with Geneen. In his foreword to Geneen's book, Sir Michael Edwardes observes: 'He was, of course, an exceptional manager who dealt with each situation in an exceptional way. The flair required to prosecute his style of management without, apparently, undermining the managers concerned, must be unique. Indeed, Geneen's presence and personality was a central factor in ensuring that this unusual approach succeeded.'

Wickham Skinner, reviewing a book about Geneen in the *Harvard Business Review* (September–October 1985), wrote: 'Geneen emerges an extraordinary person and, above all else, a single-minded executive. He rose above a mediocre start as a public accountant by learning very early of the power of business data analysis. Because of his intense scrutiny of facts from every source (not just financial data but also production, labor, sales, and logistical information), he could quickly take over any discussion in which decisions were being made. His insights were usually ideas that no one else had thought of, which gave him a one-up position and an arsenal for persuasion.' An arsenal he may have had, but its weaknesses were exposed following his departure in the 1970s. He left a vacuum, a management style beyond emulation.

In his authoritative book *Geneen* (1985), Robert Schoenberg provides a valid assessment of Geneen's contribution to management practice:

> He apotheosised the rational and analytic. It was not just that before, accountants were bean-counters, and after, they could be chairman. Planning, analysis, and control had always been recognised as Good Things . . . that are not necessary for real life. Geneen showed they were essential for his kind of assured results. . . . The other side of the coin was a ruinous tendency to overprize management-by-the-numbers. The analysts, the accountants, the dealmakers, the lawyers, the controllers – all number crunchers – they took over and no one was left to do any honest work. Production and the product were no longer glamorous. It was reason run amok, effacing the purpose of the enterprise. . . . The sadness of Harold Geneen's story is not that he missed his goal but that such gifts served so narrow a purpose.

Warren Bennis

Born New York City, 1925
Professor of Management, University of Southern California

In *Future Shock* Alvin Toffler claimed: 'If it was Max Weber who first defined bureaucracy, and predicted its triumph, Warren Bennis may go down as the man who first convincingly predicted its demise and sketched the outlines of the organizations that are springing up to replace it.' Bennis, a disciple of management pioneers Douglas McGregor and Joseph Scanlon, predicted the rapid demise of bureaucracy in his book *The Temporary Society* (1968). Temporariness and participation were the key words, he claimed, in the organisation of the future.

Bennis became associated with the organisational development movement in the late 1950s when it was gaining momentum. Organisational development aimed to provide a long-range programme for improving the effectiveness of a total organisation. When he abandoned it later, Bennis observed: 'I think the field is in something of a cul-de-sac. I find organizational development intellectually kind of barren.'

His career has covered education, administration, consultancy and writing with the production of fifteen books and a massive five hundred articles. He has been described as 'the poet-philosopher-scholar of organisational life . . . like the legendary Don Quixote bruised and battered with scars but undaunted'. Psychologist Abraham Maslow called Bennis 'one of the Olympian minds of our time'. In the 1970s, an article by Bennis prompted a critic to recommend that 'everybody connected with Vietnam, Watergate and other major sins of the republic' should read it.

Bennis has carried his message around the globe. He has spent time working in Switzerland, France and India as well as at the Massachusetts Institute of Technology's Sloan School of Management, the State University of New York and as president of the University of Cincinnati for six years in the 1970s. In recent years, he has become best known for his work on leadership. The foundations of this interest were laid at MIT's Sloan School of Management where he came under the influence of Douglas McGregor, creator of Theories X and Y. 'McGregor was my key mentor, because he made it clear that I could have a career in an area that always interested me, but wasn't actually a vocation.' His belief in McGregor's work remains strong: 'The McGregorian chant is still profoundly true. If you look at the work of Peters and Waterman and others, they all grow out of that initial McGregor theory.' At MIT, Bennis also had six years of analysis. 'Not a lot of people say it, but my psychotherapist was another major influence. He taught me all about myself.'

The fruits of Bennis's thoughts on leadership have produced two books: *The Unconscious Conspiracy: Why Leaders Can't Lead* (1976) and *Leaders* (1985). It was *Leaders*, co-written with

Burt Nanus, that cemented Bennis's success. Bennis spent time with ninety of America's leaders researching common factors before emerging with the much-quoted aphorism 'Managers do things right. Leaders do the right thing.' It is not, Bennis makes clear, as simple as that. There are, after all, over four hundred definitions of leadership. 'It is probably the most studied and least understood of any management subject. It is an argument without an end,' says Bennis.

Bennis is widely attributed with a strong influence in the leadership field. Tom Peters, co-author of *In Search of Excellence*, has said: 'Warren Bennis saw twenty-five years ago what has only now come into view for the rest of us. He is the embodiment and guru of the current revolution in Western management. . . . Our first revolution in forty years. His new leadership writing is the very best I have ever been exposed to.' Theodore Levitt has also expressed enthusiasm: 'Not since Chester Barnard has anyone combined so well the learning from practice with the learning from study and thought to give the world so much about becoming and being an effective leader.'

The French painter Braque once said the only thing that really mattered about painting can't be explained. The same, according to Warren Bennis, can be said of leadership. He sees the subject as all-embracing and, in the late 1980s, all-important. He works around a definition of leadership as: 'The capacity to create a compelling vision and translate it into action and sustain it.' The leaders Bennis spent time with were extremely varied, including astronaut Neil Armstrong, the coach of the Los Angeles Rams, orchestra conductors and businessmen such as Ray Kroc of McDonald's and William Kieschnick, chief executive of ARCO. 'I felt the responses pour over me,' recalls Bennis.

Obvious links between such a diverse group of successful leaders were, Bennis admits, difficult to find. 'They were right-brained and left-brained, tall and short, fat and thin, articulate and inarticulate, assertive and retiring, dressed for success and dressed for failure, participative and autocratic.' The vast majority were white males – the six women and six black men had to be sought out. The only surprise among the group was that almost all remained married to their first spouse and eagerly supported the institution of marriage.

Despite the apparent disparity in their skills and occupations, Bennis eventually identified four common abilities among the ninety leaders: management of attention, meaning, trust and self. A literary enthusiast, Bennis is quick to point out that this bears out Tolstoy's lines in *Anna Karenina*: 'All happy families resemble each other, while each unhappy family is unhappy in its own way.'

Management of attention is, Bennis continually emphasises, a question of vision. Successful leaders have a vision which other people believe in and treat as their own. 'What I discovered was they all had a strong, plausible and compelling vision of where they wanted their company to go,' he says. 'The best leaders are ideas people, conceptualists.'

Putting a vision into practice is a long-term process. The short term is determined by the market, Bennis says, while strategies bridge the gap between the short and long term. 'With a vision, the leader provides the all-important bridge from the present to the future of the organisation.' He points to the strength of Lee Iacocca's vision at Chrysler and those of President Kennedy and Martin Luther King saying, 'I am concerned with the narrow vision of soulless Geneen-like managers, who are dominating the scene – the recovery experts, the numbers people, almost morally mesmerised by the bottom line. I think it's very dangerous.' Bennis foresees imminent change: 'I think there's going to be a turn-round to more visionary leadership. I see the hunger for it. But there is an awful lot of good leadership being subverted.'

The second skill shared by Bennis's selection of leaders was management of meaning, the ability to continually communicate successfully. A vision is of limited practical use if it is encased in four hundred pages of wordy text or mumbled from behind a paper-packed desk. Bennis points to the difference between Presidents Carter and Reagan. Jimmy Carter immersed himself in detail. He was one of the best-informed presidents since Woodrow Wilson but was conspicuously unable to communicate his message effectively. One of Carter's aides told Bennis: 'Working for him was like looking at the wrong side of a tapestry – blurry and indistinct.' Reagan, on the other hand, is a master communicator. One survey showed support for the US invasion of Granada to have doubled after Reagan's explanatory speech.

His first budget speech graphically compared the size of $1 trillion to the Empire State Building. The images are simplistic but communicate a vision. Reagan was re-elected; Carter was not.

Bennis also provides corporate examples. Johnson and Johnson has a regularly updated credo and the effect is described by the company's chief executive: 'Too often, in this and other businesses, people are inclined to think, "We'd better do this because if we don't, it's going to show up on the figures over the short term." This document allows them to say, "Wait a minute. I don't have to do that. The management has told me that they're really interested in the long term, and they're interested in me operating under this set of principles. So I won't." '

At General Motors, chief executive Roger Smith took the top nine hundred executives on a five-day retreat to discuss the company's vision and make sure it would be truly shared throughout the company. Bennis believes effective communication relies on use of analogy, metaphor and vivid illustration (as exemplified by Ronald Reagan) as well as emotion, trust, optimism and hope.

The third aspect of leadership identified by Bennis is trust, 'the emotional glue that binds followers and leaders together'. Leaders have to be seen to be consistent. He believes Margaret Thatcher has provided a good example of this. 'She has been focused, constant and "all of a piece" – and she has been re-elected as a result,' says Bennis. He cites the consistency of Pope John Paul II in expressing ideas which are not necessarily popular. At one press conference, the Pope was asked how he could defend building a swimming-pool at the papal summer palace. The Pope's reply was straightforward. 'I like to swim. Next question.'

What Bennis labels 'deployment of self' is the last common bond between the leaders he has studied. The chosen ninety, he recalls, did not talk about the clichés usually associated with leaders. Charisma and time management were not glibly put forward as the essence of success. Instead, the emphasis was on persistence and self-knowledge; taking risks; commitment and challenge; but, above all, learning. 'The learning person looks forward to failures or mistakes,' says Bennis. 'The worst problem in leadership is basically early success. There's no opportunity to learn from adversity and problems.'

The recession of the late 1970s and early 1980s provided the adversity and problems that brought many of the current leaders to the fore. In Britain, Michael Edwardes, Christopher Hogg and John Harvey Jones have taken on large-scale restructuring jobs, as have Iacocca and Roger Smith of General Motors in the United States. Bennis sees his message getting through. 'Leadership has to start at the top. Until the mid 1970s we had such a technological lead that leadership was not crucial,' he says. 'Industries that were once boring and routine are now amongst the most exciting. Rapid change is causing people to ask what sort of leadership they require.'

The sort of leadership which Bennis would provide has already been put to the test. He left the University of Cincinnati in 1977 after six years as its president. With 70,000 students and 2600 faculty members, the challenge of university administration to Bennis's ideas was enormous. 'My theory disappointed my practice,' he remembers. 'I found two things most difficult. My theories were based on an interpersonal model but, leading a large organisation, I found it very difficult to connect on the interpersonal level. It was difficult to create, implement and orchestrate a vision in a fragmented organisation only held together by a central heating system.'

At the time, Bennis told one interviewer: 'As a supposed leader, I watch with envy the superior autonomy of the man mowing the university lawn, in complete control of the machine he rides, the total arbiter on which swath to cut, where and when. I cannot match it.' Platonic stuff, Bennis now admits, but the problems are equally applicable to business. 'As a believer in participation I found myself asking how to get everyone in on the act and still get some action,' he says. 'Especially in the public sector, the number of stakeholders to take into account is awesome.'

Bennis learned from the experience. The lesson he says was: 'You can be very bold as a theoretician. Good theories are like good art. A practitioner has to compromise.' He has tried to link theory and practice with a double-entry diary which compares the two. 'I never know how I think or if I compromise until I write it. Writing a diary keeps me honest. It helped me to understand the difference between observatory and participative truth. A journalist or a social psychologist is in the balcony and can see things participants can not.'

Bennis continues to prefer the boldness of theorising and is now professor of management at the University of Southern California. Like his friend Peter Drucker, he claims, 'I'm a newspaperman basically,' and is wary of becoming isolated: 'There's a danger of becoming so distant from experience that it becomes pornographic.' But with a broad range of interests and pursuits, Bennis has never been far away from the actual process of leading. He has been an adviser to four American presidents. 'I find most management writing really boring and dull. I'm interested in going out talking and meeting top leaders,' he says, 'I take most of my cues from successful practitioners rather than from things I read. My reading is in philosophy, history, the theatre.'

His next book, *On Becoming a Leader*, aims to provide insights into putting leadership skills into practice. 'The new book will deal with three questions – how do people learn how to lead, what do organisations do to promote or stifle it, and how can you teach it?' He firmly believes leadership can be learned. Bennis's optimism shines through conversation. 'Every person has to make a genuine contribution in their lives. The institution of work is one of the main vehicles to achieve this.' But work demands leaders. 'I'm more and more convinced that individual leaders can create a human community that will, in the long run, lead to the best organisations.' He finishes with a quotation from Churchill – one which he fervently supports and globe-trots to preach: 'The emperor of the future will be the emperor of ideas.'

CHAPTER 6

Culture, Quality and Excellence

Try as we might, it has proven impossible to separate these three skeins of modern management thinking. The search for their roots takes us to Murphy (of Murphy's law), Rolls-Royce and the founders of Marks and Spencer, but as they have developed and influenced each other they have fused into a single broad approach and set of theories.

Culture

Defining exactly what we mean by corporate culture is almost as difficult as defining leadership. One definition which seems to meet with a fair degree of acceptance is 'a set of behavioural and attitudinal norms, to which most or all members of an organisation subscribe, either consciously or subconsciously, and which exert a strong influence on the way people resolve problems, make decisions and carry out their everyday tasks'.

There are various claims to the first use of the term corporate culture, but one of the strongest is by Stanley Davis, whose book *Comparative Management: Organizational and Cultural Perspectives* was published in 1970. Certainly, the term didn't come into common use in companies until the late 1970s; then the concept received a boost in 1980 when *Business Week* ran a cover story about it. Davis, who has taught at Harvard and Columbia, is now research professor at Boston University's School of Management.

Davis makes a distinction between *daily beliefs* and *guiding beliefs*, explaining the distinction in these terms: 'Guiding beliefs, themselves, come in two varieties. There are external beliefs about how to compete and how to direct the business, and there are internal beliefs about how to manage, how to direct the organisation. Taken together, they are the roots and principles upon which the company is built, the philosophical foundation of the corporation. As fundamental precepts, guiding beliefs rarely change. They are held in the realm of universal truths and are broad enough to accommodate any variety of circumstances.

'Daily beliefs, on the other hand, are a different species. While they are equally part of a corporation's culture, they should not be confused with guiding beliefs. Daily beliefs are rules and feelings about everyday behaviour. They are situational and change to meet circumstances. They tell people the ropes to skip and the ropes to know. They are the survival kit for the individual.'

Guiding beliefs either work for or work against strategic objectives. In setting strategy, he argues, it is important to measure the degree of 'cultural risk'. One way of doing this is to match how important each element of the strategy is to the company's health and objectives against how compatible each element is with the culture. A strategy with high importance and low cultural compatibility will present great difficulties in implementation and will, says Davis, be an unacceptable risk.

Edgar Schein of the Massachusett's Institute of Technology's Sloan School of Management has looked at culture from a number of perspectives. He was one of the first writers to investigate in detail the conflict between work, career and family that we now more popularly call corporate bigamy. He has also studied the role of culture in strategy-driven change. He believes the most useful definitions of culture are those that emphasise its role as 'social learning'. He explains: 'An organization's culture is what it has learned as a total social unit over the course of its history.' Culture is made up, he suggests, of three main elements:

- artefacts: physical layout, dress codes, office landscape, slogans, 'the emotional climate as a stranger would feel it'; artefacts are frequently visible but are often not decipherable
- values: these are the principles upon which people base their behaviour, often reinforced by stories and myths, and people are sufficiently aware of them to discuss them when pressed
- underlying assumptions: these are the source from which the values and behaviours in the organisation derive; they may cover the relationship of the organisation to its

environment, the nature of human nature, how people should relate to each other, and they are usually taken for granted, less visible and operate much lower in the consciousness.

Schein suggests that culture will support the organisation's strategy when there is a large measure of consensus among employees and managers. He details five main areas where this consensus is essential:

- consensus on the core mission or primary task – what business are we in and why?
- consensus on goals – what specifically is everyone meant to do?
- consensus on the means to accomplish the goals – how the tasks should be divided up; the kind of reward and incentive systems to use; how all the separate activities will be integrated
- consensus on how to measure progress – the nature of the reporting and feedback systems
- consensus on remedial or repair strategies – when and how to intervene when things go wrong.

In effect, Schein has managed to tie corporate culture to management by objectives.

Charles Handy (see pages 86–91) has also had a strong influence on how managers (in Europe at least) conceive their corporate cultures. In *Gods of Management* he reaches back to classical analogies to describe the cultural factors at work in four types of organisation, which he describes as 'the club culture' (Zeus), 'the role culture' (Apollo), 'the task culture' (Athena) and 'the existential culture' (Dionysus).

Max Boisot, a Frenchman, started out as an architect and then changed his mind, deciding to study management at MIT. His research at INSEAD led him to study companies in a variety of national cultures, particularly in South-east Asia. (He is currently dean of the China–EEC Management Programme in Beijing.) Boisot suggests that much study of corporate culture could be better called 'managerial anthropology'. His approach to culture revolves around the types of knowledge or information within an organisation and how they are used. Among his classifications are:

- Public knowledge such as textbooks and newspapers, which is codified and diffused
- Proprietary knowledge such as patents and official secrets, which is codified but not diffused – here barriers to diffusion have to be set up
- Personal knowledge, such as biographical knowledge, which is neither codified nor diffused
- Common sense – that is, what 'everybody knows', which is not codified but is widely diffused.

These can be represented on a matrix, which he describes as the organisation's culture space or 'C-space'. Knowledge will not necessarily be static in any box in the C-space; it may move to another, as, for example, *ad hoc* procedures become written down.

This basic representation helps to explain many of the 'cultural' differences between, say, Japanese and American firms. Each type of organisation (Boisot classifies these as bureaucracies, clans, fiefs and markets) is most comfortable with one type of knowledge and the kind of relationships that implies. The same is true, in general terms, of national cultures. US firms, with their strong market awareness, gravitate towards public knowledge; Japanese firms, being more fief-like, gravitate towards personal knowledge.

Terrence Deal, a professor at Peabody College, Vanderbilt University, and Allen Kennedy, a former McKinsey consultant now running his own computer company in Boston, are joint authors of *Corporate Cultures: The Rites and Rituals of Corporate Life*, published in 1982. Previous books on this theme – for example, Graham Cleverly's *Managers and Magic* – had tended to focus on the peculiarity and anomalies of corporate behaviour. Deal and Kennedy, however, start from the premise that a strong culture is an important ingredient in business success. They proved the point by profiling eighty companies; the eighteen companies which had clearly articulated qualitative values or beliefs 'all were uniformly outstanding performers'.

The culture of these organisations was underpinned, they found, by:

- the values themselves
  For those who hold them, shared values define the fundamental character of their organisation, the attitude that distinguishes it from all others. In this way, they create a sense of identity for those in the organisation, making employees feel special. Values are a reality in the minds of most people throughout the company, not just the senior executives. It is this sense of pulling together that makes shared values so effective.
- heroes
  Heroes are action-oriented visionaries, much in the mould of Leavitt's pathfinders. They help to create strong corporate values by:
  - making success attainable and human
  - providing role models
  - symbolising the company to the outside world
  - preserving what makes the company special
  - setting a standard of performance
  - motivating employees.
- rites and rituals
  These companies make a great deal of use of play, rituals and ceremonies to emphasise key values.

If some of these themes sound conspicuously similar to those of the excellence movement, so they should. The authors say, 'Tom Peters is the intellectual and spiritual godfather of this book' and go on to acknowledge other McKinsey figures, including Bob Waterman. But the influence was by no means a one-way affair – Peters admits that his own thinking was heavily influenced by Kennedy in particular.

Geert Hofstede would probably be amused by the description 'a wandering Dutch misfit'. Many of his university colleagues have difficulty placing his challenging research into a neat academic niche. Yet Hofstede is widely regarded as the father of 'cross-cultural management' – an approach that recognises that national or regional cultures have a strong influence on the behaviour of people in businesses. Hofstede explains his concept of culture as follows:

'Culture consists of the patterns of thinking that parents transfer to their children, teachers to their students, friends to their friends, leaders to their followers, and followers to their leaders. Culture is reflected in the meanings people attach to various aspects of life; their way of looking at the world and their role in it; their values – that is, in what they consider as "good" and as "evil"; their collective beliefs – what they consider as "true" and as "false"; their artistic expressions – what they consider as "beautiful" and "ugly". Culture, although basically resident in people's minds, becomes crystallised in the institutions and tangible products of a society, which reinforce the mental programmes in their turn. Management within a society is very much constrained by its cultural context, because it is impossible to co-ordinate the actions of people without a deep understanding of their values, beliefs and expressions.'

Currently Hofstede is at the University of Limburg – an appropriate venue for cross-cultural management, being at the borders of Holland, Germany and Belgium. His concepts developed partly out of his wartime experiences in occupied Holland, partly out of global travels with his close-knit family and partly out of a massive fifty-country study of 116,000 employees in similar jobs within a large multinational company. Of his wartime experience, he writes: 'Our family relationships were reasonably harmonious. My father had a modest but fixed income, so that we did not suffer from the 1930s economic crisis. There was enough of everything but not luxury; money was unimportant and rarely spoken of. What was important was knowledge and intellectual exercise, at which we were all quite good. I went to regular state schools and liked them. We lived through the German occupation (1940–45) without physical suffering but detesting the occupants. I was too young at the time to understand the full scope of the ethical issues involved in Nazism, but I had seen my Jewish schoolmates being deported never to return. Only in the years after 1945 did I fully realise that for five years we had lived under a system in which everything I held for white was called black and vice versa; which made me more conscious of what were my values, and that it is sometimes necessary to take explicit positions.'

After qualifying as an engineer, Hofstede wrote his doctoral thesis on 'The Game of Budget Control'. Of his thesis adviser, Professor Herman Hutte, Hofstede says: 'He succeeded in changing a mechanical engineer into a psychologist; a miracle not unlike changing water into wine.' Then, to learn how factories really worked, he spent six months incognito working on factory floors, observing the behaviour of managers and operators. His career with Dutch companies took him through work study to personnel research, before he joined IMEDE, the Swiss business school, in 1971.

It was at IMEDE, and afterwards at the European Institute for Advanced Studies in Management in Brussels, that Hofstede carried out his classic study of the values that lay behind the cultures of employees in different countries. The study identified four dimensions of values where there were significant and relative constant variations between people of different cultures. These were:

- Collectivism – Individualism
  Some cultures prefer a tightly knit social system; others a much looser system. At the collectivism end of the scale, people look after each other and are heavily dependent on each other; individualistic cultures, on the other hand, stress independence and self-sufficiency.
- Power distance
  Cultures differ in how comfortable they are with inequalities of power distribution. People who can accept such inequalities (that is, who expect and tolerate large power distances) tend to be comfortable with a tall hierarchy and with paternalistic leadership. People who are most comfortable with small power distances take well to consultation, participation and techniques such as management by objectives (MBO). One of the reasons MBO does not work in many countries is that it is incompatible with large power distances.
- Uncertainty avoidance
  Cultures with strong uncertainty avoidance are uncomfortable with ambiguity and unpredictability. They tend to react to uncertainty by creating formal rules and procedures. Cultures with weak uncertainty avoidance do not need so many rules, because they have higher tolerance for ambiguity.
- Femininity – Masculinity
  Feminine values emphasise caring and nurturing;

masculine values emphasise assertiveness. Hofstede describes Japan as masculine; in Japan, the role difference between the sexes is extreme. Sweden, by contrast, is a 'feminine' culture; although men still dominate its society, there is far less differentiation between sexual roles. Masculine cultures place great importance upon performance and productivity; feminine cultures also value job satisfaction and quality of working life.

The importance of Hofstede's work lies in demonstrating that there is no universal 'right' style of management: 'The nature of management skills is such that they are culturally specific: a management technique or philosophy that is appropriate in one national culture is not necessarily appropriate in another.'

Quality

Ever since Murphy, quality in the West (and particularly in the United States) had been an engineering activity. Along with work measurement came a variety of techniques of quality assurance. But in post-war Japan, under the guidance of two Americans who could not find an audience at home, the idea of 'total quality management' began to develop. Those two Americans were W. Edwards Deming (born 1901) and J. M. Juran (born 1904).

'Deming is to management what Benjamin Franklin was to the Republic,' one commentator has observed. He has preached the quality gospel throughout the world, developing fierce loyalty among his disciples and antagonism from those companies which do not go the whole way down his prescribed path to quality. Yet it was only in 1980 with the NBC White Paper 'If Japan Can, Why Can't We?' that he established his reputation in the United States. This may well be the reason for Deming's dim view of management standards in his native country. 'Export everything to a friendly country except American management,' he once said.

In Japan it was altogether different. Deming was embraced as a far-sighted visionary offering practical means of revitalising Japanese industry. His ideas were greeted with enthusiasm and, by the 1950s, he was reputed to be the most revered American in

Japan after General MacArthur. In 1951 the Deming Prize for quality improvement was instituted; it has been won by Nissan, Fuji and Mitsubishi among others, and continues to be one of the most sought-after awards in Japanese industry. In 1960 Deming received the Second Order of the Sacred Treasure, the first American to do so.

Deming had gained a Ph.D. in physics from Yale in 1928 and spent time working at the Hawthorne Western Electric Plant in Chicago in the 1920s. (J. M. Juran, the other well-known quality guru, also worked there.) He went on to become a US government statistician and his approach to quality improvement remains firmly statistical. The idea is simple: all processes are subject to some level of variation which reduces quality; if the level of variation is managed and decreases, quality standards will improve. Implementing this and other Deming theories has proved successful in some of the world's largest companies. Ford, for example, has given Deming much of the credit for its turnaround in the early 1970s. Procter and Gamble, AT&T, NEC and Irving Bank are among the many companies that have benefited from Deming's work. Ford has estimated that 95 per cent of its employees became aware that quality was their first priority; Nashua improved efficiency and lowered prices by up to 20 per cent while still increasing profit margins.

Deming claims only 15 per cent of production faults are the fault of employees; 85 per cent are down to management. He has developed fourteen points of management. Failure to adhere to one of them can, he warns, be catastrophic. The priorities he first preached in Japan – precision, performance and attention to customers – remain. Deming's fourteen points of management are:

1. Create constancy of purpose for improvement of product and service – 'It is no longer sufficient to have customers not complain. It is necessary for good business to have customers that boast about your product or service, stay with you and bring in a friend with new business.'
2. Adopt the new philosophy
3. Cease dependence on mass inspection – cost of 'rework' businesses is often as high as 25 or even 40 per cent of total operating costs

4. End the practice of awarding business on price tag alone – 'Time-honoured operating policies can serve as barriers to improvement.'
5. Improve constantly and forever the system of production and service – 'If you wait for people to come to you, you'll only get the small problems. You must go and find them. The big problems are where people don't realise they have one in the first place.'
6. Institute training – managers and workers must work together to identify opportunities for improvement
7. Institute leadership
8. Drive out fear
9. Break down barriers between staff areas – workers simply want a chance to take pride in their work; managers should be seen as coaches not judges
10. Eliminate slogans, exhortations and targets for the work-force
11. Eliminate numerical quotas
12. Remove barriers to pride of workmanship
13. Institute a vigorous programme of education and retraining
14. Take action to accomplish the transformation.

However, J. M. Juran has suggested that Deming is more at home with statistics than with management and that he delivers 'far-out statements and platitudes' about management. But Deming expressed his theories at Utah State University School of Business in the George S. Eccles Distinguished Lecture Series in 1983:

Some of you are students of finance. You learn how to figure and how to run a company on figures. If you run a company on figures alone you will go under. How long will it take the company to go under, get drowned? I don't know, but it is sure to fail. Why? Because the most important figures are not there. Did you learn that in the school of finance? You will, ten or fifteen years from now, learn the most important figures are those that are unknown or unknowable.

What about the multiplying effects of a happy customer, in either manufacturing or in service? Is he in your figures? What about the multiplying effect of an unhappy customer? Is that in your figures? Did you learn that in your school of finance?

What about the multiplying effect of getting better material to use in production? What about the multiplying effect you get all along the production line? Do you know that figure? You don't. If you run the company without it, you won't have a company. What about the multiplying effect of doing a better job along the line?

People all over the world think that it is the factory worker that causes problems. He is not your problem. Ever since there has been anything such as industry, the factory worker has known that quality is what will protect his job. He knows that poor quality in the hands of the customer will lose the market and cost him his job. He knows it and lives with that fear every day. Yet he cannot do a good job. He is not allowed to do it because the management wants figures, more product, and never mind the quality. They measure only in figures. The factory worker is forced to make defective products, forced to turn out defective items. He is forced to work with defective material, so no matter what they do, it will still be wrong. The worker can't do anything about it. He is totally helpless. If he tries to do something about it, he might as well talk to the wall. Nobody listens. . . .

A dean of a school of business wrote to me to complain that I was a little rough in a speech that I gave to 2400 purchasing managers in New Orleans. It was a meeting of the International Benevolent Protective Order of Purchasing Managers. They could hear what I was saying. The acoustics were good in the auditorium. There was just one difference between me and the dean. I get around to see what materials come in; he does not. Teamwork is needed between the purchasing department and production and sales. They won't get it, though, because the mandate handed down from management to the purchasing department is to get the lowest price. Top management has to learn something about the entire company. They can no longer play solos or be prima donnas. There has to be teamwork, but the annual system of rating destroys teamwork. How could someone in purchasing get a good rating for paying a higher price? Even if it saves ten times as much in production, you do not get a good rating by paying a higher price.

The foreman had better not stop the line. He'll hurt production if he does, and he may not be here tomorrow. Fear governs almost everybody. Only perhaps one in 200 is not governed by fear. A millwright, feeling a bearing, informed the foreman that it was getting warm. He suggested that they stop and take care of it before the bearing froze up and scored the shaft. If that happened they would be down for sure. The foreman knew that the proper thing for the company to do was to stop and work on the bearing. His answer was, 'We can't stop now, we must get these castings out today.' He didn't make it. The bearing froze and scored the shaft. The line was down for four days, but the foreman did his job.

Even in his eighties Deming continues to challenge many of the fashionable management practices of the time. Leveraged buy-outs, management by objectives and management by walking about have all been, at some time, subjects of his derision.

Rumanian-born J. M. Juran has similar fascinations and a background which, remarkably, parallels that of Deming. Now it is said that 'he is a prophet whose time is come', but throughout a lengthy career he has had to struggle for acceptance in the United States.

Juran's pioneering work on quality control began in the 1920s when he joined American Telephone and Telegraph's manufacturing arm. He became corporate industrial engineer before branching out alone as a quality consultant. In 1951 he edited, and to a large extent wrote, *The Quality Control Handbook*. Since then, he has attempted to develop quality into a complete corporate philosophy though, again like Deming, it was not until the 1980s that his message gained any popularity in the West. But since 1954 Juran has preached his message in Japan and claims some of the credit for overturning the poor reputation of Japanese goods.

Central to Juran's quality philosophy is that impetus must come from the top. He has been critical of the use of quality circles in the West, predicting, 'We went about it the wrong way. We'll come back and do it better within twenty years.' He continues to preach the gospel of quality throughout the world. His 'Management of Quality' course has been attended by over twenty thousand managers in more than thirty countries. His clients include Motorola, Texas Instruments, Du Pont, Monsanto, Xerox and the IRS.

Companies in the United States had not entirely ignored Deming and Juran. As corporate vice-president of ITT, Philip Crosby was responsible for international quality programmes. His approach was developed further when he established his own consultancy company with its notion of a 'Quality College'. Crosby recognised that organisations, as productive flow systems, were built up of multiple customer–supplier relationships. In an assembly operation, for example, an operator is the supplier to the next station in line. By focusing on customer expectations, all the way along the flow system to the real customer in the market-place, it was possible to remove many of the errors and much of the wastage that occurred.

The Japanese soon established their own quality gurus and also developed the notion of cycle time reduction – minimising the time from a customer's order to the time it is delivered. In particular this was developed by Toyota, the car manufacturer, which demonstrated that it was possible to extend the concept of quality management as prevention of waste to include waste of time. From this conceptual leap was born the just-in-time (JIT) approach, now widely used across Japan, in which production is organised for constant flow, without buffer stocks, and in which materials and components are delivered to each process only as they are needed for a specific order. (Henry Ford I had developed a similar approach for his Model T car, but his process allowed for minimal product variation, whereas in theory, JIT allows for batches of one.)

The ideas of JIT have been taken further in recent years. George Stalk and others of the Boston Consulting Group realised, while researching a book, that the idea of JIT could, and would, be expanded to apply to more than simply manufacturing – research and development, distribution and a whole range of operations could be adapted to the theory.

The concept of cycle time has been furthered by quality consultant, Philip Thomas (born 1934). Thomas developed his approach, 'Total Cycle Time', during a career of over twenty-five years in the electronics industry working for integrated circuit pioneers RCA, Fairchild and the General Instrument Corporation. His consultancy group, established in 1978, now consists of over fifty 'problem solvers' in Dallas, San José and Frankfurt. Its clients include some of America's largest and most prestigious companies from General Motors and Xerox, to General Electric and IBM.

Total Cycle Time focuses on the three elements, which Thomas regards as driving competitiveness: customer service ('ability to satisfy a customer's need in a timely manner'), time to market ('the period between the moment a new product is identified and the point at which it can be produced cost-effectively') and total asset utilisation ('effective employment of plant, equipment, inventory and people'). In order to measure a company's performance within these elements Thomas has created three levels of business performance which he calls baseline, entitlement and benchmark.

- Baseline is the company's current level of performance and can be expressed in terms of cycle time, profits, productivity and quality.
- Entitlement is the performance level a business should be able to achieve with its current resources of plant, equipment, process and people. To calculate entitlement, Thomas has developed a frame of reference involving more than 100 business and industrial processes. Historical analysis, theoretical analysis, process databases and specific competitive analysis all help to establish a company's entitlement.
- Finally, benchmark applies to the best competitive performance a business can achieve. This involves comparisons with companies in similar or even completely different businesses and may result in recommending that certain resources or technology are added.

Bringing about the changes recommended by Thomas normally involved a major cultural transformation in companies. There are five steps to achieving this, he says: inspiration, identification, information, implementation and institutionalisation. It can take from nine months to four years to move through these steps successfully.

In his book *Making American Business Unbeatable* (1989), Thomas presents a typical case study of how his theory translates into practice. Visiting a production line in a company he gains his first insights into likely opportunities for cycle time reduction. At one section he notices people working at a leisurely pace and is told, 'You should see them in a couple of weeks; it'll be nothing but go, go, go.' The orders, he discovers, usually arrive at the end of the month and clearly lengthen the cycle time. The cycle time is made even worse by reworking. 'Half the orders that come in here have only about 80 per cent of the details we need,' complains one employee. There is also the question of interdepartmental rivalries. Thomas is told: 'Those orders are on hold because of pricing or engineering questions, matters beyond my control. It wouldn't be fair to include them in my department's cycle time.' Thomas, however, makes sure he includes them.

From this example, Thomas points up some of the usual obstacles to shortening time cycles – large lot sizes, long set-up times, high re-work levels and a high percentage of idle equipment. The result is a baseline for design development of thirty months, and sixteen for entitlement. For the make-market cycle, baseline is 125 work-days against an entitlement of forty-eight. Thomas estimates that moving to entitlement levels would take two years with a resulting 24 per cent gain in productivity. Generally, Thomas says, cycle time reductions result in 20 per cent improvements in blue-collar productivity and white-collar gains of 25 to 50 per cent.

It is in white-collar productivity that Thomas finds the largest gulf between baseline and entitlement. The reasons go back to the scientific management methods of Frederick Taylor, which concentrated on the productivity of blue-collar workers. 'The whole industrial engineering movement grew up to develop blue-collar productivity. When you go to white-collar workers it's virgin territory.'

Excellence

As has happened elsewhere, the bridge between philosophy and a practical management approach of potential general application came in part from satire. Robert Townsend's irreverent *Up the Organization* (1970) contained a great deal of blunt advice, from how to encourage other people to own up to mistakes, through the principles of delegation, to heresies such as 'fire the whole personnel department', as a means of getting line managers to take proper responsibility for people problems.

Townsend (born 1920) based his idiosyncratic theories on his work as president of Avis, where he was responsible for the company's revival until it was absorbed into the ITT empire (derided by Townsend as an 'inhuman' company run by an 'accountant'). *Up the Organization*, despite its aphoristic levity, laid down many of the guiding principles of the later excellence movement.

> People don't hate work. It's as natural as rest or play. They don't have to be forced or threatened. If they commit themselves to mutual objectives, they'll drive themselves more effectively than you can drive them. But they'll commit themselves only to the extent they can see ways of satisfying their ego and development needs. Get to know your people. . . . And then try to create an organisation around your people, not jam your people into those organisation-chart rectangles. The only excuse for organisation is to maximise the chance that each one, working with others, will get for growth in his job. You can't motivate people. That door is locked from the inside. You *can* create a climate in which most of your people will motivate themselves to help the company reach its objectives.

The emergence of excellence as a management philosophy was in part a US reaction to the success of the Japanese in seizing markets through quality. Peters and Waterman's *In Search of Excellence* appeared in 1982. The book, Peters admits candidly, succeeded to a large extent because it came out at the right time. Unemployment was rocketing, manufacturing declining rapidly and people, especially in once self-assured America, were anxiously looking for solutions. The Japanese seemed to have it right, but how could their best practices be brought to the Western world? The answer Peters and Waterman gave was to look at the best companies in the United States, companies where the simple things were done well. They looked for success stories and found them. 'There is good news from America,' said the book. 'Good management practice today is not resident only in Japan.'

In Search of Excellence was followed by studies in Britain,

France, Belgium and elsewhere. The British study, published as *The Winning Streak*, took note of academic criticisms of Peters and Waterman's book and included parallel studies of unsuccessful companies and of small companies. It placed even greater emphasis on the calibre of leadership as the key characteristic of excellent companies – an emphasis reflected in Peters's next book, *A Passion for Excellence*. The British study identified some differences relating to national culture. The French and Belgian studies found even more. It seems that the characteristics of excellence are not only influenced by corporate culture but by national culture as well.

The excellence movement has not been an unprecedented success story. Columbia University's Professor Kathryn Harrigan explains: 'Americans are into cults, particularly the cult of the personality. They are all looking for the recipe of success and Tom Peters made the best job of that. People know exactly where to place him.'

Rosabeth Moss Kanter, whose book *The Change Masters* appeared in 1983, also points out that Peters and Waterman's book 'stresses simple rather than complex structures'. (Kanter's book was labelled by critics as 'the thinking man's *In Search of Excellence*'.) Another critic acerbically noted: 'Tom Peters, in his much acclaimed book, *In Search of Excellence*, accidentally discovered mediocrity.'

Huge numbers of book sales are not, of course, indicative of the book's effect on managers. Peters says: 'The book has not changed anything in itself, but it's part of something big that has.' In the foreword to *A Passion for Excellence*, Peters's sequel with Nancy Austin, the authors noted of *In Search of Excellence*: 'If history is any guide, two or three million probably opened the book. Four or five hundred thousand read as much as four or five chapters. A hundred thousand or so read it cover to cover. Twenty-five thousand took notes.'

One book does not change the way a country does business. But what *In Search of Excellence* achieved, almost single-handed, was to put management and business on the agenda. Suddenly it was talked about in circles where it had never been seriously discussed before. This, in itself, cannot be underestimated. The manager of a small company was as likely to be interested as the president of an international conglomerate.

Popcorn makers were talked of in the same breath as the president of IBM, because all were involved in management.

The companies featured in the book have found it hard work to maintain their levels of success. Even IBM, perhaps the most obvious choice in the book, suffered one of the worst slumps in its history during the early 1980s. People Express, the company considered a model by many readers of *In Search of Excellence*, also collapsed dramatically.

Given the unprecedented commercial success of *In Search of Excellence*, it was hardly surprising that there would be dozens of pale imitations. Very few of these have any research base or add anything to the debate. However, this flurry of publications did help (in parallel with the quality movement) to spawn the current global interest in customer care. Jan Carlzon, chief executive of Scandinavian airline SAS, was one of the first to spell out the potential for the company balance sheet in a determined push to put the customer first.

The growing awareness of how an organisation's culture can contribute or detract from its performance, combined with the global depression of the late 1970s, helped to swell interest in the issues of leadership and change management. In the previous chapter we considered how leadership relates to excellence; managing change and managing culture are equally closely linked. One recent book dominates the latter issue – Rosabeth Moss Kanter's *The Change Masters* – but recently both Peters and Waterman have separately produced books that emphasise the importance for corporate survival and growth, of developing organisations that can not only live with change but can embrace it as an opportunity rather than as a threat.

Robert Hayes

Born Wakenney, Kansas, 1936
Professor at Harvard Business School

In the introduction to *A Passion for Excellence*, Tom Peters and Nancy Austin wrote: 'The landmark *Harvard Business Review* article by Bob Hayes and the late Bill Abernathy, "Managing Our Way to Economic Decline", is the piece that we think of as the cornerstone of the corporate revolution. It attacked the

MBA/numbers only mentality of American managers and the lack of concern in American corporations for such basics as manufacturing.'

Formally in technical sales with IBM and operations research at McKinsey, Robert Hayes is fascinated by manufacturing and productivity management. His message is forthright. In the 1980 *Harvard Business Review* he and Abernathy roundly criticised the short-term orientation of American managers, citing a 'broad managerial failure . . . of both vision and leadership'. A *Review* editor said: 'They were willing to stand up and say the Emperor has no clothes.' Hayes describes the situation: 'At that time America was facing what President Carter called a malaise: a lack of direction and a failure of will. The dollar was falling and there was great concern that something was wrong with America. Within the US people were all saying it was due to the government, OPEC or labor unions.' The article cast aside such misconceptions and provided a challenge for American industry. It gained the academic duo immediate attention and some notoriety.

Hayes and Abernathy overturned the conventional wisdom on why Japan had emerged to challenge markets once the preserve of American companies. The factors regarded as uniquely Japanese – lower labour costs, more automated and newer factories, strong government support and a homogeneous culture – were, Hayes argued, a fallacy. In a later article (*Why Japanese Factories Work*) he wrote: 'The modern Japanese factory is not, as many Americans believe, a prototype of the factory of the future. . . . Instead, it is something much more difficult for us to copy; it is the factory of today running as it should.'

The genesis of the Hayes–Abernathy article occurred at Harvard's research centre at Vevey in Switzerland, where the two worked together in 1978. At the time Abernathy was studying the world automotive industry. In conversation with Hayes it became clear that their results and thinking were along similar lines. Hayes recalls: 'If I had been alone I would have felt uneasy with the conclusions I was drawing, but when Bill Abernathy said he saw exactly the same things we buttressed each other's confidence.'

The isolation of Switzerland provided a fresh perspective

on the plight of American industry and clarified their ideas. American business, they argued, was caught in an insular and complacent time capsule. 'At that time most Americans were looking at the problem from within the United States. The manufacturing people didn't see any problem, because everyone they could see was doing things the same way,' says Hayes. The standardisation of approaches to manufacturing and technology management meant that American companies compared themselves with virtually identical companies. 'Companies had essentially stopped competing on the basis of their superior manufacturing. They'd standardised manufacturing – buying equipment from the same suppliers, using the same kind of experts for advice, buying parts from the same suppliers, having the same unions. If you blindfolded someone and put them into an auto company they wouldn't have been able to tell if it was Ford, Chrysler or General Motors. They all looked the same.'

A degree of complacency had entered into industry. 'Many of the kinds of things we accept as good management in the United States are no longer accepted in other parts of the world. There's too much reliance here on theories and techniques that worked during the 1950s and 1960s when markets were expanding rapidly,' Hayes said at the time the article came out.

What Hayes and Abernathy observed in Europe, however, was quite different. Hayes's background in operations research was an advantage. 'I was the right person in the right place at the right time. I was trained as a field observer, so when I went to Europe I was trying to look as objectively as possible at what was happening in factories and in companies.' What was happening in Europe provoked his immediate concern. It was far less standardised and more technologically advanced than he had anticipated. 'In Europe there was greater variability and a much wider range of options. Europeans are more isolated – the French, Germans and British all had their own ways. There was also much more emphasis on technology and they were becoming quite advanced.' The argument that the US was failing to utilise fully its technical or manufacturing resources did not go down well when Hayes and Abernathy first tried it out on audiences of Harvard alumni. It was like preaching to atheists.

Undaunted, Hayes and Abernathy decided to shake things up with a hard-hitting article. 'We needed to do something which would shock people into wakefulness, if not action.' When it was published in July 1980 after a number of rewrites ('The article which emerged was different, much more provocative and less academic, from the one we originally wrote'), Hayes was unsure what the reaction would be. 'I was uneasy about the article as it appeared because I didn't think it was academically respectable. It was very much dedicated to changing the way business people thought about the problem. Until they felt that pressure there was no reason to change anything.'

The article quickly became one of the most talked about and controversial in the *Review*'s history. Hayes recalls: 'The impact in the business community was immediate and astonishingly supportive. It seemed to trigger an outpouring of people who agreed and rather violent discussions with those who disagreed.' Within a week of publication, it was attracting attention in Japan. Hayes was inundated with requests for interviews.

What most concerned Hayes and Abernathy was how their colleagues at Harvard would regard the punchy, almost journalistic style. But its immediate success clearly affected their response. Hayes confirms: 'My colleagues probably saw the article rather differently when they saw the impact it was having.' Elsewhere Hayes and Abernathy were accused of being involved in 'advocacy' rather than 'research'.

As for its actual impact, Hayes is sceptical. 'I don't think any single article has an effect. It can crystallise and focus the way people see things but they have to be feeling the pressure to change.' In his view, the arguments included in the article still hold. 'What I have done since that article is much more significant but I'm still proud of it. Most of what I said has now become part of conventional wisdom.'

In his books and articles since 1980, Hayes has reinforced and bolstered his argument with academic depth and some fervour. 'In a sense I've spent the last seven or eight years trying to give more academic respectability, more evidence to the arguments as well as expanding them,' he says. He sees the factory floor and the assembly line as crucial and neglected areas and points to 'managerial remote control' and an over-reliance on financial analysis. 'We must compete with the Japanese, as they do with us: by always putting our best talent and resources to work doing the basic things a little better, every day, over a long period of time. It is that simple – and that difficult.'

In the book *Restoring Our Competitive Edge* (1984), which he wrote with Stephen Wheelwright, Hayes argued that well-run factories around the world share many similarities: 'a well-run German factory is more like a well-run Japanese factory than German society is like Japanese society. And well-run American factories have important similarities to both.' The book calls for the development and implementation of coherent manufacturing strategies and provides a comparison between German, Japanese and American companies. In Japanese factories Hayes and Wheelwright found:

- cleanliness, quiet and orderliness
- attention to the care and maintenance of equipment
- pressure to reduce inventory
- attempts to eliminate uncertainty (reduce the number of things that can go wrong)
- quality consciousness.

(Hayes had not been to Japan prior to the 'Managing Our Way to Economic Decline' article.) In the German plants Hayes and Wheelwright saw:

- emphasis on a technically strong management
- high levels of competence in the work-force
- strong customer orientation
- consciousness of competitive pressure
- long-term orientation.

Similar characteristics were identified by Peters and Waterman (Hayes worked with Waterman whilst at McKinsey) in *In Search of Excellence*. Hayes and Wheelwright conclude by exhorting American industry to build:

- the capability of its work-force
- the technical strength of its managers
- the quality of its processes and products
- a participative relationship among all levels of management and labour

- process (manufacturing) engineering capability
- patiently in small, but frequent steps.

American managers' preference for short-term rather than long-term planning is a common theme in Hayes's work. In a *Harvard Business Review* article in 1985 he wrote: 'Most companies select goals that are too short term. It is almost impossible for a company to create a truly sustainable competitive advantage – one that is highly difficult for its competitors to copy – in just five to ten years (the time frame that most companies use). Goals that can be achieved within five years are usually either too easy or based on buying and selling something. Anything that a company can buy or sell, however, is probably available for purchase or sale by its competitors as well.'

He is critical of the common process of evaluating performance on financial grounds alone. It encourages short-term thinking. To counter this, he encourages businesses to put more money into research and development, even though it may have detrimental effects on short-term returns.

Though based at Harvard, Hayes is not afraid of attributing some of the blame for America's economic decline to its business schools. He explains: 'Business schools in the US had undergone a period of rapid change in the 1960s. MBAs became desirable things and there was a huge explosion in numbers. Before 1960 business schools here were very field- and institution-orientated. It was "this is how banks are run, this is how businesses are run". They were descriptive not prescriptive.'

He believes short-term financial orientation was bolstered by the business schools. 'Faculties became dominated by quantitatively trained people. The danger with the quantitative approach is that you tend to focus on topics that lend themselves to that sort of analysis and not on those that don't. There are a lot of important things that don't fit in.' Hayes provides an example: 'Mathematics has its own attraction. If you find a problem and develop a mathematical framework for solving it, the next step for a mathematician is to try to apply the framework to another problem. The mathematical framework starts driving your research agenda, rather than the problems themselves.'

This quantitative approach has meant that Hayes's field of operations management has been eliminated at many schools. But at Harvard the study of nitty-gritty practicalities of manufacturing is encouraged. 'Harvard really forces you to ask what the implications are for practising managers. We probably have the largest group of people focused on operations management of any graduate business school in the world.'

This insistence on relating research to industrial practice provides a guide to Hayes's future interests. His current research concerns the US and Japanese semiconductor businesses as well as a comparative international design project. 'I've become concerned that we aren't teaching anything about design,' says Hayes. His perception is broadening. 'If I analyse why my outlook changed it's because I began doing comparative studies.'

Tom Peters (born 1942)
and Robert Waterman (born 1936)

Consultants

In 1982, Tom Peters and Robert Waterman's book *In Search of Excellence* transformed the management book market virtually overnight. It has now sold over five million copies world-wide and has spawned the money-spinning excellence movement. Whether this book and its successors have changed management is still open to question. In *Frontiers of Management* Peter Drucker writes: 'The great virtue of the Peters and Waterman book is its extreme simplicity, maybe oversimplification. But when Aunt Mary has to give that nephew of hers a high school graduation present and she gives him *In Search of Excellence*, you know that management has become part of the general culture.' Later in the same book Drucker observes: 'The book's great weakness – which is a strength from the point of view of its success – is that it makes managing sound so incredibly easy. All you have to do is put that book under your pillow, and it'll get done.'

Peters himself has expressed some disquiet about the book's effects on managers. However, Waterman argues: 'I don't think we did more harm than good. Tom says things like that to grab attention. We had no reason to believe it would be different from any other business book.' He admits the up-beat, emphasising-the-positive approach of *In Search of Excellence* could have had its drawbacks. 'There is a danger that people may take a popular book as a prescription. We helped move forward something that was already happening anyway. Up until then, most management models were very derivative of Taylor – line and staff. Even though other models had been written about, there was no concrete evidence that other models were working and that they were associated with success.'

The book challenged much conventional wisdom and management practice. CBI director-general John Banham says: '*In Search of Excellence* overturned all the sacred cows of management. It told people what they wanted to hear – that there was nothing in Japan that wasn't already available in the United States. It's counter intuitive: they weren't teaching any of that stuff at Harvard.'

In Search of Excellence came out of Peters and Waterman's work with management consultants McKinsey. One colleague explained: 'The original clients of the organisational effectiveness study were European multinationals with US operations that were not doing too well. They wanted to know how the best companies in the United States were run. When they were presented with the results of the study, they rejected them. Only when they were shown back to the US companies that participated in the research did the results obtain an enthusiastic response.'

Peters explains: 'McKinsey had to become more intellectual and invest in R&D – in part, because a lot of strategies were coming a cropper in the nasty real world. I got the job of doing this. I went to work on that in March 1977. It was a survey of companies, not meant to be in search of anything, just to see what companies were doing.' Presenting the initial findings to Royal Dutch Shell in Holland, Peters got a cool response – 'undaunted, we decided to feed back the research to the people we'd talked to. John Young at Hewlett Packard was turned on by it.'

Eventually, the research was boiled down to eight essential points, identifiable characteristics of excellent companies:

- *A bias for action*, for getting on with it
- *Close to the customer*, a genuine belief that the customer is king
- *Autonomy and entrepreneurship*, an environment that encourages innovation
- *Productivity through people*, treating the rank and file as the root source of quality and productivity gains
- *Hands-on, value-driven management*, leaders who make their presence known, who tell employees about the values they hold
- *Stick to the knitting*, staying close to the business they know
- *Simple forms, lean staff*, very simple structures and a minimum of headquarters bureaucrats
- *Simultaneous loose-tight properties*, they are both centralised (around their core values) and decentralised (as regards other values).

The timing of *In Search of Excellence* was perfect, Peters admits: 'It arrived the month unemployment hit 10 per cent in the United States. That was of great symbolic influence. Within weeks we saw business books in all the bookshops.' A magazine article led to the book – the book to an industry. 'People thought it was a tribute to US excellence. We didn't tell about the bad side. It was a conscious decision to write about the good things. Books didn't have chapters on customers. We introduced words like customer,' says Peters. 'The book has not changed anything in itself, but it's part of something big that has. We see it continuously developing. The biggest change has been in the past two years. Flexibility is the word. I think we did a service to industry by reintroducing customers into the language.'

The lengthy list which was the backbone of the original book was gradually condensed in Peters's subsequent writings until, in *A Passion for Excellence*, co-authored with Nancy Austin, the concept was encapsulated in a simple triangle. On the three sides of the triangle are the key concerns of care of customers, innovation and people; central to all of these is leadership, exercised in large part by what Peters calls 'Management by Walking Around' (MBWA).

It was during two years working at the Pentagon that Peters became, in his own words, 'completely and hopelessly fascinated by complex organisations'. He recalls: 'I watched people being vilified by bureaucracies; people slithering through bureaucracies. I watched a huge organisation from a small corner.' Working in the capital was clearly an important experience. 'In Washington, when I was twenty-nine, Kennedy created a caucus of young people with no experience to run operations. Heads the size of melons – I look back with disgust at myself. I became a garden-variety mathematically adept executor of strategic projects.'

After the Pentagon, Peters went to Cornell where he became a bachelor and master in civil engineering before joining the navy in Vietnam. In 1970 he went to Stanford for an MBA and received a Ph.D. in 1973 for his work on organisational behaviour. Then, in his own words, he 'went back to Washington because I didn't have anything to write about and I was tired of eating lentils'. He worked with the Office of Management and Budget and later joined the anti-narcotics campaign.

In December 1974 Peters joined McKinsey. Five years later he started work on what was to become *In Search of Excellence* with the study of forty-three companies. From this work an article appeared in *Business Week* on 22 July 1980. Peters remembers it as 'the last day of peace I ever had'.

Peters left McKinsey before the book was published. 'I left because I never fitted into an institution very well. They made me a partner, but I was never comfortable,' he says. His co-author, Robert Waterman, remained with the company.

Peters's talents are undoubted. Waterman says: 'Tom believes in huge amounts of commitment. He's almost fanatical.' His colleague Lennard Arvedson adds: 'What I'd like people to understand about Tom is how hard he works. He never gives a standard presentation. Some stories or slides are the same, but he always tailors things to the audience.'

As with other management thinkers, it is not only hard work which is identified as a secret of success. Arvedson continues: 'He has a very genuine curiosity – wanting to learn and discover; a deep empathy with people (although he can rant and rave at his staff). He is very demanding of himself and it doesn't come easy. . . . He has a driving force to produce. I once asked him what he enjoyed most. He said the writing.'

Waterman, once described as 'the Indiana Jones of a white-collar, six-figure consultant's world', has remained the low key half of the duo. While Peters has travelled the world preaching excellence, Waterman prefers small, intimate meetings. Assessing his own motivation, he says: 'You are never quite sure what drives you. It goes back to why I got into consulting at McKinsey in the first place. I can have more impact and more fun working with a variety of companies. I've done line management – I prefer consulting.' Strangely enough, it was McKinsey which provided Waterman with management experience. 'My first major line management job was after I was made a principal at McKinsey. I was sent to Australia to get the office there going again. I was then half consultant/half manager. I proved to myself I can run a business. I most enjoy acting as an adviser, helper.'

Initially, Waterman's consultancy work with McKinsey focused on restructuring and decentralising, a process many companies had completed by the mid 1970s. 'What became intriguing to me was how few really good strategies were getting implemented. The ideal was: first you got strategy right, then the structure would follow. I couldn't see any close relationship between strategy and structure,' recalls Waterman. 'I took a leave of absence to teach at IMEDE and had the chance to view the world outside McKinsey. When I returned I met Tom Peters. For some different, some similar reasons we both felt organisation issues were far more important than consultants had been recognising.'

These shared concerns formed the basis of the partnership behind *In Search of Excellence*. It is, on first appearances, a curious match – Peters the gregarious opinion-maker; Waterman the contemplative water-colour artist concentrating on high-level consultancy. Waterman says it was a 'symbiotic relationship – I had a lot of rich examples from consultancy. Tom was intellectualising and opening my eyes to a lot of literature I had not heard of before.'

In the latest of his books, *Thriving on Chaos*, Peters begins 'Excellence isn't. There are no excellent companies.' Called by one reviewer 'a cook book for the 1990s', *Thriving on Chaos* tackles the problems and demands of change. 'The times demand that flexibility and love of change replace our long-standing penchant for mass production and mass markets based upon a relatively predictable environment now vanished. No firm can take anything in its market for granted.'

Again, Peters tackles managerial complacency head on, calling for quality, flexibility and training of the highest order. His new recipe for success requires 'products or services, which emphasize innovative design, tailored for narrow markets and resulting from more intense listening to customers; superior quality; exceptional service and responsiveness to customers'.

Five major themes emerge in *Thriving on Chaos*:

- obsession with responsiveness to customers
- constant innovation in all areas of the firm with risk and some failures encouraged
- partnership: 'achieving flexibility by empowering people'
- leadership, which loves change and shares an inspiring vision
- control by means of simple support systems aimed at measuring the right things – innovation frequency, boundary bashing, quality, expenditure on skill upgrading, rate of change – with financial controls reviewed to make sure they are not running counter to this dynamism.

Peters has now turned to organisation structure as a means of explaining the difference between excellent companies and also-rans. The traditional structure, he says, is an 'inflexible, rule-determined mass-producer'. It is characterised by a small ('shrivelled') corporate centre with narrow scope and separated from the rest of the organisation by thick walls – that is, the centre has relatively little interaction with the real, day-to-day happenings in the divisions and in relationships with the customers. Communications tends to be one way, via rules and procedures. Protecting the wall around the corporate centre is 'the praetorian guard of central corporate staffs' who are frequently 'brilliant, MBA-trained, analysis-driven staffs without line operating experience'. The middle manager in traditional organisations tends to be a narrow, functional specialist, whose role is akin to cop – he passes orders and information up and down rather than makes things happen horizontally. The whole structure is enclosed by another thick wall between operators and customers. The wall is breached only at formal points, where sanctioned information is passed out or specified information is collected by designated functionaries.

By contrast, Peters believes the firm of the future will be 'flexible, porous, fleet-of-foot . . . [where] every person is paid to be obstreperous, a disrespecter of formal boundaries, to hustle and to be fully engaged with engendering swift action and constantly improving everything'. In this organisation, the central core is much larger, embracing a wide variety of people who assist in creating and developing the corporate vision. The boundaries to the centre are not fixed – people wander in and out according to need. Top management, in particular, spends much of its time outside the centre, looking at what really happens and crossing boundaries both within and outside the firm. Middle managers follow suit, spending much of their time communicating across, rather than within functional boundaries. Unlike their counterparts in traditional structures, who are frequently defensive, their communications across functional barriers are 'natural, informal, proactive and helpful'. This example set by all layers of management sets the pattern of the behaviour of operators and other front-line people. Frequently multi-skilled, they get things done by using networks to go directly to the person who can best help them. That person may be horizontal to them within the organisation, or several layers above.

The new structure also has very thin walls dividing it from the outside world – 'a thin, transparent, permeable barrier' as Peters describes it. Not only do employees at all levels interact constantly with customers and suppliers, but these outsiders are drawn in as much as possible to become insiders. This involves more than just exchanging information. 'They must become part of [the firm's] most strategic internal dealings.'

Achieving this kind of organisation requires a very different outlook and 'an astonishing amount of hard work . . . perpetually clarifying the vision, living the vision, wandering, chatting, listening and providing extraordinary and continuous training'.

Waterman's *The Renewal Factor* (1987) pursues similar themes. It carries on from *In Search of Excellence* with the idea of learning from the best. 'The key word today is change and so many things can happen so fast that, unless one is relying on informed opportunism, change can overcome and defeat the

best set of predictions about what will happen in the market-
place,' says Waterman.

Waterman regards *The Renewal Factor* as 'a more balanced
book'. Producing it was clearly an arduous task; it took an
estimated seven person-years and over twenty drafts. The result
is eight essential points on how to make a company 'renewable':

- informed opportunism
  'The renewing companies treat information as their main
  strategic advantage, and flexibility as their main strategic
  weapon.'
- direction and empowerment
  'The renewing companies treat *everyone* as a source of
  creative input. . . . Their managers define the boundaries
  and their people figure out the best way of doing the job
  within these boundaries.'
- friendly facts, congenial controls
  'The renewing companies treat facts as friends and
  financial controls as liberating.'
- a different mirror
  Executives of these companies are able to step out of their
  business and put it into perspective well enough and
  frequently enough to anticipate crisis.
- teamwork, trust, politics and power
  The first two of these words are common parlance in these
  firms; the latter two are taboo. This represents the reality
  of how their people behave.
- causes and commitment
  'Commitment results from management's ability to turn
  grand causes into small actions so everyone can
  contribute.'
- attitudes and attention
  'Visible management attention, rather than exhortation,
  gets things done.'
- stability in motion
  They have 'a habit of habit breaking' that involves constant
  reviewing of courses.

Don Burr, founder and former chairman of People Express,
said of *The Renewal Factor* in *Inc.*, February 1988:

Waterman's book is inspiring – perhaps too much so. It is elegant in its simplicity. It is powerfully persuasive. And therein lies the danger. My experience is that many managers will not understand the degree of difficulty involved in implementing these ideas. If they are so sound, then they should go down easily, right? Wrong. The danger then is that people will all too quickly dismiss this brilliant work as a piece of utterly romantic, unrealistic stuff. Our experience is that it is profoundly, creatively productive material that requires great, even heroic commitment, or it is easily lost to the strong forces of conservative bureaucracy.

Waterman told us: 'I'm very satisfied with what I've done so far. Doing new things is important in life – I've changed dimensions every three years or so. I've now formed a consulting firm, trying to focus on the whole question of implementation. It seems that a lot of the real action in the future in why companies can and can't get things done is "How do they get people way down the line to adopt these things on their own?" '

Rosabeth Moss Kanter

Born Cleveland, Ohio, 1943
Consultant and Professor at Harvard Business School

In 1985 *Ms* magazine made Rosabeth Moss Kanter one of its 'Women of the Year', along with Geraldine Ferraro and Olympic champion Joan Benoit. While the careers of the other two have not captured the world's attention, Kanter has gone from strength to strength. Her consultancy skills are sought out by some of the world's leading companies: IBM flew her to London for the day; CBS sent a jet to pick her up; while General Electric offered to place an obstetrician on call when she was eight months pregnant, so she wouldn't miss a speech. The *New York Times* has referred to her as 'a superwoman of sorts' and it is claimed she is among the most sought after speakers on management in the world. At a Management Centre Europe conference in 1986, Kanter was introduced in highly flattering terms: 'If you think of Tom (Excellence) Peters as the right brain and Peter Drucker as the left brain, then Rosabeth Moss Kanter has to be the whole brain!' Now a Harvard professor she is, in the words of a BBC documentary on her work, 'a fearless critic of management tradition'.

Kanter graduated from Bryn Mawr before taking a Ph.D. at the University of Michigan. Remaining in academia, she joined Brandeis University as an associate professor of sociology before arriving at Harvard's Organisation behaviour programme in 1973. Forsaking Harvard for Yale and the Massachusetts Institute of Technology between 1977 and 1986, she rejoined Harvard as a professor of business administration with an endowed chair dedicated to innovation and entrepreneurship. In 1977 she also began a consultancy career, setting up Goodmeasure management consultancy with her husband. Goodmeasure's clients have included Procter and Gamble, Honeywell, IBM, Digital, General Electric, Apple and Xerox.

Kanter's non-traditional interests are illustrated by early books on Utopian groups such as kibbutzim and the Shakers and one on feminist perspectives of society.

Her first book to make a real impact was *Men and Women of the Corporation* (1977). It was based on five years' close association with a company in a consultant capacity and won an award for the best book of the year on social issues. But it was the 1983 book, *The Change Masters* ('the thinking manager's *In Search of Excellence*'), which elevated Kanter to star status. The *Harvard Business Review* commented: 'The depth of reach here is great. Kanter's deservedly popular book is concerned not merely with the detail, which is rich, but also with the theory. And it's in this latter regard that Kanter offers a real service. She integrates the opposites that bedevil business managers – the individual versus the group, personal motivation versus the environment, getting things done versus being nice.'

Kanter defines change masters as 'literally – the right people in the right place at the right time. The right people are the ones with the ideas that move beyond the organisation's established practice, ideas they can form into visions. The right places are the integrative environments that support innovation, encourage the building of coalitions and teams to support and implement visions. The right times are those moments in the flow of organisational history when it is possible to reconstruct reality on the basis of accumulated innovations to shape a more productive and successful future.' The question Kanter poses is how constantly to change reality. Her solution is that reality is not fixed, though our perceptions of it may well be. Her aim, she claims, is to help executives stay ahead of change rather than become its victims.

The Change Masters examined 115 cases of significant innovation within US companies in order to discover the structures necessary for innovation and change. To bring about change Kanter provides the following prescription:

'First, the organisation must put in place the systems, practices, culture and rewards that will encourage people to be enterprising – to solve problems and to see and take advantage of opportunities.

'The second characteristic of change master companies is that they have a structure that's built around small working teams. The teams have autonomy to act in local areas and are functionally complete – that is, they have representatives from every function, every discipline, that's required to get the end job done. It's the opposite of dividing the process into infinite numbers of departments and specialists, each with a territory to manage.

'The third noteworthy aspect of change master companies is in their culture. Those organisations that tap people's problem solving abilities and enterprising skills have what I call a culture of pride, rather than a culture of mediocrity or inferiority.'

In *The Change Masters* Kanter offers characteristically forthright opinions on the state of American industry. In 1987 she went on to tell the magazine *Quality Progress*:

We are under siege as a nation, and many of our companies are under siege, because we're playing a very new game. . . . I think the game that best describes most businesses today is the croquet game in *Alice In Wonderland*. In that game nothing remains stable for very long. Everything is changing around the players. Alice goes to hit a ball, but her mallet is a flamingo. Just as she's about to hit the ball, the flamingo lifts its head and looks in another direction. That's just like technology and the tools we use. Just when employees have mastered them, they seem to change, requiring different learning and competence.

Kanter challenges the attitude of businesses to change. 'Change is always a threat when it's done to me or imposed on me, whether I like it or not. But it's an opportunity if it's done by me. It's my chance to contribute and be recognised. That's the simple key to all of this: make it an opportunity for people and reward them for it. Throughout every rank of American organisations, we must think about problem-solving as entrepreneurs do. They think of every problem as an opportunity to do it better. This is the kind of attitude we need,' she says.

As one would expect of a woman who has written books on community life, Kanter believes everyone should become involved in developing ideas. The traditional and compartmentalised attitude towards problems merely encourages the attitude 'it's not my job'. Setting up a committee is not the way to achieve change, she argues; it requires a leader with a vision. 'It was striking for me to learn that in the late 1970s *Fortune* magazine applauded General Motors for having a "council of elders" – retired top executives who stayed around to advise new management. My question to them as they were suddenly being shocked by incredible foreign competition and change was "Where is your council of youth? Where is your input for new ideas, for people who don't already share the assumptions of your business?"' she told *Personnel Management* (September 1986).

Kanter also challenges the modern method of rewards: 'What's capitalism about except the fact that people should be earning what they get, instead of having it automatically handed to them, because they occupy a certain desk all the time?'

She has provided a blue-print for successful and unsuccessful harnessing of change. Her rules for stifling innovation are:

1. Regard any new idea from below with suspicion – because it's new and because it's from below.
2. Insist that people who need your approval to act first go through several other levels of management to get their signatures.
3. Ask departments or individuals to challenge and criticise each other's proposals. That saves you the job of deciding; you just pick the survivor.
4. Express your criticism freely and withhold your praise.

That keeps people on their toes. Let them know they can be fired at any time.

5. Treat identification of problems as signs of failure, to discourage people from letting you know when something in their area isn't working.
6. Control everything carefully. Make sure people count anything that can be counted, frequently.
7. Make decisions to reorganise or change policies in secret and spring them on people unexpectedly. That also keeps people on their toes.
8. Make sure that requests for information are fully justified and make sure that it is not given out to managers freely. You don't want data to fall into the wrong hands.
9. Assign to lower-level managers, in the name of delegation and participation, responsibility for figuring out how to cut back, lay off, move people around, or otherwise implement threatening decisions you have made. And get them to do it quickly.
10. And above all, never forget that you, the higher-ups, already know everything important about the business.

In contrast, Kanter's guidelines for building commitment to change are:

1. Allow room for participation in the planning of the change.
2. Leave choices within the overall decision to change.
3. Provide a clear picture of the change, a vision with details about the new state.
4. Share information about change plans to the fullest extent possible.
5. Divide a big change into more manageable and familiar steps; let people take a small step first.
6. Minimise surprises; give people advance warning about new requirements.
7. Allow for digestion of change requests – a chance to become accustomed to the idea of change before making a commitment.
8. Repeatedly demonstrate your own commitment to the change.

9. Make standards and requirements clear – tell exactly what is expected of people in the change.
10. Offer positive reinforcement for competence; let people know they can do it.
11. Look for and reward pioneers, innovators, and early successes to serve as models.
12. Help people find or feel compensated for the extra time and energy change requires.
13. Avoid creating obvious 'losers' from the change.
14. Allow expressions of nostalgia and grief for the past – then create excitement about the future.

Kanter has been active in trying to achieve change in the United States and worked with Michael Dukakis in his presidential campaign. Together they produced a book, *Creating the Future* (1988), which recounts Dukakis's economic success in the state of Massachusetts. It is this 'miracle', based on encouraging entrepreneurs, which Kanter would like to bring about elsewhere in American industry. Her newest book examines how companies are indeed starting to adapt to the challenging global business environment.

CHAPTER 7

The Misfits

Difficult to categorise, though far from light-hearted, are two iconoclastic British-based thinkers: E. Fritz Schumacher (1911–77) and Edward de Bono (born 1933).

E. Fritz Schumacher

Born Bonn, 1911
Died 1977
Economist

German born, Schumacher first came to England in 1930 as a Rhodes Scholar to study economics at New College, Oxford. By the age of twenty-two, he was teaching the subject at Columbia University in the United States. He returned to Britain in 1937, after a brief spell in Germany where his lack of sympathy with the rise of Nazism made it difficult for him to work. In Britain during wartime Schumacher's abilities guaranteed him privileged treatment and, instead of being imprisoned, he worked for five years as a labourer in Oxfordshire. His services were also used by the government and he was involved in formulating economic strategy in Whitehall. After the war he returned to Germany as economic adviser to the British Control Commission.

His talents recognised, in 1950 Schumacher was recruited by the National Coal Board as its economics expert. When he left the NCB twenty years later he was proud to report that he had exactly the same number of staff – two – as when he started.

It was in the early 1960s that Schumacher's ideas began to come together. He established a close working relationship with Lord Robens, chairman of the NCB, and began to question basic economics and his own approach to life. Inspired by eastern religions, he accepted a post as an adviser to the Burmese government. 'I went to Burma a thirsty wanderer and there I found living water,' he later commented.

Schumacher formed the International Technology Development Group in 1965 and travelled extensively, advising third world countries on overcoming the economic problems they faced. He advocated small-scale production, working with nature and using 'intermediate technology', which he regarded as more relevant to third world needs. 'Organizations should imitate nature, which doesn't allow a single cell to become too large. When it grows big, it splits,' he argued. Later he became a director of the Scott-Bader Institute.

Schumacher's *Small is Beautiful* (1973) is a collection of essays encapsulating his theories and, perhaps more significantly, capturing the mood of the time. It proved itself an antedote to the prevailing corporate mentality of the early 1970s. Widely read – by Jimmy Carter amongst millions – and influential, the book was the fruit of Schumacher's varied experience as a businessman, farm labourer, civil servant and economist. Says Harold Bridger of the Tavistock Institute: 'Schumacher produced an idea which people could build on. A lot of his ideas were picked up.'

Edward de Bono

Born Malta, 1933
Thinker

Edward de Bono introduced the phrase 'lateral thinking' into the English language. It now features in the *Oxford English Dictionary*: 'seeking to solve problems by unorthodox or apparently illogical methods'.

De Bono recently observed, in *International Management* (February 1988), that 'I am not a teacher or an author. I am what philosophy stopped being 600 years ago. I am a thinker about thinking. Things such as linguistics, psychology, information theory impinge on what I am doing. But none of them actually encompasses it.'

His twenty-eight books have constantly provoked surprise and, from time to time, criticism. Whatever the response there is always interest in the latest concerns and developments in thinking of de Bono. His books have been translated into twenty-one languages from Russian to Korean, Hebrew to Japanese. The most well-known remains *The Use of Lateral Thinking* (1967), reprinted thirteen times.

With degrees in medicine, psychology and physiology, de Bono has taught at the Universities of London, Harvard, Oxford and Cambridge. The Cognitive Research Trust, which he developed in Cambridge, is the largest institution of its kind in the world. De Bono has been its director since 1971. Much of the rest of his time is spent working for the Supernational Independent Thinking Organisation (SITO), based in The Hague.

CONCLUSION

What Makes a Management Guru?

In the past decade, management thinking has, to a large extent, emerged from the shadows of academia. Management books are now aimed at a far wider and less specialised audience. With managers such as John Harvey Jones and Lee Iacocca taking a higher profile individual management styles are far more accessible than ever before. However, this entrepreneurism of ideas means that marketing and self-promotion can be as important as original thought. If the packaging is right there are rich pickings. 'Some gurus simply package things to the lowest possible taste. As a result, they have more influence than sophisticated writers like Drucker,' says Tom Horton of the American Management Associations.

The rewards are high as managers continue to flit from trend to trend in search of a universal panacea. But what makes a management guru? The management thinkers themselves have little time for the term (in Sanskrit 'guruh' means weighty) – 'I detest the word guru and feel that it puts an unprofessional stamp on things,' Robert Blake, originator of the managerial grid, once claimed. 'I ascribe the popularity of this hideous word to its fitting more easily into a headline than its older synonym – charlatan', says Peter Drucker. Frederick Herzberg also takes a cynical view: 'You can tell whether someone is a guru by the degree of academic jealousy and hostility he engenders.'

According to John Banham, director-general of the Confederation of British Industry, gurus require brains, courage and luck. It may even be being in the right place with the right idea at the right time – 'There are few people who have the self-confidence and guts to look the fashion of the day in the eye and say that's nonsense and be right.' This luck factor is confirmed by John Chadwick, director of Britain's Sundridge Park Management Centre. 'It's because they're there at the time that they become gurus,' says Chadwick. And Valerie Hammond, director of research at a rival institution, Ashridge Management

College, agrees: 'It's about being spot on with the time – answering today's problems rather than yesterday's or tomorrow's.'

Perceptions differ widely, yet there is clearly a difference in stature between intellectual powerhouses such as Peter Drucker, Lyndall Urwick or Michael Porter at one extreme and people who have merely exploited one good idea at the other. There is also a difference between the true management guru and the business hero. Sir Michael Edwardes, for example, had a timely influence on British management by epitomising the kind of leadership qualities needed for renaissance from crisis and encapsulating them in his biography, but he is not seen as a management guru.

Kirsty Ross, managing director of IBP Consultants, draws two distinctions between gurus: 'I believe there are two kinds of guru. The far-away one whom one probably only meets through her/his books and teachings and whose impact is world-wide and world changing. The other is the guru whom one knows, whose impact is very personal and who can also be a world changer but not necessarily. The dominant characteristics of the first are the intellectual ability; the visionary appeal; the ability to talk at quite a high level. The second is a much more anecdotal teacher. Human and humane; one who hangs in there with you; one who is the source of many a-ha moments.'

One academic we talked to defines a guru as 'Somebody who was or still is successful in the practice of management and has efficiently changed an organisation so that it serves as a model for others.' Or, alternatively, 'A scholar, often previously a successful executive or consultant, who contributes enormously to the development of management.'

For one of the most thoughtful analyses of what makes a guru we are indebted to Britain's John Humble, who identifies six essential characteristics:

1. Integrative power
    'Even if his topic is highly current, the guru is able to put it into context within the broader picture of economic development and business trends.'
2. An extraordinary and intuitive sense of timing
    'They have remarkable early warning systems that alert

them to trends long before they become obvious to other people. They usually don't know how it happens, but they become convinced they should devote themselves to investigating it and spreading their insights.'

3. Longevity
'You have to be around for quite some time. One good idea is not enough. The key question is: do they keep on coming up with the goods?'

4. International influence
'The really valuable management ideas tend to achieve rapid dissemination across the globe. In most cases, this is because an enthusiast has taken them up, whose mental horizons are international, rather than domestic.'

5. A missionary zeal for what he believes in
'The exhaustive tours undertaken by the top management gurus are not motivated by money – most become comfortably well off quickly, or can find much easier ways of earning their high daily fees. The real gurus are genuinely concerned to tell other people about their discoveries. Years after the event, they are still excited about them and keen to spend time talking to people about what they have learned, in or outside the paid seminar.'

6. An ability to listen
'All the gurus I've known, including Urwick, Drucker, Levitt and Schumacher, have combined a confidence in the rightness of what they have to say with a humility that allows them to keep learning. They never closed their minds to ideas from students, peers or anyone who had an idea to discuss.'

Others highlight the need for a strong personality, integrity and good communication. Intense competition means presentation and platform skills are critical. 'If you don't get an audience in the first sixty seconds, you're lost,' says Peter Drucker. Evangelical fervour is increasingly common among the gurus. 'Publicity makes a guru. He must have something to say in an interesting way,' says Martyn Hobrough of PA Consulting Group.

The pressures of competition mean that topicality is also of prime importance. Michael Goold, of Ashridge Management

College's Strategic Management Centre, says, 'The emergence of a guru requires the interaction of a topical issue of management concern and an individual with some fresh thinking on that issue.' The fresh thinking may not necessarily be comprehensive. Tom Peters has said that much of what he wrote in the best-selling *In Search of Excellence* can be found in Drucker's *The Practice of Management* published nearly thirty years before.

'Genuinely new thinking on the perennial problems of management is rare. There are many aspiring gurus and reams of research output, but little of it really succeeds in catching the attention of busy managers,' says Goold. 'In part this may reflect the quality of the aspiring guru's public relations; but even more it depends on whether he truly has something to say. The disappearance of yesterday's gurus is equally understandable. Issues do not remain topical for ever, and fresh ideas are soon well known. It is only the super-gurus who can continually come up with further new thinking addressing the changing agenda of top management year after year.'

The practitioners of management can find it difficult to distance themselves from day-to-day problems. 'Quite often gurus have the ability to articulate what a lot of practitioners know intuitively and have never been able to articulate,' says PA's Hobrough. 'The ability to identify emerging issues is something gurus do well. They have good antennae – they look at the outside world and see the patterns.'

Practising managers, being constantly short of time, want ideas that can be grasped and put into practice. John Chadwick points out that intensive research is all very well, but managers are wont to ask, 'What's that to do with selling fork-lift trucks against the Deutschmark?'

A number of observers credit the successful management gurus with a particular talent. A director of the Urwick Management Centre, Rodney Morton, expressed it: 'One thing all the gurus have is an easily understood conceptual framework addressing a current problem. They make people feel strongly about it. Their wisdom sounds like common sense.' Similarly, Ashridge's Valerie Hammond concludes: 'Gurus are people who encapsulate in a few words something you know to be true. They set down a complete philosophy which makes sense to others both in business and the man in the street.'

The perennial question remains – can good management practices be learned? Business schools remain the prime source of managerial knowledge and they are far from being universally accepted as the fount of wisdom. Peter Drucker has little time for them, Henry Mintzberg even less for the traditional MBA offering. Harold Geneen is equally scathing: 'You can be taught the tools of your trade in a school of business administration. In fact, if you pass all your examinations, you are rewarded with the title "Master of Business Administration". But the legion of young men and women who come out of the business schools each year, armed with calculators and computer science, are at best enlightened business administrators, not leaders.' Experience, Geneen argues, is all.

There is a regrettable paucity of women among the management gurus. Of the women we feature, Mary Parker Follett has remained an unsung heroine of management thinking. A recent biography has helped promote her ideas, but in general she has remained a minor and neglected figure. Most prominent women management thinkers tended to be part of a male–female team – Lilian Gilbreth for example, or Jane Mouton, co-author of *The Managerial Grid* with Robert Blake.

In recent years, women have clearly played a far larger role in management thinking and practice. In the United States, we have highlighted the work of Rosabeth Moss Kanter and Kathryn Rudie Harrigan. In Britain, Joan Woodward and Rosemary Stewart have been highly influential in relatively confined circles. Rather more contentiously, Anita Roddick, founder of the Body Shop, is using business success as a platform to raise business awareness about environmental issues. But it appears that men will remain the source of the bulk of management thinking as long as they dominate the top positions in universities and businesses.

Less obvious, but equally striking, are the truly international backgrounds of the leading management thinkers. Though most of the contemporary thinkers are American, a significant number have foreign, usually European, origins – quality expert J. M. Juran was born in Rumania, Theodore Levitt in Germany, Peter Drucker in Austria, Igor Ansoff in Russia, Harold Geneen in England, Elton Mayo in Australia.

One possible explanation for the dominance of the United States in innovative management thinking is given by John Banham. 'The idea of management as its own discipline or profession is a peculiarly American characteristic. The nearest thing to a management guru in Japan is Ken Ohmae. In Germany, management is engineering; in the United Kingdom it has been associated with accountancy. Only in the United States has it been seen apart from these disciplines.'

Among the Britons, there is also a strong foreign influence. De Bono and Schumacher were born in Malta and Germany respectively. Lyndall Urwick spent his later years in Australia, while C. Northcote Parkinson gained many of his insights teaching in the Far East. If the huge amount of international travelling management thinkers experience is added, the pattern becomes even more pronounced. Virtually all have had some experience of living and working abroad. An international perspective helps point out the essential differences from which major insights can be drawn.

Apparently inexhaustible, these people are compulsive achievers with an extraordinary range of attainments. The phrase 'renaissance man' has been used of quite a number of them. Warren Bennis has also been compared to Don Quixote, Bob Waterman to Indiana Jones. Self-educated Frederick Taylor took out patents for over a hundred inventions and managed to find time to win the US tennis doubles championship. Reg Revans held the record for the Cambridge undergraduate long jump and was in the 1928 UK Olympic team. Recent gurus continue this trend. Michael Porter has backed or managed several musical acts. He is also an excellent golfer and could have played professionally. Kathryn Harrigan has run a theatre and was the model for actress Diane Keaton in the film *Baby Boom*, while Bob Waterman is an acclaimed painter.

Workaholism is rife. Their publications, no doubt helped by teams of enthusiastic researchers and students, are enormous in number. Warren Bennis has written fifteen books and over five hundred articles. Edward de Bono wakes at 6 a.m. and begins an average daily production of twenty-six pages. Peter Drucker, now aged seventy-nine, is booked up for the next two years with speaking and writing commitments. Harold Geneen has gained an international reputation for hard work. He has said that an executive's work should begin at 5 p.m. – nine to five was for meetings.

Despite this incredibly heavy work-load, gurus live for an uncommonly long time. Their momentum is such that they seem to find it difficult to stop. Even the early management pioneers reached ripe old age. Robert Owen lived until he was eighty-seven, Fayol to eighty-four, Sloan ninety-one, Urwick ninety-two. Of the present crop, Deming is eighty-seven, Juran eighty-four and Revans eighty-one.

The academic world still produces the majority of management gurus. American universities provide salaries for a large proportion of our selection. At Harvard alone there are Porter, Hayes, Argyris and Levitt of our major profiles and numerous others whom we have profiled in less detail. Bennis, Herzberg and Mintzberg are also based at universities throughout America and Canada. Cynically, one might argue that academia does not provide the life-shortening pressures of the business world. It is easier to theorise with a university chair, condominium and a weekend place in New Hampshire.

Those management thinkers not lured into academia can generally be found in their own consultancies. From our list Lyndall Urwick is perhaps the first who can be truly categorised as a consultant, though Taylor and Fayol practised it to some extent when their business careers were over. Now consultancy is lucrative – a vital PR front to getting theories across to a broader audience. Ansoff, Waterman, Peters and Kanter all have their own companies offering consultancy in their personal theories. Virtually all the academics spend some of their time as consultants.

These consultancies are usually small and personality based. Those gurus who have worked in large consultancies usually find they can only emerge from the chrysalis outside the organisation. Either big consultancies stifle innovative thinking or it becomes a collective process, not attributable to individuals. This is a notable development from the early figures in management theory. Owen was a mill owner, Fayol in charge of a large mining and metallurgical company, Taylor a steel company manager. Alfred Sloan spent his career with General Motors and Chester Barnard forty years with Bell Telephones. But their theories were only postulated on retirement.

Business heroes are not necessarily intellectual giants. People have been managing for as long as history; they have been intellectualising about it for a much shorter time. The most successful managers often find it difficult to articulate their principles of management – for one thing, it is likely they have not fully thought them through but they are also unlikely to have the time, being men of action rather than reflection. However, many of today's gurus do have 'hands-on' business experience. Robert Hayes worked with IBM before joining McKinsey; Igor Ansoff with Rand and Lockheed.

John Chadwick makes the point that managers are more likely to listen to someone speaking from similar experience to their own. 'In the late 1980s, gurus have to have the credentials of having done it,' he says. 'Management at the moment has been through a difficult process of discontinuity. Steady-state management gurus are now rejected. The Iacoccas have been through the chaos.' As for the future, he predicts: 'It will be more analytical – less about personalities and what they did; more about how the team was made to function.'

Kirsty Ross of IPM Consultants predicts: 'Tomorrow's gurus need to be aware of the world and its environment in the widest sense. They need to be well rounded people – not just intellectuals. They need to care for things in a wider sense. They need to be aware of how humans are changing. They need to be aware of both genders too. Tomorrow's gurus can't just speak for men with a male perspective. They need to be aware of the gender conditioning of women and men and they need to teach leadership in a tomorrow sense in a rapidly changing world.'

Brian Patterson, director of management and corporate development at Ireland's Waterford Glass Group, adds: 'They'll need to be able to integrate more diverse factors and handle more complexity, but with simplicity. Because the airwaves are getting invaded, they'll have to compete more for space through sustained, high quality output and energetic communication using all the media.'

Management thinking, like business itself, is now highly competitive. Whatever the nature and talents of tomorrow's management gurus, they cannot survive – or even emerge – without the active acclamation and acceptance of managers in the real world. As the challenge of managing complex, turbulent businesses increases, tomorrow's managers will have to learn to be more discriminating, separating the glib and theoretical from the profound and practical. Books like this one will, we hope, help them achieve such a level of discrimination by helping them recognise some of the distinctions between the real long-term innovators and movers and the unoriginal, uninspired fast-talkers who will next year peddle a different brand of snake oil. For the true management guru, his or her work transcends geographical or business sector barriers; it is a lifetime's devotion, a long-term fascination with the nature of business problems and with helping people within businesses overcome them.

Appendix:

Chronology of Management Thinking

Sixteenth century Machiavelli's *The Prince* and Thomas More's call for greater specialisation of tasks

1776 Adam Smith's *The Wealth of Nations*

1798 Eli Whitney secures a gun-making contract which leads to one of the first experiments in interchangeable parts

Late eighteenth century French economist, Jean Baptiste Say, examines entrepreneurship and in Britain James Watt and Matthew Robinson Boulton introduce control techniques at their Soho foundry

1800 Robert Owen moves to New Lanark as factory manager and begins his experiments in more humane personnel management

1825 Owen's New Lanark experiment comes to an end

1832 Charles Babbage's *On the Economy of Machinery and Manufactures*

1853 Titus Salt established Saltaire

1861 John Stuart Mill's *Representative Government*

1888 Henri Fayol becomes managing director of French mining company Comambault

1895 Frederick Taylor's *A Piece Rate System*

1903 Taylor's *Shop Management*

1911 Taylor's *The Principles of Scientific Management*; Frank Gilbreth's *Motion Study*

1912 Gilbreth sets up his own consultancy company

1914 $5 day introduced by Henry Ford

1916 Henri Fayol's *Administration Industrielle et Générale*

1917   Death of Frederick Taylor

1918   University of Manchester College of Technology established a department of industrial administration

1919   Mayo published his first book, *Democracy and Freedom*

1920   Ford producing a car per minute

1923   Alfred Sloan becomes president of General Motors

1924   Thomas Watson Senior renamed his company International Business Machines

1927   Beginning of Hawthorne Investigations

1933   Elton Mayo's *The Human Problems of an Industrial Civilisation*

1934   British consultancy Urwick, Orr and Partners established

1936   President Roosevelt's Committee on Administrative Management established with Luther Gulick and Louis Brownlow

1938   Chester Barnard's *The Functions of the Executive*

1939   Peter Drucker's first book *The End of Economic Man*; Fritz Roethlisberger and W. J. Dickson's *Management and the Worker*

1941   Mary Parker Follett's *Dynamic Administration*

1945   Mayo's *The Social Problems of an Industrial Civilisation* and development of T-group training at National Training Laboratories in Bethel, Maine

1946   Urwick and Brech's *The Making of Scientific Management*

1947   Urwick Report on Education for Management; the establishment of Tavistock Institute

1948   Beginning of the Tavistock Institute's Glacier Project

1949   Norbert Wiener's *Cybernetics*

1950   Marvin Bower becomes managing director of consultants McKinsey

1951   The Deming Prize for quality improvement instituted in Japan; Elliott Jacques's *The Changing Culture of the Factory*

1954   Drucker's *The Practice of Management*

1957   Chris Argyris's *Personality and Organization*

1958   Establishment of consulting company Kepner-Tregoe; James March and H. A. Simon's *Organizations*

1959   Frederick Herzberg, Mausner and Snyderman's *The Motivation to Work*; Harold S. Geneen becomes president and chief executive officer of ITT

1960   Douglas McGregor's *The Human Side of Enterprise*; Abraham Maslow's *Motivation and Personality*; Theodore Levitt's 'Marketing Myopia' article in the *Harvard Business Review*

1961   Rensis Likert's *New Patterns of Management*

1962   Alfred Chandler's *Strategy and Structure*

1963   Robert Cyert and James March's *A Behavioral Theory of the Firm*

1964   Blake and Mouton's *The Managerial Grid*

1965   Alfred P. Sloan's *My Years with General Motors*; Igor Ansoff's *Corporate Strategy*; opening of first two business schools in Britain in London and Manchester

1966   Drucker's *The Effective Executive*

1967   Edward de Bono's *The Use of Lateral Thinking*; Paul Lawrence and Jay Lorsch's *Organization and the Environment*

1970   Stanley Davis's *Comparative Management: Organizational and Cultural Perspectives*; Robert Townsend's *Up the Organization*

1971   Geert Hofstede joins IMEDE and begins his classic study of international employee values

1972   Stafford Beer's *Brain of the Firm*

1973   Henry Mintzberg's *The Nature of Managerial Work*

1974   Peter Drucker's *Management*

1977   Abraham Zaleznik's *Harvard Business Review* article 'Managers and Leaders: Are They Different?'

1978   Charles Handy's *The Gods of Management*

1979   Reg Revans's *Action Learning*; Igor Ansoff's *Strategic Management*

1980   Robert Hayes and William Abernathy's *Harvard Business Review* article 'Managing Our Way to Economic Decline'. The NBC White Paper 'If Japan Can, Why Can't We?' which marked the resurgence of quality awareness in the United States

1982   Peters and Waterman's *In Search of Excellence*; Kenichi Ohmae's *The Mind of the Strategist* and Terence Deal and Allen Kennedy's *Corporate Cultures: The Rites and Rituals of Corporate Life*

1983   John Adair's *Effective Leadership*; Theodore Levitt's *The Marketing Imagination*; Rosabeth Moss Kanter's *The Change Masters*

1984   Robert Hayes and Steven Wheelwright's *Restoring our Competitive Edge*; Paul Hersey's *The Situational Leader*; Ralph Kilmann *Beyond the Quick Fix*

1985   Warren Bennis and Burt Nanus's *Leaders*; Michael Porter's *Competitive Advantage*; Kenichi Ohmae's *Triad Power*

1986   Drucker's *The Frontiers of Management*; Edward Lawler's *High Involvement Management*

Bibliography

Abernathy, W.J. and Utterback, J.M. 'Patterns of Industrial Innovation', *Technology Review*, **80**, 7, 1978

Abernathy, W.J., Clark, K.B. and Kantrow, A.M. *Industrial Renaissance*, New York, Basic Books, 1983

Ackoff, R. *The Art of Problem Solving*, New York, Wiley, 1978

Adair, J. *Effective Leadership*, London, Gower, 1983

Ansoff, H.I. *Corporate Strategy*, New York, McGraw-Hill, 1965

    Business Strategy, Harmondsworth, Penguin, 1969

    Strategic Management, London, Macmillan, 1979

    Imparting Strategic Management, Prentice-Hall, 1984

Argyris, C. *Personality and Organization*, New York, Harper and Bros, 1957

    Understanding Organizational Behavior, Homewood, Ill., Dorsey Press, 1960

    Integrating the Individual and the Organization, New York, Wiley, 1964

    Intervention Theory and Method, Reading, Mass., Addison-Wesley, 1970

Argyris, C. and Schon, D.A. *Organizational Learning: A Theory of Action Perspective*, Reading, Mass., Addison-Wesley, 1978

Barnard, C.I. *The Functions of the Executive*, Cambridge, Mass., Harvard University Press, 1938

    Organization and Management, Cambridge, Mass., Harvard University Press, 1948

Beer, S. *Brain of the Firm*, Harmondsworth, Penguin, 1972

Bennis, W. *Organization Development: Its Nature, Origins and Prospects*, Reading, Mass., Addison-Wesley, 1969

Bennis, W. and Nanus, B. *Leaders*, New York, Harper and Row, 1985

Bennis, W. and Slater, P.E. *The Temporary Society*, New York, Harper and Row, 1968

Berne, E. *Games People Play*, London, André Deutsch, 1964

Blake, R. and Mouton, J. *The Managerial Grid*, Houston, Texas, Gulf Publishing, 1964

Boisot, M. *Information and Organizations*, London, Fontana, 1987

Bower, J.L. 'Simple Economic Tools For Strategic Analysis', Harvard Business School Case Study No. 9-373-094

Burns, J.M. *Leadership*, New York, Harper and Row, 1978

Burns, T. and Stalker, G.H. *The Management of Innovation*, London, Tavistock Institute, 1966

Chandler Jr, A.D. *Strategy and Structure*, New York, Doubleday-Anchor, 1966

Coverdale, R. *Training for Development*, London, Training Partnerships, 1967

Cyert, R.M. and March, J.G. *A Behavioral Theory of the Firm*, Englewood Cliffs, NJ, Prentice-Hall, 1963

Davis, S.M. *Managing Corporate Culture*, Cambridge, Mass., Ballinger Publishing Company, 1984

de Bono, E. *Lateral Thinking for Management*, Maidenhead, McGraw-Hill, 1971.

Deal, T.E. and Kennedy, A.A. *Corporate Cultures: The Rites and Rituals of Corporate Life*, Reading, Mass., Addison-Wesley, 1982

Drucker, P.F. *Concept of the Corporation*, New York, John Day, 1946

The Practice of Management, New York, Harper and Row, 1954

The Effective Executive, New York, Harper and Row (Harper/Colophon Books), 1967

Management: Tasks, Responsibilities, and Practices, New York, Harper and Row, 1973

Management, London, Pan, 1977

Managing in Turbulent Times, New York, Harper and Row, 1980

Innovation and Entrepreneurship, New York, Harper and Row, 1985

Fayol, H. *Administration Industrielle et Générale*, Paris, 1916, 1925, English translation by Coubrough, Geneva, 1930, and translation by Storrs, London, Pitman, 1949

Fiedler, F.E. *A Theory of Leadership Effectiveness*, New York, McGraw-Hill, 1967

Fiedler, F.E. and Chemers, M.M. *Leadership and Effective Management*, Glenview, Ill., Scott, Foresman and Co., 1974

Follett, M.P. *The New State: Group Organization – The Solution of Popular Government*, London, Longmans, Green and Co., 1918

  Creative Experience, London, Longmans, Green and Co., 1924

  Freedom and Coordination, London, Pitman, 1949

Geneen, H. *Managing*, New York, Doubleday, 1984

Gilbreth, F.B. *Motion Study*, New York, D. Van Nostrand, 1911

  Primer of Scientific Management, New York, D. Van Nostrand, 1912

Gilbreth, F.B. and Gilbreth, L. *The Psychology of Management*, New York, Sturgis and Walton, 1914

Goldsmith, W. and Clutterbuck, D. *The Winning Streak*, London, Weidenfeld and Nicolson, 1984

Goold, M. and Campbell, A. *Strategies and Styles*, Oxford, Basil Blackwell, 1987

Graham, P. *Dynamic Managing – the Follett Way*, London, Professional Publishing, 1987

Handy, C.B. *Understanding Organizations*, Harmondsworth, Penguin, 1976

  Gods of Management, London, Pan, 1979

  The Making of Management, London, Longman, 1988

Harrigan, K.R. *Strategies for Declining Businesses*, Lexington, Mass., Lexington Books, 1980

  Strategic Flexibility, Lexington, Mass., Lexington Books, 1985

  Revitalising Troubled Operations, Lexington, Mass., Lexington Books, 1988

Hayes, R. 'Why Japanese Factories Work', *Harvard Business Review* (July–August 1981)

Hayes, R. and Abernathy, W.J. 'Managing Our Way to Economic Decline', *Harvard Business Review* (July–August 1980)

Hayes, R., Clark, K.B. and Wheelwright, S. *Dynamic*

Manufacturing: Creating the Learning Organization, New York, Free Press, 1988

Hayes, R. and Wheelwright, S. *Restoring Our Competitive Edge*, New York, Wiley, 1984

Herzberg, F. 'One More Time: How Do You Motivate Employees?', *Harvard Business Review* (January–February 1968)

Herzberg, F., Mausner, B. and Snyderman, B. *The Motivation to Work*, New York, Wiley, 1959

Hofstede, G. 'Motivation, Leadership and Organization: Do American Theories Apply Abroad?', *Organizational Dynamics*, **9**, 1, 1980

Culture's Consequences (abridged edn), London, Sage Publications, 1980

Hunt, J. *Managing People at Work*, London, Pan, 1981

Iacocca, L. *Iacocca: An Autobiography*, New York, Bantam Books, 1984

Jacques, E. *The Changing Culture of a Factory*, London, Tavistock Publications, 1951

Equitable Payment, London, Wiley, 1961

A General Theory of Bureaucracy, London, Heinemann, 1976

James, B. *Business Wargames*, Tunbridge Wells, Abacus Press, 1984

Kanter, R.M. *Commitment and Community*, Cambridge, Mass., Harvard University Press, 1972

The Change Masters, New York, Simon and Schuster, 1983

Kotter, J.P. *The General Manager*, New York, Free Press, 1982

The Leadership Factor, New York, Free Press, 1988

Lawrence, P.R. and Lorsch, J.W. *Organization and Environment*, Cambridge, Mass., Harvard University Press, 1967

Leavitt, H.J. 'Some Effects of Certain Communicative Patterns on Group Performance', *Journal of Abnormal Psychology* (1951)

'Unhuman Organizations', *Harvard Business Review* (1962)

'Applied Organizational Change in Industry', in March, J.G. (ed.) *Handbook of Organizations*, New York, Rand McNally, 1965

Managerial Psychology, 4th edn, Chicago, Ill., University of Chicago Press, 1978

Levitt, T. 'Marketing Myopia', *Harvard Business Review* (July–August 1960)

Innovation in Marketing, New York, McGraw-Hill, 1962

The Marketing Mode, New York, McGraw-Hill, 1969

The Marketing Imagination, New York, Free Press, 1983

Lewin, K. *Resolving Social Conflicts*, New York, Harper and Row, 1948

Likert, R. *New Patterns of Management*, New York, McGraw-Hill, 1961

The Human Organization: Its Management and Value, New York, McGraw-Hill, 1967

Lindblom, C. E. *Politics and Markets*, New York, Basic Books, 1977

McClelland, D. C. *The Achieving Society*, New York, Van Nostrand, 1961

Maccoby, M. *The Leader*, New York, Simon and Schuster, 1981

McGregor, D. V. *The Human Side of Enterprise*, New York, McGraw-Hill, 1960

McGregor, D. *The Professional Manager* (ed. W. E. Bennet and C. McGregor), New York, McGraw-Hill, 1967

MacGregor Burns, J. *Leadership*, New York, Harper and Row, 1978

Machiavelli, N. *The Prince* (trans. G. Bull), Harmondsworth, Penguin, 1967

Mant, A. *Leaders We Deserve*, London, Martin Robertson, 1983

March, J. G. *Handbook of Organizations*, New York, Rand McNally, 1965

March, J. G. and Simon, H. A. *Organizations*, New York, Wiley, 1968

Maslow, A. H. 'A Theory of Human Motivation', *Psychological Review*, **50** (1943)

Motivation and Personality, New York, Harper and Row, 1954

Mayo, E. *Democracy and Freedom*, Melbourne, Macmillan, 1919

The Human Problems of an Industrial Civilization, New York, Macmillan, 1933

The Social Problems of an Industrial Civilization, Cambridge, Mass., Harvard University Press, 1945

Mill, J.S. *System of Logic*, London, Longman, 1971

Mintzberg, H. *The Nature of Managerial Work*, New York, Harper and Row, 1973

    The Structuring of Organizations, Englewood Cliffs, NJ, Prentice-Hall, 1979

    Structure in Fives, Englewood Cliffs, NJ, Prentice-Hall, 1983

    Power In and Around Organizations, Englewood Cliffs, NJ, Prentice-Hall, 1983

Naisbitt, J. *Megatrends*, New York, Warner, 1983

Nelson, D. *Frederick W. Taylor and the Rise of Scientific Management*, Madison, Wisconsin, University of Wisconsin Press, 1980

Ohmae, K. *The Mind of the Strategist: The Art of Japanese Business*, New York, McGraw-Hill, 1982

    Triad Power: The Coming Shape of Global Competition, New York, Free Press, 1985

    Beyond National Borders, New York, Dow-Jones Irwin, 1987

Ouchi, W. *Theory Z, How American Business Can Meet the Japanese Challenge*, Reading, Mass., Addison-Wesley, 1981

Parkinson, C.N. *Parkinson's Law and Other Studies in Administration*, London, Murray, 1958

Peters, T.J. *Thriving on Chaos*, New York, Alfred A. Knopf, 1987

Peters, T.J. and Austin, N. *A Passion for Excellence*, London, Collins, 1985

Peters, T.J. and Waterman, R.H. *In Search of Excellence*, New York, Harper and Row, 1982

Pettigrew, A.M. 'On Studying Organizational Cultures', *Administration Science Quarterly*, **24** (1979)

Porter, L.W. and Lawler, E.E. *Managerial Attitudes and Performance*, Homewood, Ill., Irwin-Dorsey, 1968

    'What Job Attitudes Tell About Motivation', *Harvard Business Review* (January–February 1968)

Porter, M.E. *Competitive Strategy: Techniques for Analyzing Industries and Competitors*, New York, Free Press, 1980

    Competitive Advantage, New York, Free Press, 1985

Porter, M.E. (ed.) *Competition in Global Industries*, Cambridge, Mass., Harvard Business School Press, 1986

Prahalad, C. K. and Doz, Y. L. 'Managing Managers: The Work of Top Management', seventh NATO Conference on Leadership, 12–17 July, St Catherine's, Oxford, 1982

Quinn, J. B. *Strategies for Change: Logical Incrementalism*, Homewood, Ill., Richard D. Irwin, 1980

Reddin, W. *Managerial Effectiveness*, Maidenhead, McGraw-Hill, 1970

The Best of Bill Reddin, London, Institute of Personnel Management, 1985

Revans, R. *Action Learning*, London, Blond and Briggs, 1979

Roethlisberger, F. J. *Man-in-Organization*, Cambridge, Mass., Belknap Press of Harvard University Press, 1968

Roethlisberger, F. J. and Dickson, W. J. *Management and the Worker*, Cambridge, Mass., Harvard University Press, 1939

Scanlon, B. *Principles of Management and Organizational Behavior*, San Francisco, Jossey-Bass, 1973

Schein, E. H. *Process Consultation*, Reading, Mass., Addison-Wesley, 1969

'Management Development as a Process of Influence', *Industrial Management Review*, May 1969

Organizational Psychology, 3rd edn, Englewood Cliffs, NJ, Prentice-Hall, 1980

Organizational Culture and Leadership, San Francisco, Jossey-Bass, 1985

Schein, E. H. and Bennis, W. G. *Personal-Organizational Change Through Group Methods*, New York, Wiley, 1965

Schoenberg, R. *Geneen*, New York, W. W. Norton, 1985

Schon, D. *Beyond the Stable State*, New York, Random House, 1978

Schumacher, E. F. *Small is Beautiful*, London, Blond & Briggs, 1973.

Simon, H. A. *Administrative Behavior: A Study of Decision-Making Processes in Administrative Organization*, New York, Macmillan, 1947

The New Science of Management Decision, New York, Harper and Row, 1960

Sloan, A. P. *My Years with General Motors*, New York, Doubleday, 1954

Smith, A. *An Inquiry into the Nature and Causes of the Wealth of Nations*, New York, Modern Library, 1937

Stewart, A. and Stewart, V. *Tomorrow's Managers Today*, 2nd edn, London, Institute of Personnel Management, 1981

Stewart, R. *The Reality of Management*, London, Pan, 1970
Choices for the Manager, Maidenhead, McGraw-Hill, 1983

Tannenbaum, R., Weschler, I. R. and Massaryk, F. *Leadership and Organization*, New York, McGraw-Hill, 1961

Taylor, F. W. *A Piece Rate System*, New York, McGraw-Hill, 1985

Shop Management, New York, Harper, 1903

The Principles of Scientific Management, New York, Harper, 1911

Tichy, N. M. and Devanna, M. A. *The Transformational Leader*, New York, Wiley, 1976

Toffler, A. *Future Shock*, London, Bodley Head, 1970

Townsend, R. *Up the Organization*, London, Michael Joseph, 1970

Trist, E. L., Higgin, G. W., Murray, H. and Pollock, A. B. *Organizational Choice*, London, Tavistock Institute, 1963

Urwick, L. *Scientific Principles of Organization*, New York, American Management Association, 1938

Urwick, L. (ed.) *The Golden Book of Management*, London, Newman Neame, 1956

Urwick, L. and Brech, E. F. L. *The Making of Scientific Management*, London, Management Publications Trust, 1946

Vroom, V. H. *Work and Motivation*, New York, Wiley, 1964

Vroom, V. H. and Deci, E. L. (eds) *Management and Motivation*, Harmondsworth, Penguin, 1970

Vroom, V. H. and Yetton, P. *Leadership and Decision-Making*, Pittsburgh, University of Pittsburgh, 1973

Waterman Jr., R. H. *The Renewal Factor*, New York, Bantam, 1987

Watson, T. *A Business and Its Beliefs: The Ideas That Helped Build IBM*, New York, McGraw-Hill, 1963

Weber, M. *The Theory of Social and Economic Organization*, New York, Free Press, 1947
The Protestant Ethic and the Spirit of Capitalism, New York, Charles Scribner's Sons, 1958

Weber, M. in *Economy and Society*, ed. G. Roth and C. Wittich, New York, Bedminster Press, 1968

Wiener, N. *Cybernetics*, Cambridge, Mass., MIT Press, 1948

Woodward, Joan. *Industrial Organization: Theory and Practice*, Oxford, Oxford University Press, 1965

Zaleznik, A. *The Managerial Mystique*, New York, Harper & Row, 1989

'Power and Politics in Organizational Life', *Harvard Business Review* (May–June 1970)

'Managers and Leaders: Are They Different?', *Harvard Business Review*, **55**, 5, 1977

'The Leadership Gap', *Washington Quarterly*, **6**, 1, 1983

Index